POLICING UNREST

Policing Unrest

On the Front Lines of the Ferguson Protests

Tammy Rinehart Kochel

NEW YORK UNIVERSITY PRESS

New York

NEW YORK UNIVERSITY PRESS
New York
www.nyupress.org

References to Internet websites (URLs) were accurate at the time of writing. Neither the author nor New York University Press is responsible for URLs that may have expired or changed since the manuscript was prepared.

Please contact the Library of Congress for Cataloging-in-Publication data.

ISBN: 9781479807352 (hardback)
ISBN: 9781479807369 (paperback)
ISBN: 9781479807383 (library ebook)
ISBN: 9781479807376 (consumer ebook)

New York University Press books are printed on acid-free paper, and their binding materials are chosen for strength and durability. We strive to use environmentally responsible suppliers and materials to the greatest extent possible in publishing our books.

Manufactured in the United States of America

10 9 8 7 6 5 4 3 2 1

Also available as an ebook

CONTENTS

Introduction

I was there every night, every night. I can tell you everything
that happened every night. . . . It's just, you had to be there.
—Dylan, Black police supervisor

At 12:02 p.m. Central Daylight Time on August 9, 2014, White Ferguson
police officer Darren Wilson shot and killed 18-year-old Black suspect,
Michael Brown, in Ferguson, Missouri, located in St. Louis County. The
fatal confrontation occurred near Canfield Green Apartments (since
sold and renamed Pleasant View Gardens), an area composed of predominantly Black, low-income residents. Drawing on a professional
arrangement for addressing officer-involved shootings, Chief Thomas
Jackson of the Ferguson Police Department contacted Chief Jon Belmar of the St. Louis County Police Department to conduct an official
investigation. During that moment, neither chief executive imagined
the sequence of events that would ensue and the impact the incident
would have on policing and communities for years to come. Michael
Brown's fatal police shooting in 2014 was the first of a series of twenty-
first-century Black suspect deaths in police custody in the United States
that has invoked national and even international debate, scrutiny, protest, and impassioned calls for police reform.

Brown's police shooting death, the way it was investigated, and the
social and news media coverage it received sparked an intensive three
weeks of protest, vigils, looting, violence, and large civil demonstrations
in and around Ferguson. People were angry, passionate, and even desperate. Events were replete with overt racial tension as evidenced by ve-
hement and poignant wording on protestors' signs (e.g., F*** the Police;
Justice for All; Hands Up Don't Shoot; Stop Killing Us; No Justice No
Peace; Black Lives Matter), media's repeated references to Brown as "an
unarmed Black man," and ignition of the "Black Lives Matter" movement featuring the phrase "Hands up don't shoot." Protests persisted

intermittently through to the grand jury verdict months later and even through the one-year anniversary of Brown's death. Ferguson—as the shooting incident and protests that followed are commonly referenced—was the most intense and prolonged period of civil unrest in US history.

Scholars have suggested that Ferguson ushered policing into a heightened crisis of confidence—a struggle for police to restore legitimacy and police-community relations in the face of renewed, vigorous, and widespread criticism about police discrimination against Black Americans. That moment, 12:02 p.m. on August 9, 2014 in Ferguson, Missouri, was a flash point that initiated a new era of activism and protest in response to police killings of Black suspects in the United States. Protest policing has drastically increased during the twenty-first century (Baker, Bronitt, and Stenning 2017), following years of relative calm in US demonstrations, since the Civil Rights era protests. Brown's death and the Ferguson protests are pivotal events in police-community relations. Thus, it is important to explore what led to the protests, to understand the police and public response to them, and to use this knowledge to improve policing and public safety.

The Role of Police in Society

As a society, we expect much from police. A primary role for police in the United States has been and continues to be to handle "something that ought not to be happening, about which somebody ought to do something right now" (Bittner 1990: 249). Police rush to the scene of a crisis, assess its needs, and promptly impose solutions. Policing scholar Egon Bittner recognized that society has assigned this role to police because police are the only agency available to the public 24 hours daily who also have been uniquely authorized by law to use force against members of the public to control situations and restore safety and order. Because of these two factors—their consummate availability and the authorization to use force—by default, police take on a variety of provisional roles in a diversity of situations, with limited information and often limited assistance and guidance.

The public has assigned police this awesome responsibility because they abhor violence and wish it to be attenuated. Even its use by police is detested, despite being legally authorized. Thus, as Carl Klockars, in his seminal article on the *Dirty Harry Problem*, astutely articulates, police must minimize their use of force in order to retain public confidence in the police authority to use force and to maintain legitimacy (Klockars 1980). So, while the role of police in society is shaped in large part by the authorization to use force, in practice, police rarely use force. According to the most recent Police-Public Contact Survey, in 2018, only 2 percent of residents who had contact with police during the prior year experienced the threat or use of force (including handcuffing) (Harrell and Davis 2020). Research suggests that most police officers, as much as 70 percent, are not involved in any use of force incidents that involve deploying a weapon or injury to a person (Brandl and Stroshine 2013). By design and in practice, police use of force is rare.

Despite its rare occurrence, police use of force, especially deadly force, is incisive. As witnessed in Ferguson and more recently following deaths or injury of other individuals while in police custody (e.g., George Floyd in Minneapolis, Minnesota; Jacob Blake in Kenosha, Wisconsin; Philando Castile in Falcon Heights, Minnesota; Walter Scott in North Charleston, South Carolina; Sandra Bland in Prairie View, Texas; Alton Sterling in Baton Rouge, Louisiana; Freddie Gray in Baltimore, Maryland), the implications of an encounter involving police use of force are far-reaching and highly impactful on police-community relations. Seeing police use deadly force against Michael Brown brought to center stage the tension between the necessary legal authority for police to use force and its application as abhorrent to public consciousness. The public reaction to seeing deadly force used against Brown increased public protests as a tool to facilitate change in policing and propelled the United States into the crisis of confidence in policing that exists today.

Current Crisis of Confidence in Policing

The way that policing matters to people differs across the spectrum of social inequality (Bittner 1990). Police spend considerably more time in communities with large minority populations, and young Black minorities are most likely to be arrested and to experience force or threat of force against them by police (Kochel, Wilson, and Mastrofski 2011; Bolger 2015). The most recent police–public contact survey shows that 5 percent of Black suspects stopped by police reported experiencing force during the encounter, compared to 2 percent of White suspects. Among suspects who experienced police use of force, 63 percent of Black suspects thought the force was excessive compared to 44 percent of White suspects (Harrell and Davis 2020).

Scholars have attributed structural inequalities and feeling mistreated and marginalized by police as the basis for why Black residents have historically and consistently held more negative views about police (Weitzer and Tuch 2004; King and Waddington 2005). This is important, because when a group has a robust reservoir of goodwill for police, as past surveys show Whites generally have, their generalized support for police tends to temper that group's reaction to a critical incident like Brown's death, and their assessment about police legitimacy will hold. When they have a basis of diffuse support, a group is more willing to assume that police had right intentions. However, a history of failure of an institution to meet a group's needs leads to frustration, mistrust, and a lower reservoir of support. Among dissatisfied Black residents, a single, highly publicized critical incident, such as Brown's fatal police shooting, drawing on weakened diffuse support for police, threatens police legitimacy (Easton 1965).

A study in Cincinnati, Ohio, found Easton's theory about diffuse support to hold true following the highly televised, violent arrest of a Black youth who resisted arrest. Nonwhite residents they surveyed were much more likely than White residents to believe that police used force inappropriately (Kaminski and Jefferis 1998). Lasley (1994) found similar results following the police beating of Rodney King, who was Black, in Los Angeles in 1991—Black residents' views about police declined twice as much as White residents. I also found this to be true among St. Louis County residents following Brown's death. Black residents' trust in police declined by 25 percent, while White residents' trust remained stable (Kochel 2019). Marginalized populations in these three studies showed greater declines in police legitimacy and trust than White populations.

Police are now experiencing a more universal sense of frustration and mistrust in the United States than previously. A series of high-profile deaths of Black suspects while in police custody occurring over a relatively short period of time has contributed to a crisis of confidence in policing. Public support has not been this low for two and a half decades. A Gallup poll in 2015 reported the lowest support for police since 1993, following the Rodney King incident, and confidence in police continued to decline through 2020 (Jones 2021). Evidence of mistrust and reduced confidence in policing have taken numerous forms. Politicians and academics have publicly criticized policing strategies, such as stop and frisk and investigatory stops, with disproportionate impacts on racial minorities. In summer 2020, then President Trump signed the Safe Policing for Safe Communities executive order, which incorporated use of force and certification requirements for law enforcement agencies pursuing federal grants. Similarly, New York's governor signed an executive order to mandate police reform. Applications to become a police officer in the United States are about half what they once were. Social equality movements, such as Black Lives Matter, have gained traction. There is an ongoing national debate about abolishing or defunding the police and reallocation of resources from police to other social services. Scenes like the protests in Ferguson are less of an anomaly than they once were. Protests touting dissatisfaction with policing in response to high-profile police use of force events against minorities are commonplace. During June 2020, cities in every state in the United States and Washington, DC, as well as in dozens of other countries, protested the death of George Floyd at the hands of police. Protests, both peaceful and violent, persisted for months. Seeing news coverage of the demonstrations provided a poignant reminder that the fatal police shooting of Michael Brown in Ferguson, Missouri in 2014, and the prolonged protests that followed, brought forth a renewed era of adversity in policing.

As has occurred frequently following crises involving the police (e.g., National Kerner Commission on Civil Disorder; Eisenhower Commission on the Causes and Prevention of Violence; Scranton Commission on Campus Unrest), after Brown's death in Ferguson, a presidential task force was convened to advise police agencies on how to restore trust and police legitimacy. The challenge to police legitimacy in the United States today returns us to the dilemmas raised by Egon Bittner and Carl Klockars—the need for police to use coercive power to do good and achieve just outcomes, but also the risk of diminished public respect for police when they do so. Bittner explains that police use of force, or minimally, the threat of force, is unavoidable—in order to achieve peace, we as a society have decided to allocate the legal, but limited, use of violence very specifically to police and for self-defense (Bittner 1970). This paradox of violence to achieve peace can only be propitiated by successful integrated application by officers of perspective and passion. Officers must understand that, while at times they must use coercive means to accomplish important outcomes like safety and social order, to successfully do so, they must impart compassion, empathy, sensitivity, and respect for people and recognize the suffering of others in order to restrain their use of coercive power, applying it in a limited capacity in a professional and unbiased manner. Klockars (1985) describes the ability to police with both perspective and passion as police professionalism.

When speaking with the officers who conducted protest policing in Ferguson, it was clear that they were wrestling with these ideas, sorting through the application of their legal roles, need to promote safety, feelings of empathy, concerns about procedural justice (behaving fairly and respectfully), and the effects of public opinion. As I was listening to the officers' stories about policing the Ferguson unrest, I realized that policymakers, politicians, law enforcement leaders, and scholars can learn from the Ferguson experience, pursue answers to the policy questions it raises, and integrate the experiences of Ferguson alongside criminal justice theory and prior research to inform debate and police reform efforts. In that pursuit, I have written this book.

Goals of This Book

Although media coverage of Michael Brown's 2014 fatal shooting by Darren Wilson and the prolonged civil unrest and conflict in and around Ferguson that followed seared lasting impressions on the minds of citizens across the nation and internationally, this book provides a lens through which to examine those events that has not yet been viewed publicly. The book provides an inside perspective of the police experience during the Ferguson protests. Based on in-depth one-on-one interviews with 45 police personnel involved in the day-to-day police actions in and around Ferguson during the unrest, and a survey of more than 200 sworn officers who worked for the St. Louis County Police Department— the agency that led the law enforcement response during much of the unrest—the book scrutinizes the challenges of police-community relations by drawing on the Ferguson experience. Adopting this perspective provides a rare opportunity to investigate how officers make sense of, draw from, and struggle with their role in communities; occupational and organizational culture; issues of race, social identity, and discrimination; and questions about procedural justice, legitimacy, and officer motives during the longest civil disturbance in US history. These issues are vital to explore and understand as the profession is focused on improving policing practice, legitimacy, and relations with the public, especially during a period in history when protest has become commonplace.

The book also provides a voice to St. Louis County residents' experiences and views about these events in their county. In the weeks following Brown's death, residents who lived near the shooting death and the protest locations, who had previously been surveyed about their opinions about police as part of a hot spots policing evaluation in 2012–2013 (Kochel and Weisburd 2017, 2019; Kochel, Burruss, and Weisburd 2016), were re-interviewed. Then, we re-surveyed residents nearly one year after Brown's death. Drawing from this three-part series of community surveys, the book describes residents' experiences during the protests, their views about the impact of the protests, their protest experiences with police, opinions about how police can improve confidence and trust, and assessments about residents' trust and perceived legitimacy of police. I integrated the community perspective into the book to complement the focus on the experiences and mindset of police officers and to provide balance.

The goal of the book is to situate the lived experiences of police officers and community residents within available empirical evidence and theory in order to raise and deliberate important policy questions about police-community relations. The book considers questions about the role of police as peacekeepers in support of social justice, the capacity of police to represent all members of society and strategies to achieve this, aspects of police occupational culture that frame the police-community experience, and changes in policing consequent to Ferguson that affect police delivery of services and engagement with the public. It is not meant to advocate a side or position, rather it strives to peer deeply and thoughtfully into the Ferguson experience and to learn from it.

The Study

The study was possible because of my long-term research partnership with the St. Louis County Police Department that allowed police leadership to trust in my ability and interest in providing a fair representation of events, showing the perspectives of police officers and community residents. My working association with St. Louis County began in 2005, when the department agreed to participate in a US Department of Justice, Office of Community Oriented Policing Services (COPS)-funded study examining the co-implementation of Compstat and community policing (Willis, Mastrofski, and Kochel 2010b; Willis 2011; Willis, Mastrofski, and Kochel 2010a). At that time and continuing today, I have been transparent with the department about the research process, engaged with police personnel from the line level to the chief, and shared the findings in reports and presentations with department personnel prior to dissemination in scholarly journals or the general public. I believe this interactive and transparent approach to applied research increased some departmental leaders' appreciation for research and willingness to seek assistance from me. When the protests in Ferguson began, the St. Louis County Police Department Director of Police Operational Support reached out to me. We discussed whether I could assess the impact of the police response to the Ferguson demonstrations on county residents' opinions about police, generate some ideas for improving confidence and trust, and identify lessons learned. Together, we brainstormed appropriate survey questions, and in September and October 2014, my team of Southern Illinois University students conducted resident telephone surveys.

In September and October 2014, within weeks of Brown's death, we surveyed 390 residents who had previously been surveyed for a National Institute of Justice–funded hot spots policing study in 2012–2013. We then re-surveyed 259 residents nearly one year after Brown's death, in April and May 2015 (see Kochel 2014, 2015a, 2018b, 2015b). The hot spots community survey provided a baseline for the current study to be able to assess the short- and long-term impact of the protests and protest policing in Ferguson on residents' perceptions about police. These data provide the basis for the community callouts in each chapter. Table I.1 provides demographic information on St. Louis County residents and survey respondents. As the table shows, since the residents surveyed were sampled from the highest crime areas of the county, the sample does not represent St. Louis County residents as a whole; rather, the survey sample best represents residents living in disadvantaged, high crime contexts, similar to the location where Michael Brown was killed.

TABLE 1.1 Community Survey Respondents versus St. Louis County Demographics

	NIJ Study 2012–2013 (Averages)	Sept–Oct 2014	April–May 2015	St. Louis County Demographics*
	(avg. n = 950)	(n = 390)	(n = 259)	(pop = 1 million)
Male (%)	39	39	36	47
Average Age	40	45	47	37
Police Officer (%)	2	0	0	<1
Own Home (%)	24	33	36	72
Race/Ethnicity				
African American (%)	72	70	70	19
Asian/Pacific Islander (%)	1	0	0	3
White (%)	21	24	25	76
Other (Includes Multi) (%)	4	8	7	3
Hispanic (%)	3	1	0	1
Marital Status				
Married (%)	23	24	27	54
Never Married (%)	51	44	46	33
Divorced (%)	18	22	18	8
Widowed (%)	5	10	8	3
Education				
College Degree (%)	14	18	23	38
Some College (%)	44	49	43	29
High School GED/Diploma (%)	30	28	29	24
No High School Degree (%)	8	5	5	9
Income				
No Income (%)	11	7	8.5	—
$1–$15,000 (%)	20	18	18	10 (includes no income)
$15,000–$24,999 (%)	19	23	21	11
$25,000–$34,999 (%)	17	18	19	12
$35,000–$49,999 (%)	13	19	19	16
$50,000–$74,999 (%)	7	10	11	21
$75,000 or more (%)	2	5	4	29

NOTE: *Based on the American Community Survey 2008–2012.

Building on that work, I sought and received support from then St. Louis County Police Chief Jon Belmar and the Board of Police Commissioners to interview key police personnel and survey officers throughout the organization about their experiences conducting protest policing in Ferguson. Chief Belmar expressed his full support for the study with police personnel, and receiving his support opened the floodgates. While I had planned to conduct interviews with 20 police personnel, instead we interviewed 45 police personnel. Officers in the department appeared cautiously enthusiastic about participating in the research, in some cases spending as much as two hours talking about their experiences. Having conducted a snowball interview sample—that is, getting referrals from interviewees about whom to interview next—likely helped to raise confidence among officers as the interviews progressed and it became evident that the information was treated confidentially and that my approach to the discussions was fair and open-minded. By the end of the interview period (targeting September through November 2015), I fielded several officer inquiries proactively requesting to be interviewed for the study. Also, the survey response rate, 31 percent of all sworn personnel, was higher than for prior officer web-based surveys that I conducted within the department (e.g., compared to 29 percent in 2013 and 18 percent in 2012). Details about the study methods and instruments are included in the appendix.

TABLE 1.2 Police Demographics

	St. Louis County Sworn Personnel 2013/2014	Police Personnel Interviewed 2015 (n = 45)	Police Officers Surveyed and Involved in Protest Policing 2016 (n = 218)
Race			
Black	10%	24%	7.5%
White	87%	76%	89%
Other	3%	0	3.5%
Gender			
Male	87%	84%	88%
Female	13%	16%	12%
Experience (avg.)	10 years	13 years	15 years
Sworn	833	43	218
Nonsworn	252	2	0

Table I.2 shows the distribution of race, gender, and experience among the interviewed officers, surveyed officers, and more generally within the department around the time of the protests. The sample of protest policing officers surveyed approximates the demographics of sworn officers in the department. Black officers were over-represented among interviewees in order to gain an understanding of the protest policing experience for that group. Average years of experience increases over time, as would be expected.

Synopsis of Events

To lay out the foundation for the book, this introduction provides a synopsis of key events that will be described in much more detail throughout the book. On August 9, 2014, on Canfield Drive, 18-year-old Black suspect, Michael Brown, was shot and killed by White Ferguson police officer Darren Wilson. Brown died immediately, lying in the street. Fulfilling a request by Ferguson Police Chief Tom Jackson, Chief Jon Belmar of St. Louis County Police Department sent investigators to conduct an independent investigation. Subsequently, St. Louis County Police Department was the target of considerable criticism and public outrage regarding the long crime scene processing time, in which Brown's body remained in the street for approximately four hours. The After-Action Assessment by the Institute for Intergovernmental Research (IIR) describes how the public interpreted the way that the scene was processed and the delay in removing Brown's body as an insult by police against the Black community (Institute for Intergovernmental Research 2015).

A key issue was that St. Louis County police investigators struggled to process the scene in the midst of chaos. Social media posts and media coverage of the incident were abundant and expedient, increasing the number of bystanders at the scene to as many as 200 within the first hours following Brown's death. Four different shots fired incidents occurred near the scene, all while investigators attempted to gather and record forensic evidence. By 2:00 p.m. on August 9, 2014 (two hours after Brown's death), St. Louis County police personnel on scene felt so overwhelmed by the crowd that they called for additional personnel from within the department and also initiated a mutual aid plan to gain assistance from other police departments in the area. Throughout the afternoon, a second wave of officers was called to the scene, including the St. Louis County police tactical unit and K-9 officers. The goal for the additional personnel was crowd control to help protect the integrity of the scene and evidence.

Crowds persisted into the early hours of August 10 and protests continued for 17 consecutive days, the longest protest of its time. For the first four days following Brown's death, St. Louis County Police Department served as the lead agency coordinating the police response to the crowds and demonstrations. Then, five days into the unrest, Missouri State Highway Patrol formally assumed this role at the governor's request. Within days of this formal change, command transitioned informally to a hybrid approach, described in the After-Action report as "unified command." Although four police agencies led the protest policing effort (St. Louis County Police Department, Ferguson Police Department, Missouri State Highway Patrol, Metropolitan St. Louis Police Department), many other agencies—just over 50—were engaged in handling the civil unrest during these initial weeks. Throughout this time, protests included large crowds, chanting and holding signs, protestors throwing frozen bottles of water, bricks, rocks, and Molotov cocktails, as well as shooting guns and even looting and arson. Police wore riot gear and used skirmish lines (a line of police officers standing close to each other), fortified vehicles, arrest, curfews, and a variety of less than lethal weapons including tear gas, a long-range acoustical device (LRAD), and bean bag rounds in their efforts to maintain public order.

Political spokespersons like activist Reverend Al Sharpton, Missouri Governor "Jay" Nixon, and President Barack Obama publicly characterized the events based on their perspectives. On August 13, 2014, the US Department of Justice initiated a Civil Rights investigation. Governor Nixon declared a state of emergency that lasted three weeks; he also brought in the National Guard. Local schools and area streets were closed over a 13-day period. Numerous businesses were looted and burned. The St. Louis County Police Department and Ferguson Police Department succumbed to a cyberattack by the group Anonymous, which shut down websites and email correspondence, disrupted communication, and placed officers at risk for identity theft.

Following the initial intensive period of unrest, demonstrations became smaller, with the next major event occurring two months later—the Weekend of Resistance October 10–12, 2014. Coalitions and activists organized the event, involving a convergence of protestors from around the country to Ferguson, Missouri to conduct rallies and marches to bring renewed attention to the shooting death of Brown and to call for officer Wilson's arrest and prosecution. One vivid image from the event was protestors carrying a coffin of mirrors in the streets and to police headquarters. This image and many other incidents described throughout the book are portrayed in photos taken by David Carson, Robert Cohen, Jim Forbes, and Huy Muck, with the *St. Louis Post-Dispatch*, and are available to review in a well-constructed montage that they title "#Ferguson in Pictures" (Anonymous 2014b).

Following the Weekend of Resistance, the next high-profile event took place a month later, on the evening of November 24, 2014. The highlight was St. Louis County Prosecutor Robert McCulloch's release of the grand jury decision not to indict officer Wilson. This prompted a new wave of protests and civil unrest, including setting fires to stores and police vehicles.

A year later, officers prepared for protests on the one-year anniversary of Michael Brown's shooting death on August 9, 2015. Following a march in honor of Brown, the occasion included gunshots, where a police vehicle took gunfire and officers returned fire. Again, stores were looted and burned.

Although this summary describes key events that happened during this tumultuous time, it does not provide insight into the lived experiences of officers or residents who participated in these events. Those details are integrated throughout the chapters of this book.

Context

Ferguson, Missouri is a small town of 21,000 people located on six square miles inside of St. Louis County—a county with more than 500 square miles, one million residents, and 90 municipalities. St. Louis County forms a half-circle around the city of St. Louis and is bordered on the east by the Mississippi River. Ferguson is located in the northern part of St. Louis County, near the intersection of Interstate highways 70

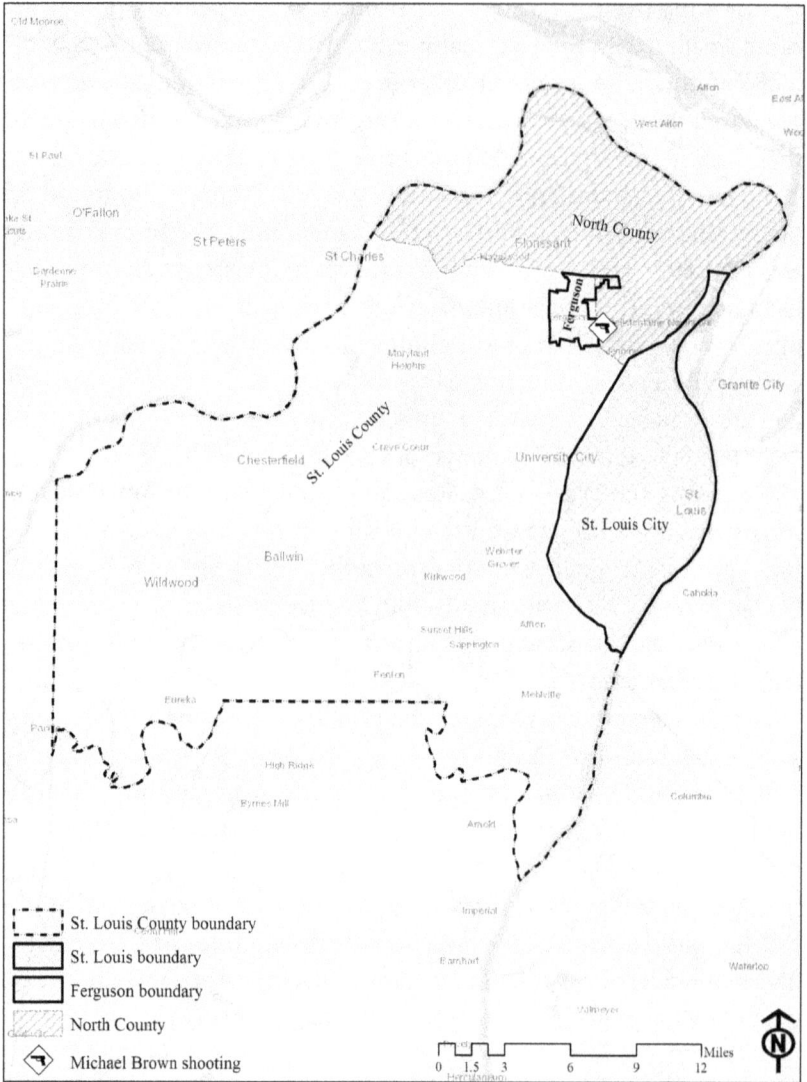

Figure 1.1 Map of St. Louis County, Missouri Denoting the Location of Ferguson.
Created by Seyvan Nouri.

and 170. The northern portion of St. Louis County is commonly referred to as North County. North County houses many predominantly Black neighborhoods (over half of area residents are Black), contains a high proportion of single-parent families with children, and struggles with high levels of crime and disadvantage. Around the time of Brown's death, the media referred to the area as "St. Louis's decaying Black suburbs" (Kendzior and Lee 2014), suffering from declining infrastructure (Schneider 2014). Although Ferguson does have a dedicated police department, St. Louis County Police Department serves unincorporated areas and numerous municipalities surrounding Ferguson and in 2014 had a formal protocol with the Ferguson Police Department to investigate officer-involved shootings for them. Figure I.1 shows the location of Ferguson within St. Louis County.

St. Louis County Police Department

Established in 1955, St. Louis County Police Department provides full policing services for the unincorporated areas of the County as well as dozens of municipalities and school districts that contract with them for full police services and some that contract only for dispatching and computer-aided report-taking services. They provide the primary police services for about 400,000 of the county's approximately one million residents. In 2014, the St. Louis County Police Department employed more than 800 sworn officers and 240 civilian personnel and fielded about 800,000 calls for service annually. At that time, police were geographically assigned to seven precincts and the city of Jennings, with commanders overseeing each police precinct and senior command staff and support units operating out of police headquarters in Clayton, Missouri. Specialized units included the Office of Emergency Management, Tactical Operations, Highway Safety, Criminal Investigations, Communications, Metro Air Support, Police Canine, Crisis Intervention, Planning and Analysis, Security Services, and Chaplains, among others. The department is certified by the Commission on Accreditation for Law Enforcement Agencies (CALEA) and operates a regional police academy.

The city of Ferguson is small and St. Louis County Police Department is only moderately large compared to jurisdictions like New York City, Chicago, Los Angeles, or Baltimore. Yet, the protest experiences in the metropolitan St. Louis area after Brown's death are highly relevant to similar recent events in major cities like Baltimore, Chicago, Minneapolis-St. Paul, Seattle, and Washington, DC. In fact, Cobbina's (2019) book, *Hand's Up, Don't Shoot*, describing protestors' experiences, makes side-by-side comparisons of the similarities of the recent protests in Ferguson and Baltimore. Furthermore, the Ferguson protests are critically important to understanding the national police/race crisis. The Ferguson experience invigorated debate and renewed action to address long-standing concerns about the racial tensions between the police and the public.

Overview of the Book

I asked officers, "If I was sitting on your shoulder and was going through this [the Ferguson protests] with you, how would I experience it, what would I see, what would be my perspective?" *Policing Unrest* tries to answer that question. As the epigraph in the beginning of this chapter shows, supervisor Dylan said to me at the outset of his interview, "I was there every night, every night. I can tell you everything that happened every night. . . . It's just, you had to be there." My hope is that by compiling the retold experiences of the police who were there, this book can provide insight even among those who were not there. *Policing Unrest* provides a rare glimpse into what the experience was like from behind the badge—through the eyes of police officers—generating a more comprehensive and also personal understanding about the events that took place and helping to inspire a more informed stance on how to further improve policing and police-community relations going forward.

During the interviews, officers discussed an extensive range of topics. They described serving on skirmish lines, use of force decisions and decisions not to use force, being a Black police officer in a struggle of overt racial tension, the contrast between media coverage and the lived experiences of officers, isolation of police, the officer self-legitimacy crisis and de-policing that followed Ferguson, personal and family impacts, and lessons learned. This book not only describes the experiences of officers, but also how police interpreted and processed those experiences, and the implications of their experiences and views for policing post-Ferguson, in relation to available research and theory. In this way, the book aims to provide relevant evidence and theory to inform discussions regarding appropriate solutions to policing in a democratic context that is fraught with waning support and trust in police.

The book adopts Tim Newburn's (2016a) life cycle model to the Ferguson protests. While prior research has focused primarily on the causes and contributors of protest, and this book touches upon that topic as well, the life cycle model also considers how the protest unfolds and changes over time, including the nature of the protest, information such as the types and number of people involved, motives of protestors and police, types of protest activities and violence, and how the unrest is policed and managed. Particularly unique to the life cycle approach is examination of the aftermath of a riot—the impacts on the public, social justice, and policing. In the book, I describe the nature of the Ferguson unrest at various key points, how it was policed and managed, the public and police motives and rationalizations for their actions, and I also consider the aftermath for police and communities.

This book makes no attempt to duplicate the COPS Office–sponsored "After Action Report" (Institute for Intergovernmental Research 2015), which details the events during the first few weeks following the shooting incident, nor does it aim to offer critiques and feedback about protest policing as reflected in the "Collaborative Reform Report" prepared by the Police Foundation (Norton et al. 2015). Additionally, it is not meant to be a global script for police reform like the "President's Task Force Report on 21st Century Policing" (President's Task Force on 21st Century Policing 2015). It is not even meant as a resource to offer recommendations for effectively conducting protest policing, which can be found in the New York University Policing Project's recently released guide on "Policing Protests to Protect Constitutional Rights and Public Safety" (The Policing Project at NYU School of Law 2020). Rather, the emphasis of this book is to complement these reports by featuring the lived and personal experiences of police officers, supervisors, and command staff framed by available theoretical and empirical knowledge. It is important to give adequate consideration of the public perspective on these topics, and quite a bit has been written regarding protestors' experiences and public opinions about the police response in Ferguson, including my own and others' research (Cobbina 2016; Cobbina, Conteh, and Emrich 2019; Cobbina, Owusu-Bempah, and Bender 2016; Kochel

2014, 2015a, 2019). To promote balance of perspectives within the book, each chapter integrates elements from a community survey of residents as "community callouts," whereby residents' views on topics related to the chapter are discussed. Jennifer Cobbina's (2019) book, titled *Hands Up, Don't Shoot*, focuses specifically on protestors' experiences and provides a uniquely perfect complement to the officers' and residents' accounts herein. When relevant, I integrate into the text references to her presentation of that viewpoint.

Chapter 1, "Serving on the Line," provides a detailed description of the frontline protest policing experience. It outlines the social conditions that created an environment conducive to protest and draws from officers' interactions with the public, the media, citizens, and with command staff during the protests to investigate what challenges arise in defining a role and expectations for police that balance the goals of safety and justice in a community. Chapter 1 shows the struggle at the skirmish line between the legal and peacekeeper roles during protests and how police viewed the crowd from these positions. The chapter integrates prior theory about crowd behaviors and empirical findings, addressing procedural justice in the protest context to establish a framework against which police and protestor actions can be considered. The community callout provides residents' testimony about their experiences during the Ferguson protests—including police use of force, the perceived rationale behind protestors using violent means (e.g., burning buildings, throwing Molotov cocktails at police) to draw national attention to concerns about discrimination, and what the protests accomplish for Black Americans.

Chapter 2, "Police Culture and Being on the Island," considers how officers engage with aspects of the police occupational culture during the protests to try to understand whether and in what ways components of culture informed officers' perspectives toward the communities they served and the coping techniques used in response. The chapter reflects upon available literature on police culture to classify remarks made by both officers and residents that demonstrate the way that elements of the police culture (e.g., noble motives and the role of police as crime fighters, situational uncertainty and danger, officer solidarity, pulling one's weight, us versus them) are featured and played out during protest policing in Ferguson. Central issues are the feelings of isolation and betrayal that followed from interactions with members of the community, protestors, the media, and political leadership. The community callout provides resident testimony about the issue of us versus them and accumulated poor treatment by police, as well as differences by race in the perceived ability to rely on the criminal justice system to gain justice.

Chapter 3, "Being Black in Blue," considers the experiences and views of Black versus non-Black officers conducting protest policing. Chapter 3 investigates how officers' experiences can inform the expectation that hiring more Black officers will improve police-community relations in Black communities. It describes the theoretical basis in representative bureaucracy theory, but discusses how double marginality may constrict the benefits. It also contrasts the self-assessments of Black versus non-Black officers on issues such as procedural justice, preparedness, self-legitimacy, and mental health, which are systematically favorable among Black officers, and so provide tentative support for increasing minority participation in policing. The community callout features the community survey finding that residents' purport that hiring more minorities in policing will improve their confidence and trust. This notion in the survey is supported by both Black and non-Black residents, but is an especially strong sentiment among minority residents.

Chapter 4, "Policing in the Aftermath of Protests," addresses officers' perspectives on how the public views them post-Ferguson, and how protest policing in Ferguson has affected and will affect policing going forward. Chapter 4 investigates how officers' assessments about how the public views their authority, while immersed in negative media attention, impacts their proactivity and ability to do the job well. This chapter features an empirical assessment of the officer survey data that examines the protective factors against the Ferguson effect, operationalized as difficulties with motivation at work, apprehension about using force, reduced proactivity, and finding the law enforcement career less enjoyable. Of special interest is that even accounting for factors that past research finds important (e.g., organizational justice), analysis of the officer survey data showed that Black officers were less likely to experience the Ferguson effect. The experiences described by officers in this chapter raise practical considerations for how the characteristics of officers, their skills and preparedness, and most important how they perceive public assessments of their legitimacy may affect the delivery of policing services post-Ferguson. The community callout summarizes the changes in public perceptions of trust and legitimacy by race in the long term as well as findings from a 2020 and 2021 survey of residents from three St. Louis County neighborhoods, whereby residents assessed whether and how policing in the area has improved or failed to improve since the protests in Ferguson in 2014.

The final chapter summarizes the etiology and dynamics of the protests as told through the police interviews and community surveys. The chapter aims to recap the prior topics into conclusions, lessons learned, and recommendations placed into the context of the current debate about the role of police and ongoing reforms to policing in society.

Housekeeping

Before jumping in to the telling of events, interpretations, and theories, I have two housekeeping items to mention. First, scholarly literature addressing protests, demonstrations, and riots has made much of how to define the behaviors of the public, the distinctions and classification of an incident as a protest versus civil disturbance versus a riot, etc. The reality of Ferguson is that it was not just one of these things; rather, there were times of peaceful protest, times of disorder or disturbance, and times of rioting, as Newburn's life cycle model infers. The descriptions that follow are of behaviors, as told by police and by residents. In my view, they speak for themselves. I will not attempt to split hairs to classify those behaviors into a typology. Thus, I apply a variety of terms to describe Ferguson (e.g., protest, unrest, demonstrations, disorder). The variety of terms does not intend to imply distinction, rather it is a convention to avoid using the same term thousands of times. I tend to avoid the term riot, not because there was no rioting occurring, but merely to avoid inflaming the reader or adding controversy to controversy.

The second housekeeping item is my use of pseudonyms. Much of the book draws from interviews with 45 police personnel. They were promised confidentiality. Yet, I want the reader to be able to connect comments made by a specific officer or supervisor to the other comments made by that same person, should you wish. Thus, I have used pseudonyms to quote or paraphrase police personnel throughout the book. The only name that I did not make up was Chief Belmar. He told me during our interview that he expected me to use his name, that it was unavoidable, and that was acceptable to him. Otherwise, I refer to officer pseudonym or supervisor pseudonym. I did not use the specific rank of the supervisors to further protect against someone trying to guess who said what. I did not create pseudonyms for residents' comments. So many residents were surveyed, and it is doubtful that I quoted or paraphrased a resident more than once. Instead of using pseudonyms, I often described qualities about a resident that I quoted, based on demographics (e.g., gender, race, age).

1

Serving on the Line

We went through an entire forty-year career in the span of
months.
—Fred, police officer

I don't think any, any police officer organization across the
country had to deal with what we had to deal with.
—Henry, police officer

Protest policing has increased dramatically during the twenty-first century due to global attention to social issues as well as the increased use
of social media to organize demonstrations (Baker, Bronitt, and Stenning 2017). In her book, Cobbina (2019: 153) describes our present-day
status as "an age of protest," following Ferguson like a "wave of protest
movements." During the summer of 2020, as I was writing this book,
the United States erupted in cross-country demonstrations and civil
unrest following the death of Black suspect George Floyd in police
custody in Minneapolis, Minnesota. Protests about Floyd's death in
May 2020 followed a pattern that imitates the Ferguson experience
and the 2015 protests in Baltimore, including national media coverage,
public outrage, demonstrations, and civil unrest. Between May and
August 2020, ACLED (Armed Conflict Location and Event Data Project) reported that 10,600 protests were held across the United States,
73 percent of which were associated with the Black Lives Matter movement, which found its voice in Ferguson. During just the few weeks
following George Floyd's death, ACLED identified 8,700 demonstrations in 74 countries in support of the Black Lives Matter movement
(ACLED 2020). As the Ferguson experience is proving not to be
unique, but rather part of a larger social justice movement addressing the relationships between the police and Black communities, it
becomes especially important to bring to bear what can be learned

from it to inform policing at future protests and to help restore police-community relations.

Protests such as those in Ferguson in 2014 or Seattle in 2020 (where protests about George Floyd's death lasted two months) that are prolonged, violent, and involve a massive police presence are an anomaly. Most of the time, police do not go to protests. They are most likely to be on scene at a demonstration when it poses a perceived threat to public order. Protests likely to garner police presence have large numbers of participants; "radical" goals—including aggrieving discrimination and police brutality; confrontational tactics like staging sit-ins, forming blockades, disrupting meetings, or making threats; property damage such as from vandalism or looting; counterdemonstrators; or violence (Earl, Soule, and McCarthy 2003). Even during summer 2020, when public outrage over George Floyd's death was most volatile, fewer than 5 percent of more than 10,000 protests involved demonstrators committing violence (ACLED 2020); it is rare. When police are present at protests, a study showed a 41 percent likelihood that they do not get involved (Earl et al. 2003). When police are on scene, the probability that they will make arrests or use force is only 31 percent, although this increases to 43 percent when the protest is about police brutality (Reynolds-Stenson 2018). Tactics police commonly use during protests include underenforcement of the law, negotiation, surveillance, and information gathering (della Porta and Reiter 1998). Police employ more aggressive approaches (barriers, arrests, and use of force) when they perceive a threat (Earl and Soule 2006; Reynolds-Stenson 2018).

Police behaviors at protests have been described in a variety of contrasts: brutal versus soft (degree of force used), repressive versus tolerant (in terms of behaviors prohibited versus permitted), diffuse versus selective (in terms of action taken against people or groups), reactive versus preventive, rigid versus flexible, confrontational versus consensual communication, formal versus informal, and legal versus illegal (della Porta and Reiter 1998). In Ferguson, the style of protest policing could be described as all of these qualities at some point in time. Tactics used fluctuated a great deal as police leaders attempted to identify the most effective approach under changing protest conditions, sometimes reacting to protestors and other times acting preemptively in an attempt to avoid disorder.

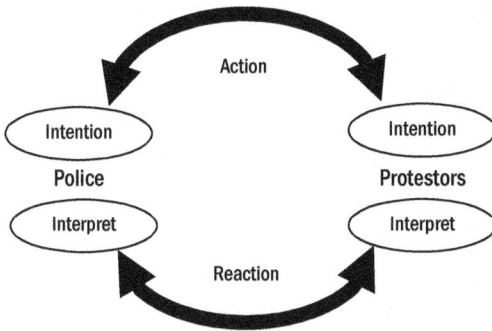

Figure 1.1 Dynamic Interactive Model of Protest Policing.

Prior studies of protest policing view police and protestor behaviors as reciprocal, meaning that the actions of the protestors are interpreted by and affect police, and the actions of police are interpreted by and affect protestors. Each are simultaneously acting, but also reacting to how they perceive the other's actions. From that perspective, protest policing is not merely a response to the protest, but rather a dynamic interaction between protestors and police, as depicted in figure 1.1. This is a helpful viewpoint from which to examine the Ferguson unrest.

Evolving Theory and Practice of Protest Policing

Protest theories postulate how the police and the public attribute meaning to each others' actions and how and why they respond to each other in the protest context. Below, I briefly describe classical crowd theory, negotiated management, and the revised flashpoints model as three major frames of thought for explaining protests and policing.

Classical Crowd Theory

The earliest protest policing theories draw on classical crowd theory (Le Bon 1895), specifically, its premise that when people become part of a crowd, they feel anonymous. As part of a group, individuals psychologically distance themselves from their sense of personal identity and accountability, which allows them to act impulsively. Because people feel personally unaccountable, they are easily persuaded to behave irrationally as part of a discontented collective.

The problem scholars have raised with this theory is that it ignores the interactive nature of protests. No consideration is given to how the crowd interprets police actions. Guided by this perspective, police apply an escalated force approach, whereby police respond to protestors' behaviors with sufficient force to dispel threats or perceived threats to social order. Police adopt equal or greater use of force than the protest crowd to disperse the crowd, enforce police directives (e.g., curfews, prohibited spaces, "keep moving"), and/or prevent disruption of the routine activities in the community (e.g., traffic flow) (Eggert et al. 2018). However, the escalated force strategy has been criticized for accelerating disorder and violence by protestors. A diffuse, indiscriminate police response to the crowd can inspire the crowd to feel united (when they had not before) in moral opposition to police, and so commit more disorder and violence in unified retaliation (Waddington and King 2005; Reicher et al. 2007; Drury and Reicher 2009). To apply the model provided in figure 1.1, there is a flaw in the interpretation of action—the meaning assigned by protestors and police to the other's behavior, which leads to the reactions of both police and protestors.

Negotiated Management

Responding to criticism of the escalated force strategy, protest policing theory and practice shifted in the 1980s. Police sought to avoid coercive intervention at protests whenever possible. Protest policing adopted a negotiated management approach, a style of policing protests that uses protest permits, prior planning, and communication with the goal of minimizing enforcement activities (della Porta and Reiter 1998). Requiring a permit application to protest gives police time to proactively assess potential threats to safety and order. The permit application facilitates communication between the police and the organizers prior to planned protests to negotiate the ground rules that protestors and police will use. The process is designed to create collaboration between the police and protestors to promote a peaceful protest, because the behaviors by protestors and the police are predictable and each party accommodates the other's goals.

Leadership in the St. Louis County Police Department described applying a negotiated management approach to a protest only months before the unrest in Ferguson. That protest was structured and predicable. Supervisor Elijah said that police knew what time the protestors would be at a specific location, protestors had pledged against committing criminal activity, and the group had arranged in advance for a subset of protestors to cross a police boundary line and be arrested. The protest occurred as scripted and the interactions between protestors and police were cordial. Of course, not all protests are preplanned, officially organized, and abide the permit process, and the protests that took place in Ferguson after Brown's death provide an example.

Revised Flashpoints Model

The revised flashpoints model provides a structure to explain why civil disturbance begins and to understand how tensions and behaviors escalate, diffuse, and de-escalate, including in response to protest policing. The model outlines seven characteristics of the social context (structure, political, cultural, organizational, contextual, situational, and interactional) that predict when protest will occur and when demonstrations will escalate into a riot or de-escalate (Waddington, Jones, and Critcher 1989; Moran and Waddington, 2016). Cobbina (2019) adopted a flashpoints model perspective when she documented the Ferguson and Baltimore protests from the protestors' viewpoints. In this way, our accounts of Ferguson concur.

The revised flashpoints model asserts that social structural conditions such as inequality, discrimination, deprivation, crime, lack of opportunity, and police-youth tensions breed discontentment with the government and contribute to collective grievance, because they disadvantage social groups. When people feel that their community voice is weak, that the government is unresponsive to their concerns, or when the media, government, or other groups ignore, vilify, or delegitimize the group's concerns or claims, group members feel a sense of injustice and marginalization. This is the political position of people of color in the criminal justice system. Black Americans are underrepresented in policing by approximately 6.4 percent (Governing 2015), composing approximately 11 percent of full-time officers from 1997 to 2016 (Hyland and Davis 2019).

Disparities in political representation and disparities for people of color as objects of police action generate estrangement from police, mistrust among communities of color, and foster a sense of powerlessness. Comparatively, politically powerful groups feel that they have alternatives to protesting as a way to facilitate government action to address collective concerns.

Cultural conditions affect group solidarity. When group members are homogenous in their beliefs and values, they feel a sense of collective identity and solidarity versus a temporary and conditional sense of membership that develops among a heterogenous group. The strength of resolve and group action will be greater and more decisive with a homogenous group of protestors versus uncoordinated, diverse, and more tentative among a heterogenous crowd. Also, police culture has a solidifying impact on officers. Willingness on the part of the group and the police to tolerate and accommodate one another's cultural differences reduces the propensity for conflict and escalation during protests.

The police organization's structure and ideology affect organizational behavior, such as systems of accountability and monitoring, training on order management, and prioritized values. Organizational values (e.g., toward crime prevention, officer safety, police-community relations) can impact the style/approach police adopt to address protest.

A key contextual factor affecting protest etiology and dynamics is the communication leading up to a triggering event. Representatives of the public or police that make controversial statements or spread rumors about pending confrontation, as well as scandalous media coverage, can set a tone that facilitates conflict and protest. Also, during protests, police intelligence and accurate knowledge about people in the crowd or lack of it affects protest dynamics, along with the extent of communication between the police and the public. The ability to communicate to agree to ground rules and common goals can prevent conflict.

Situational conditions, such as a location that is high-profile/symbolic, can encourage protest and add pressure for police to enforce social order. The layout of a location affects how many people can gather, how well police can surveil the crowd, the ability of the crowd to disperse, and the capacity for communication. For example, social media activity creates an online, mediated crowd, but it also can grow the size of the physical crowd. When officers arriving on scene have sufficient time to interpret and adjust to the situational context, this improves police tactics, reduces indiscriminate behavior, and reduces the risk of conflict.

Police and protestors evaluate and interpret each others' behaviors. Prior research supports the view that behaviors by the police and the public are shaped by how the other group behaves (Gau and Brunson 2010; Cobbina, Owusu-Bempah, and Bender 2016; Engel, Sobol, and Worden 2000; Worden and Shepard 1996; Mastrofski, Reisig, and McCluskey 2002; Terrill and Mastrofski 2002; Terrill 2003). Acts of contrition, such as if the police or the public appeases the other with an apology or other accommodation, can reduce conflict. Conversely, intensifiers include behaviors (e.g., throwing a brick at a police officer or police dispersing a crowd with tear gas) that convey a lack of accommodation or offense, which increase conflict. Protestors interpret police behaviors as fair versus unjust, and police assess protestors' actions as legitimate or criminal.

Relevant to this interactional component, the social identity model explains that participants in a group, such as a protest crowd, can change the way they see the crowd's identity based on how it is treated (Stott and Reicher 1998). In other words, the way that police, news media, politicians, social media, and even leaders from within the crowd act toward the protest crowd could alter the crowd's self-identity. The same effects can be applied to the group identity and behavior of the police.

Collectively, the seven social conditions create a milieu that is more or less conducive to protest, public disorder, and rioting, affecting the incidence and dynamics of civil disobedience. When social conditions are primed for collective action, a triggering event provides the flash point that ignites civil disobedience. When the social conditions are not primed, a critical incident leads to no response or peaceful protest (Newburn 2016b). The revised flashpoints model emphasizes that the strength of the signal from the flashpoint event is important to whether the incident is sufficient to trigger a volatile response. The event must resonate with people and their experiences and identities, as well as inspire a sense of urgency to act.

The revised flashpoints model applied in Ferguson explains the life cycle, the way that civil disturbances form, shift, and dissolve. The dynamics of protest escalate and de-escalate according to differences across the seven dimensions. One study examining 30 years of protests between

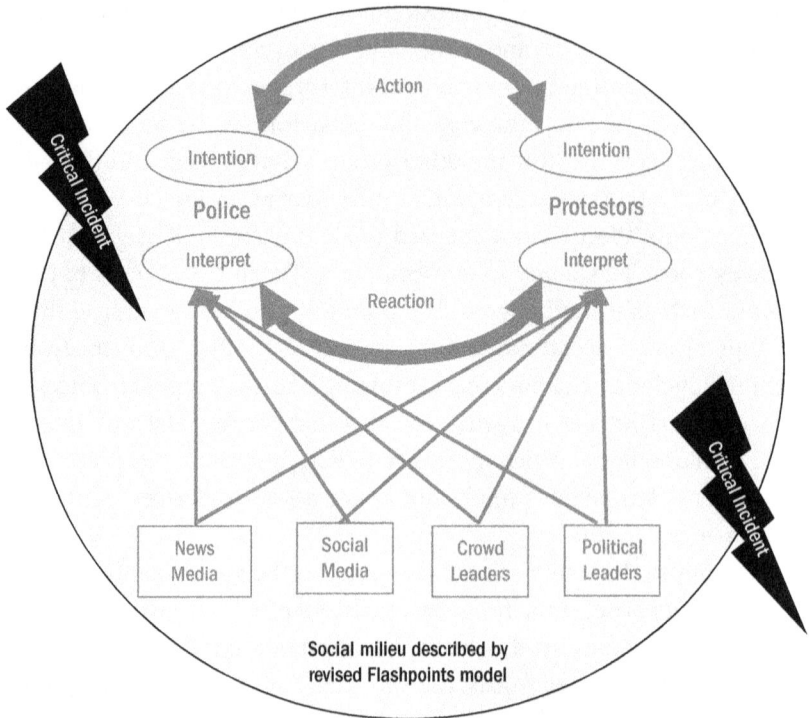

Figure 1.2 Dynamic Interactive Model with Social Identity Effects.

the 1960s and 1990s confirmed that protests manifest when a triggering event occurs in a context where social tensions are high due to economic hardships like high unemployment, social inequality, community mistrust of police, racial tensions, etc. The incident that provokes protest inspires a sense of injustice against a seemingly unresponsive government, often among groups that view themselves as powerless, at a time when tension has accumulated. Without high social tension or in a community that is relatively content, a triggering incident is viewed as a tragedy, but does not spark civil unrest. Following the spark, protest propagates when media attention, social media hype, or word-of-mouth coverage widely spreads information to increase awareness, participation, and to fuel its continuation. Factors like the strength of the shock, experiencing repeated shocks, the degree and duration of social tension, and breadth of communication impact the duration and intensity of protest activity (Berestycki, Nadal, and Rodriguez 2015).

Figure 1.2 provides a diagram of how I imagine the revised flashpoints model describes the dynamic interaction of protest policing. The grey area in which the dynamic interactions between protestors and police occur is the milieu created by the structural conditions, political power, cultural values and norms, organizational, contextual, and situational factors, that shape the atmosphere that either facilitates or suppresses a group response. One or more flash points/critical incidents are represented by the lightning bolts. If a flash point provides a strong signal and resonates with people within a milieu conducive to collective grievance, protest and civil unrest are likely. Once a collective response is initiated, then actions and reactions between the police and the public occur. Actions are made with intention by the police and protestors, motivated by aspects of the milieu such as cultural, situational, and organizational factors. Police interpret protestors' behaviors and protestors interpret police behaviors. Others, like the news media, politicians, social media, and influential members of the protest crowd act as well. These actions also are imbued with meaning by police and protestors, shaping and reshaping the group identity of each. The way police and protestors view themselves affects the actions taken by police and protestors and facilitates interpretation and reactions by the other group.

Applying the Revised Flashpoints Model to Explain the Formation of the Protests

The revised flashpoints model explains the etiology of the Ferguson protests. High social tension in Ferguson in 2014 was induced by economic and racial strain imposed on residents by the criminal justice system. A US Civil Rights investigation found that public mistrust in the Ferguson criminal justice system derived from the city using traffic violations and court fees as primary sources of revenue for the city. During the year that Brown was killed, the city had budgeted for 23 percent of its revenue to be funded through police and court-generated fines and fees. Court fines and fees made up the second largest source of income for the city in 2013. Arrest warrants (at a cost to the arrestee of $50, plus $0.56 per mile to serve it) were the primary tool used to secure payment. Those who could not pay were jailed until the next court session (and charged $30–$60 per night) (Colgan 2015). During the first week of the protests, a man approached police supervisor Dylan and told him about the traffic tickets and perceived disrespect by police officers that he viewed as the basis of the collective grievance behind the protests. The civil rights investigation, completed more than six months later, affirmed that man's impression.

Indicative of weak political power, the financial burden in Ferguson was carried disproportionately by Black residents. A two-year study found that although only 67 percent of Ferguson's population is Black, between 2012 and 2014, 85 percent of people stopped, 90 percent of those cited, and 93 percent of arrestees were Black, and suggested that officers applied racial stereotypes and violated Fourth Amendment rights when executing stops, arrests, and use of force (US Department of Justice Civil Rights Division 2015). Residents claimed that they had been unable to disrupt this practice, promoting a feeling of powerlessness against the system. The social tensions in Ferguson brought on by the economic and racial strains established an undertone of discontent among a powerless group. Even police personnel with whom we spoke refuted the validity of the practice. Chief Belmar told me, "We shouldn't be acquiring revenue for a city through traffic fines of poor people that are typically minorities, and it's become cultural to do that. That's not right. That's not what cops are here for. That ruins legitimacy and procedural justice and all that other kind of stuff."

Amidst these circumstances, Brown's fatal shooting by police provided the triggering incident in Ferguson, the flash point, while social media spread awareness in record time. The Internet erupted with tweets and posts about the shooting and displayed images of Brown, lying in blood on the yellow lines of the street, partially covered by a white sheet, his feet, arm, and top of his head sticking out, surrounded by a few orange cones, police tape, and a crowd of bystanders. According to officer Thomas, a colleague of officer Wilson told Wilson at some point after the protests began, "This is a long time coming. You just might have been what tilted it, or this incident might have just been what tilted it. If it wasn't you, it was gonna be somebody else." The remark is consistent with the etiology described in the revised flashpoint model, suggesting that Brown's fatal shooting administered the shock within a context that was already primed for collective outrage and action. As supervisor Gabe observed, "You have to look back at the last several decades in order to comprehend what the protest groups are looking to remedy." Brown's death was symbolic, it stimulated the collective response to the underlying collective grievance. What followed was a long series of dynamic interactions—protest policing.

Protest and Policing in Ferguson

As officers told us the story of protest policing, they explained that the tenor and atmosphere of the protests fluctuated across several key events: the shooting investigation, the first day of protests, three weeks of intensive protest that followed, the grand jury verdict, the shooting of two police officers at the Ferguson Police Department, and the one-year anniversary of Brown's death. Their accounts describe the environment and their involvement, interpretations, decisions, and challenges. Several themes emerge, including uncertainty and danger, logistical and leadership challenges to implementing a coordinated response with many police agencies, the challenge of using the appropriate amount of force to maintain order, defining what behaviors constitute protest, and tension across police priorities (e.g., public image and legitimacy versus providing an effective response to crimes). This chapter focuses on police experiences and behaviors, including the tactics used during the protests. Chapters 2 and 3 focus more on the interpretation by police and by citizens of the interactions between police and protestors.

Investigating Michael Brown's Death

August 9, 2014, in early afternoon, St. Louis County officers responded to Canfield Drive in Ferguson, Missouri to investigate a Ferguson police officer-involved shooting. Figure 1.3 is a map showing the location of Brown's shooting and other key locations during the protests.

Eight of the police we spoke with said that they worked on scene at Brown's death. Two themes we heard from these officers is their surprise at the public's response and the challenge of coordinating the police response. Repeatedly, police we spoke to said that on that first day, they were surprised by the public reaction to Brown's death, stating that it was completely unanticipated. For one, county police did not know about or fully appreciate the social structural strain among Ferguson

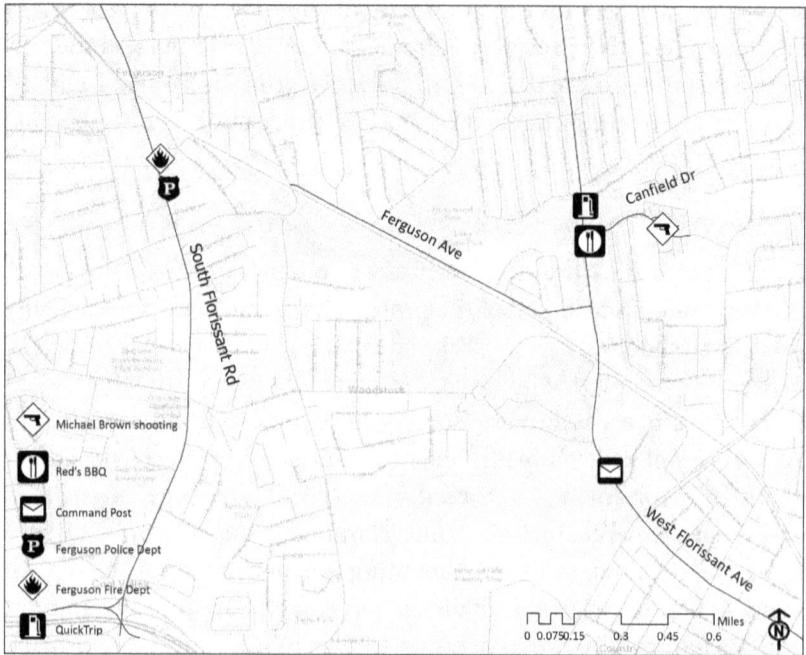

Figure 1.3 Map of Canfield Drive Where Michael Brown Was Shot. Created by Seyvan Nouri.

residents. Reflecting about the racial tension, officer William said that he felt as if, at the time of the protests, police were a better profession than when he was a young officer, that especially young officers "seldom let race affect anything" and that "we are much less racist than before, certainly." Only in hindsight was Brown's death an obvious flash point to police or anyone else.

At the scene of Brown's death, police quickly went from wondering, "Why is this happening?" to "Holy cow, my life is in danger now," according to officer Henry. Supervisor Gabe told me, "We don't deal with civil unrest . . . you're trained for it, but you know, in my two decades, it never happened! You don't really expect it to happen." Police on scene found themselves in a cycle of reactions to the public, rather than routinely securing the scene and investigating the shooting per standard operating procedures. One situational factor, according to officer Thomas, was that the location of the shooting scene was surrounded by two-story apartment buildings that overlooked the area. That meant that the scene was conducive to widespread public observation and communication about the incident, and the space could accommodate a crowd. Additionally, the shooting took place on a sunny summer Saturday, midday, so there was foot traffic in the vicinity. Due to the building locations, officers did not have a long line of sight. People could be close to the scene before officers could see them. Police surveillance was limited, creating heightened awareness about officer safety. Together, the situational conditions were ripe to draw a crowd and to put police on edge.

Supervisor Jacob said that what the crowd saw at the scene, before a coordinated and effective response could be made, painted a bad picture, with Brown being shot and lying in the street. Brown's fatal shooting resonated strongly with residents when they saw him, a young Black male, lying on the street.

Although the initial request from Ferguson Police Department to investigate the officer-involved shooting was made only to St. Louis County police, per the established protocols for officer-involved shootings, very soon after, many other police agencies were also engaged. Police agencies in the St. Louis area had an established plan for requesting mutual aid in the event an incident required additional police. The protocol demonstrates an institutional ethos supporting public order. Numerous mutual aid requests were made within the first hours of the investigation. The requests were broadcast as code 1000, then code 2000, code 3000, etc., as more help was needed. The situation escalated faster than police could contain it.

This process added police resources to the scene, but also added confusion due to poor quality of communication and unclear lines of command among police—an important situational constraint. Officer Henry estimated that as many as 50 officers from different agencies were on the scene by the end of the night, but as officer Thomas explained, when dispatch called for additional assistance, little detail was provided. Thomas was not even aware, when he responded to the mutual aid request, that the shooting involved a police officer. Officer Sebastian had been working midnights and so was awakened by dispatch and just told to go to Ferguson and seek out a supervisor. Fairly new to policing, he was with six or seven other police cars arriving on scene, and he was startled by what he saw. "Nobody said that people are violent or angry. . . . We see a sea of people." Sebastian was first in the line of cars that then began "inching through the crowd, because people wouldn't move . . . people are banging, trying to break the windows, spitting, kicking the cars" and yelling threats at the officers. He feared that the crowd was trying to pull the officers from the cars. He was worried enough that he reacted by pulling out his gun and laying it on his lap. So did his partner. Then, Sebastian saw a big man (someone "huge") push through the crowd, and he moved people out of the way, including a kid, probably around 10 years old, who had stood in front of Sebastian's car and would not move. The intervention by this person in the crowd allowed the police cars to pass through the area. As officer Sebastian explained, "There wasn't any thought or plan or anything like that," at first. It is clear from officers' descriptions at the investigation scene that arriving officers did not have time to scan and acclimate to the situational conditions. Instead, they had to immediately act, which put them at a disadvantage.

Of the investigation scene, Lincoln said,

> We're logging people [police officers] in; they're coming from different departments. I'm gathering resources. I'm making arrangements for water. We had to have a big enough area to get all these people and their cars. We had them form up in teams. We had team leaders. We had to figure out if they could even talk to us, depending on their radios. Could they talk to their dispatcher who in turn would go point to point? Do we have phone numbers for these people? Do they have any riot equipment? What do they have? How do we park these cars? Because if you respond in your police car and you go run off with a team, let's say that I need to move your car or where is your car?

It was a chaotic scene. Agencies not operating on the same radio systems meant that police used a relay system to share information. Officers communicated with their own dispatchers, who relayed the information to the corresponding dispatcher(s). Then those dispatchers could share the information with their own officers. It generated delays in communication and added to the confusion on scene.

Supervisor Connor arrived on scene around 1:30 p.m., and by that time, there were two scenes: (1) the investigation scene where Brown was killed on Canfield Drive, and (2) the spot where a large crowd had gathered outside of the police tape on West Florissant, at the end of Canfield Drive (see figure 1.3). Connor described the situation as "hectic." Tactical units with their armored trucks were positioned at West Florissant while investigators worked the death scene. Upon arrival, Connor asked, "Who is in charge of this?" It turns out, no one could tell him. He said, "At one point, someone pointed at me and said, 'You are.'" He replied, "No, no, I am not, this is not my scene." Unable to find the person in charge, he said it was difficult to make decisions about how to best use their resources. The struggle to determine who was in charge rippled across the responding officers as more and more were brought to the scene for mutual aid. At the investigation, there wasn't unity of command, said Lincoln. Officer Sebastian stood on a skirmish line with officers from towns in Missouri that he had not even heard of, and he said, "No one is giving orders." He wondered, "What are we going to do if they [the crowd that had formed] get past us?" He said no one knew.

Supervisor Connor, who had worked in North County his entire law enforcement career, more than a decade, said that the scene felt different from other shooting scenes that had occurred in the area. He felt a tension and anger in the crowd. The first thing that he did upon arrival was replace Ferguson police officers who were standing at the police tape on West Florissant, blocking access to the crime scene, with county police officers. This provided a visual and symbolic shift from blue uniforms (Ferguson Police) to brown uniforms (County Police). He also had K-9 officers put the dogs away. He felt that this shift in tactics helped to calm the crowd. Once the crowd was calm, he brought Brown's family and clergy down to the scene on Canfield. While that is atypical, the family had expressed concern that when police flipped Brown's body, that police were going to plant a gun on him. Connor felt that allowing the family to witness that moment might help to de-escalate the growing tension in the crowd.

Delays in removing Brown's body from the scene proved to be an intensifier that helped fuel the public's anger and sense of injustice. Supervisor Jason said that crime scene processing happened at a "snail's pace," because of gunshots fired by individuals in the crowd. Officer Anthony explained, "You can't process once, you know, you're getting shot at." Supervisor Dylan described that when they went in to try to remove Brown's body, they heard gunshots and had to pull back from the scene. He said, "And then it was like, man, what do we do? We gotta get it done because if we don't get it done this crowd is going to grow and grow and grow." At the scene of Brown's death, investigators faced crowds forming, four different shots fired incidents, and a dumpster fire. Supervisor Gabe estimated that there were at least a hundred or so people at the scene, "angry people." People even jumped on the fire trucks that had come to put out the dumpster fire.

Supervisors Connor and Dylan recognized that Brown's body lying in the street was agitating the crowd and making things worse. Supervisor Dylan said that people in the crowd shouted questions at law enforcement, and, he said, "We didn't have answers for them. And when you don't have answers for people, that's when they get more angry, they get upset, and they think you're hiding things. And, honestly, we didn't have any answers . . . we didn't know what happened." Supervisor Thomas, in hindsight, wishes that they could have adequately explained to the crowd about crime scene preservation so they could understand that police were not being insensitive, not letting Brown "lay out in the street like a cat had been run over," but rather their motive was to try to perform a quality investigation, that they were being careful and thorough.

Recognizing the many competing issues of protecting the crime scene, processing the crime scene, and managing the crowds, at one point that first day, supervisor Connor decided to re-open West Florissant Avenue to foot and vehicle traffic while the investigation was ongoing. This was the major cross street to Canfield Drive, where Brown was killed (see figure 1.3). Connor explained that his reasoning was that if the road was reopened, even though police had not finished processing the scene, the crowds might disperse. He was wrong. Instead, "As soon as we dropped the crime scene tape, they tried to rush Canfield." Supervisor Gabe said, "Everyone knew that there had been an officer-involved shooting where a young man was dead, and they wanted to go see." After the crowds approached the scene, rather than dispersing as Connor had hoped, police once again had to set up crime scene tape at the end of Canfield Drive, near the intersection with West Florissant Avenue and a restaurant called Red's BBQ (shown in figure 1.3).

Supervisor Connor and supervisor Jason talked about the crowds of people facing the line of officers at the police tape by Canfield Drive, near Red's BBQ. Connor estimated a crowd of about 50 to 75 people. Connor said that people there were "amped-up," stood very close to police, and yelled things at the police like, "F*** the police." At that point, supervisor Connor called down to the supervisor at the crime scene and pressed them to hurry up, fearing that if the investigators did not finish and allow police to open the road soon, the public might rush the skirmish line and police would have to use force.. According to supervisor Connor, by approximately 6:00 p.m., the tow truck arrived to tow the Ferguson police vehicle involved in the shooting, and the medical examiner was on scene. At that time, the police reopened Canfield Drive.

According to supervisor Connor, by about 8:30 p.m. that first day, the tactical unit moved away from the shooting scene and relocated to a hill overlooking the main road, West Florissant Avenue. Several of the tactical officers had arrived at work early that morning, he said, so they had been working for about seventeen or eighteen hours. They stayed with their vehicles, eating pizza and waiting to see if they would be needed further. As they sat there, they saw marked police cars driving down Canfield Drive. Since St. Louis County was on a different radio channel than Ferguson Police, who had primary jurisdiction in the area, the officers were not sure of the nature of the calls until dispatch could relay them. While they were sitting there, they received a call for aid, saying several police cars were trapped by the cars and people along the road. The officers involved called by radio to say that they were trapped and that "they didn't think that they were going to be able to get out." Connor called Chief Belmar to tell him about the problem and said, "They're gonna have to fight their way out. They are boxed in down there; they can't get out." Supervisor Jason explained that a gate blocked the responding police from going forward, so cars were being bricked, kicked, and punched. At that point, Connor said, we used the dogs to push people back as they were rocking the police car. Supervisor Jason, defending the decision, said "Dogs are not meant to go bite people, they are to keep people from coming in and hurting the officers." Jason described the incident as the most frightening of his two-decade career. At the time, Connor saw K-9 use as an alternative to lethal force. However, images of the dogs with bared teeth became famous in the media, leading to criticism of police. Yet, Jason attested to me, "Those dogs kept us from getting seriously injured or killed that night." Eventually, the fire department arrived at the location, the gate was unlocked, and the officers were able to drive forward out of the crowd. By 10:30 p.m., Connor said, the crowd filtered away and things quieted down. Connor said that as he departed, he wondered what tomorrow would bring because he felt that people were more upset than at any other police shooting he had seen.

Viewing the investigation through the revised flashpoints model lens, Brown's shooting and his body lying in the street provided the critical incident, that, along with the collective economic and racial grievances among marginalized groups in Ferguson, resonated deeply with people. This flashpoint event was intensified by the images of the Ferguson police standing in a line along the police tape blocking access to the crime scene, of K-9 units being deployed, and of tactical units with their armored vehicles positioned near the death scene. The visual cues conveyed police authority and their commitment to maintaining order. These actions were grounded in the police institutions' standard operating procedures, their organizational ethos, which also led police on scene to utilize an existing mutual aid plan to increase their resources on scene when the crowd numbers began to swell. Numerous situational and interactional factors boosted the likelihood of the scene developing into a civil disturbance. The high density of residents in the area (an apartment complex on a summer Saturday) facilitated rapid communication among residents about the critical incident. The location also provided spaces where large numbers could gather. Public communication was bolstered by the mediated crowd; people shared the incident on social media immediately, offering a critical interpretation of events. The location worked against police because it was a difficult place to surveil the public. The mutual aid plan added further confusion, with poor command structure on the scene, poor communication capacity across police on scene, differences in public disorder training backgrounds and equipment across responding agencies, and officers on scene who were not familiar with local culture and customs. The speed with which additional officers were called to the scene afforded no opportunity for arriving officers to develop situational awareness. These challenges were coupled with intensifiers by the crowd—people attacking patrol vehicles, shooting guns, setting a dumpster on fire, and shouting F*** the police—signaling their unwillingness to cooperate with and abide police authority. However, two acts of contrition are noteworthy among the officers' retelling of events. For one, a bystander emerged from the crowd to assist police by convincing a youth who had blocked the path of police vehicles to move out of the way. This pacifier event spared the crowd from an aggressive police response. The other act of contrition was by a police supervisor who extended an invitation to Brown's parents to observe the police turning over Brown's body, attempting to allay their mistrust of police and to de-escalate tension over the police investigation.

The Initial Intensive Weeks of Protest

THE FIRST DAY

When the crime scene investigation concluded, protest activities had only just begun. Officer Anthony, who had responded to assist the day Brown was shot, told me, "Sunday [the day after Brown's death] is when it started getting really dangerous. That is when the attacks on us, that's when they really started." As officer Fred noted, "You don't think that the longest, most violent period of civil unrest is gonna happen here, you know, 10 miles from where you grew up." But, August 10, 2014, one day after Brown's death, marked the beginning of a prolonged period of protests and civil unrest.

Forty percent of the officers with whom we spoke said that the unrest was unexpected. The unplanned nature of the protests triggered an all-hands-on-deck approach by police, who wanted to have sufficient personnel to manage the crowd. Officer Teresa was scheduled to be off that Sunday, but she had heard about the protests so she called dispatch, who asked for her help. Dispatch told her to go to the command post (located at a police substation near a large Target store parking lot; see figure 1.3) and "grab a helmet and a stick or a shield and whatever you can get and just go." They were desperate for help. She said that although county officers had trained for policing civil unrest, it was not a skill she ever thought she would use. Supervisor Al described that the night of August 10, 2014 lasted forever, it seemed, and they had no relief, no food, no water, no bathroom breaks. Officer Karen was also scheduled to be off that Sunday, but was called in to help. She describes being told to drive to the command post and do whatever they ask. "So I drive down there, they hand me a helmet, they take off my name tag, and they say, 'Okay get in a group of guys, we're going down [to the protests].'" She arrived at the designated area and realized that she was surrounded by officers that she did not know, not even from the same agency or surrounding agencies with whom she had previously worked. She had not watched the news that weekend and so was amazed by what was going on. It was unsettling and so unlike her typical work environment.

Also, on that first night of protests, in the evening, the tactical team congregated in the command post area in preparation for a scheduled candlelight vigil for Brown. A few hours before it was due to begin, St. Louis County tactical personnel were joined by the chief and deputy chief of Ferguson Police Department. While they were talking, aid calls came across the Ferguson police radios. Because the Ferguson chief and deputy chief were there with them, they heard the request for help come live rather than relayed by dispatchers. County tactical personnel were dressed for normal patrol, per instructions from Chief Belmar. As supervisor Connor described,

> So, we geared up real quick . . . they [the officers requesting aid] were getting rocks and bottles and things thrown at them. The only thing that we had available to us were the shin guards that we normally wear with our full callout uniforms, so the guys strapped on their shin guards and we came down that hill, came underneath the railroad tracks, and I'll never forget what I saw from in front of me when I get to see the crowd for the first time. I don't know how many people, it looked like thousands.

Officer Henry, part of the same group of responding tactical officers, more conservatively estimated the crowd to be 250–300 people, walking down the road and "chanting, 'F*** the police,' all in unison." Connor recalled,

> There were police cars in the middle of the crowd that were getting rocked, you had officers running up towards us, as we were coming downhill and, and remember, we're 16, 17 Tahoes coming down the hill. That's it, you know. It's not the big, big line of the armor trucks that you saw much later on. And we got down there and the very first thing that happened . . . was a cinderblock or a big brick bounced off the front of my Tahoe.

Henry estimated that about 20 officers from Ferguson and St. Louis County SWAT were there and the crowd was close, shouting at police.

According to Connor, another supervisor who was with him called Chief Belmar at that point and stated, "I don't think we can hold this. I think we're gonna have to go straight to [CS] gas," and requested several hundred additional officers be sent. But the chief wanted to hold off on tear gas, according to Connor, and he asked the tactical officers to delay using it until he arrived. As Connor tells it, "So, we formed a line right there, we got the officers back, we couldn't get the patrol cars back, there were probably four or five patrol cars up in the crowd that just got stuck up there . . . There were people all the way around, 360 degrees."

During the confusion and fast-paced evolution of the civil unrest, officer Henry said that some police stepped off the skirmish line to remind the other officers to remember their training on civil disturbance—what to look for and who to look for—to be attentive to bricks, backpacks, baggy clothes, and distraction techniques. Sebastian said that when he received training on civil unrest, he thought it had been a waste of time, thinking, "We're never going to need this." Henry described the tense situation on the skirmish line as "one nervous cop away or one idiot protester away from, uh, a total shoot-out." According to Connor,

It was almost surreal because you, you have people yelling and screaming at you right face-to-face. And, 30 yards away, you watched them [protestors] back their truck up and burglarize the business and empty everything out and you just, you could not do anything about it. Could not get to them, it wasn't safe for us to move, we could barely hold ground that we had. It was just kind of waiting for more help to get there until we could do anything. And that happened all up and down West Florissant, you can watch all those businesses being looted. QuikTrip, by this point, is on fire, couldn't do anything about that, it was kind of a helpless feeling as a police officer to just kind of have to stand there and watch all this happen and not be able to do anything about it. . . . I knew we couldn't do anything . . . because we just didn't have the resources.

Officer Henry described August 10 as "my most fearful night . . . of being a police officer . . . one of the most nerve-racking nights I ever, ever had." The problem was feeling "exposed," because he felt that police did not have the proper protection and equipment to deal with the situation. He described that they were wearing standard bulletproof vests, effective against small-caliber weapons, rather than plate carriers, effective against higher caliber bullets. Police feared an attack with a rifle and had no head protection. But, before the end of the night, fire department personnel picked up tactical equipment and brought it to the area. That evening, for safety, officers began responding to calls, mainly looting events, in teams of three or four.

Officer Henry told me that responding to a call at the Walmart that Sunday was like stepping into the movie *Zombieland*. I could not relate, I had not seen the movie, but he explained, "It's basically like three people that are still alive and everyone else is just gone, and they walk into a supermarket and just everything is off the shelves . . . there's trash everywhere, just chaos, but quiet." In the Walmart, they found televisions ripped off the walls, cash registers ripped out, and things laying everywhere. All that they found throughout the entire store were remnants—broken bits dropped as people ran from the store. In a storage room they found one employee who just said, "I had no idea what to do."

Then, police were getting calls for looting at the Shoe Carnival, at the K-mart, "business after business." Henry tried to describe the amount of damage and desolation, but he struggled to convey the sheer magnitude. In the midst of the looting calls, he also described a truck that pulled into the parking lot and someone in the truck shooting at police, and of having rocks thrown at them.

When the QuickTrip convenience store was reported burning that night (see figure 1.3 for the location), the fire department felt it was too dangerous to respond, according to officer Henry. Before fire trucks responded to the fire, police tactical units were dispatched on scene to ensure the safety and protection of the fire equipment and personnel. This became a common strategy. A nearby store, Sam's Meat Market, also caught fire that night, and again, fire trucks were not dispatched until police secured the scene. Henry said of the evening that it was so surreal and that, "I don't think any, any police officer organization across the country had to deal with what we had to deal with that night of just trying to stop looting in so many different locations after a candlelight vigil."

The officers' retelling of the protests on Sunday suggests several factors that prior studies of protests indicate would generate an aggressive or repressive police response during the first day of protests.

Organizationally, police on scene were decentralized, operating in a chaotic environment, in small, geographically located units, with little oversight and direction, and no time for officers to acclimate to the situational context. Police had insufficient communication—officers in the field were not even operating on the same radio frequency, therefore limiting real- time communication. There were no articulated goals for the police role at the protest and an unclear command structure. Then, while in this state of confusion and disorganization, police faced an intensifying event whereby a large group of hundreds of protestors mobilized, attacking and vandalizing police vehicles. Chants of "F*** the police," looting and arson incidents, and projectiles being thrown at police all further intensified the situational context. The police felt especially vulnerable to the threat because they lacked riot protection gear. Factors like these have historically increased the likelihood of an escalated police response (della Porta and Reiter 1998; Earl and Soule 2006; Earl 2003). Yet, despite supervisor Connor's in-the-moment appeal to the chief that the police would need to use CS gas to disperse the protestors, on the first day, the primary response to protestors by police was to establish a command post, flood the area with officers wearing standard police uniforms (instead of riot gear) and form skirmish lines, and to watch and respond to looting incidents. Based on these accounts, on the first day, police action in Ferguson could be described as reactive and tolerant, applying soft techniques.

A study of 30 years of protests identified a typology of four interactional conditions at protests: (1) peaceful demonstrations, in which both the public and police are cooperative and nonviolent; (2) nontolerated demonstrations, whereby police use repressive tactics even though the public style is cooperative; (3) paternalistic handling of demonstrations, when police use soft techniques even when protestors are violent or committing property damage; and (4) crisis demonstrations, when both the police and public use violence (della Porta and Reiter 1998). The status of a protest can modulate from one typology to another. I believe it did during Ferguson. Based on officers' descriptions, the first day in Ferguson emulates the third typology. Police found themselves using soft tactics while protestors looted, burned, and threw projectiles at police.

THE WEEKS THAT FOLLOWED

The weeks that followed shifted largely to the fourth typology (at least during the night), with both protestors and police using violence, despite media coverage, according to police, that featured only police violence. Media coverage during the first weeks of protests portrayed the police as aggressive and militaristic, repeatedly focusing on images of officers on skirmish lines, wearing riot gear, and deploying tear gas, but largely failed to show violence committed by the protestors. Prior research explains that portraying protestors as nonviolent is important to drawing support to the cause and providing the collective action with a sense of legitimacy (Hsiao and Radnitz 2021). The media portrayal of police as malevolent was a contextual aspect of the protests with the potential to escalate protestors' behaviors.

One such escalation was described by a quarter of the police we interviewed. In revised flashpoint model terms, it was an intensifying incident. Police described protestors rushing the police command post (a symbolic target) en masse. For supervisor Oliver, the incident was the biggest challenge for him during the protests, because it happened so suddenly, unexpectedly, and police were unprepared to handle it. Dispatch radioed that a large number of protestors, 200 or 300 (maybe more, officers' estimates varied widely, up to as many as 1,000), were approaching the command post on foot and were nearly there, and they planned to rush the command post. Supervisor Oliver remembered worrying that if the protestors gained access to the command post, they would also be able to loot the stores in the strip mall where the command post was situated (e.g., Target, Radio Shack, Cricket). There were many police vehicles parked at the command post as well, that were vulnerable to vandalism. The command post was stocked with weapons that needed to be protected. Following the radio call, Oliver recalled seeing police scramble to deploy out of the command post. Supervisor Wyatt saw personnel in the command post grabbing shotguns and putting on their vests. Police quickly formed a skirmish line around the command post and the tactical teams helped push back the protestors after they had reached within a few hundred feet of the post. Protestors did not overtake the command post, however, Oliver recalled thinking about the incident, "We got very lucky tonight."

Another major event occurred three days after Brown's death, on August 12, 2014. That night, an officer-involved shooting took place near where Brown had been shot. Officers working the unrest described hearing a call on the radio about several men wearing ski masks and carrying guns. At least four police cars went in search of the men. When police found the vehicle with the men, a foot pursuit ensued. One suspect was shot and the others got away. When officer Karen arrived at the scene, she remembered fearing what might happen if the protestors on West Florissant walked up the hill and saw a Black suspect lying on the ground shot and wounded. Then a large crowd did run up the hill, but about ten officers quickly formed a line and blocked off the road and the crowd's view of and access to the scene. Shortly after that, an additional 30 or so officers arrived to help secure the scene, and no violence occurred. It was dark at that point and hard to see—a factor that helped prevent additional conflict. Chief Belmar recalled expecting that the officer-involved shooting incident was going to spark new protests—provide a new flash point—but it did not. It stood out to police leadership that this officer-involved shooting did not lead to public backlash. Police offered several possible explanations, but communication between the police and the public seemed key. After the incident, police promptly provided the public with the details, including that a gun was found at the scene and had the subject's DNA inside of it. Also, although the subject was wounded, he did not die, diminishing the strength of the potential shock as a flash point.

So many officers told me that they were surprised by the protests, but after a week of intense protests (on an average night that week, 100–200 people showed up to protest, according to supervisor Larry), officer Ryan said, "You're *still* like, I can't believe this is happening!" Supervisor Hugh thought maybe it would last a week, thinking, "They can't keep this up forever." He found himself believing, "Tonight's the night that they're going to stop . . . and boom, it happens, we're standing [on the skirmish line] another day." The uncertainty surrounding the duration of the protests was a stressor for many officers. One-quarter of police personnel talked about how challenging it was to not know how long the demonstrations and riots would last.

Shootings and fights among protestors were rampant during these weeks, according to officers. Supervisor Dylan said that they had to extract multiple shooting victims from protest crowds to get them medical attention. Supervisor Luke relayed a story of four White teens, two boys and two girls, who were, they said, just wanting to be a part of history and so drove their jeep down into the protest crowd. However, protestors shot up their jeep. 'How am I going to tell my dad?' said the one teen. Officer Karen noted that too often, civilians who were shot just "wanted to see what was going on," and simply did not appreciate the level of danger at the protests. Officer Teresa saw a protestor get shot in the neck by another protestor right near her police vehicle—Teresa had been the intended target. Police who saw the situation from outside the police vehicle (including supervisor Jason) said that a group of about ten protestors had just emerged with guns from inside of Red's BBQ (near where Brown was shot; see figure 1.3), when a police car came by with lights and sirens. The protestors fired at the police vehicle as it entered the intersection, but none of the rounds hit the police vehicle. A protestor was hit instead.

Fights among protestors felt commonplace among officers. Police, like officer William, talked about feeling helpless standing on the skirmish line and watching people get attacked by others in the crowd. He bemoaned that it was not possible to walk off the line to go into the crowd to protect one person, that, "It is just a larger situation than that." Some days were relatively calm, but others were not.

Officer Henry thought that after the first few weeks of protest, the tenor of the protests shifted. During the day, he thought, the crowds were smaller, maybe 20–30 protestors, and he described the atmosphere as "a party atmosphere. It was hanging out in the street, there was music being played, people were drinking, it was, it was a hangout time, it was a social thing." Officer Alexander noticed the same transition, like a block party emerged with barbecue pits, coolers, and chairs. So, while the protests did not end prior to the grand jury verdict, they did become less intense, according to police.

The Verdict

County police felt as if they were kept wondering when the grand jury's verdict would be released. The news media repeatedly called the department public information officer saying that they heard the verdict would be released "today," almost every day for a while, but the police did not know the timing. The verdict was released to the public about three and one-half months after Brown's death, during Thanksgiving week 2014, on November 24. Officer Henry said that police did not know what to expect in terms of the outcome of the verdict or how the protestors might react to it. A common phrase repeated of every major protest event—the investigation, the candlelight vigil, storming the command post, etc.—this time came from Officer Henry, who said of the night of the verdict, "I think we were just taken off guard."

According to supervisor Larry, a calm came over the large crowd gathered by Ferguson Police Station (see figure 1.3 for the location) as people strained to listen to the grand jury decision by radio. Brown's parents were on top of a car. Supervisor Dylan said that what stood out in his mind after the verdict not to pursue charges against officer Wilson was announced was Brown's stepfather standing up and saying, "Burn this bitch down." Dylan said it felt like the crowd had been waiting for him to give the word, and they reacted. It was another evening of looting and burning. People threw chunks of the cement parking curbs at police, someone threw a brick through the Ferguson Fire Department door, gunfire erupted within the first five minutes, and protestors began smashing glass storefronts, described supervisor Larry. Officer Sebastian said of that night, "It was just bad tactics on our part." He felt that police did not have enough human resources and then they parked their police cars alongside the road. In hindsight, that seemed like an obviously bad idea to him and led to protestors burning the police cars.

Officer Joseph had been at St. Louis County police headquarters in Clayton (ten miles from Ferguson) when the verdict was announced. Immediately after the verdict was released, he responded with lights and sirens, driving over to Ferguson. When he arrived, he was stopped by an estimated 500 people in the street. Gunshots were ringing out. A reporter came up to him just south of the Ferguson Police Department and said he had been hit by a brick, and then Joseph turned around and two police cars were on fire.

For supervisor Ben, this was "the most violent, busy, potentially dangerous day of my career," standing at the Ferguson Fire and Police Departments. Officer Owen remembers being called to respond to officers asking for assistance at the Ferguson Police Station. He said that they were immediately surrounded. Police cars were broken into. At least a dozen buildings burned that night (e.g., O'Reilly Auto Parts, Title Max, Little Caesars, a beauty salon), windows were broken at city hall. "That verdict night, it was like walking through the end of days. Like I was in a movie, just buildings going [burning], it was crazy. I've never seen anything like it," officer Teresa commented. Supervisor Connor said that police deployed twice the amount of tear gas during the verdict night than they had during any night in August. Officer Fred said that he grew up seven minutes from Ferguson Police Station, and 15 years ago, when he lived nearby, the area was "beautiful." But, when he looked around the night of the grand jury verdict, "Everything was on fire, and by everything, I mean everything was on fire . . . I could not believe what I was seeing." Officer Henry said, "It's heartbreaking watching it . . . watching businesses get burned, you know, for a reason just because the verdict didn't go the way people wanted it to go." Yet, because the protests had devolved into what he described as a social atmosphere, including drinking and hanging out, Henry also felt that even if the grand jury had voted to pursue charges, that also would have led to violence. He likened the situation to what sometimes happens in college towns after winning a national championship or when a team wins the World Series. He said that the atmosphere of the protests had shifted from social justice to just social.

Several officers expressed disappointment at the lack of National Guard presence in Ferguson for the verdict release. Officer Henry said that Twitter was showing National Guard presence in the county seat of Clayton and in St. Louis City, but not in Ferguson, not where the protestors were located, near the Ferguson Police Department. As officer Henry observed, "I think if their presence were there, I don't think a lot of that stuff [looting, burning] would have happened." By the night after the grand jury verdict—the unrest perpetuated overnight—police found 60–70 shell casings from 23 different guns in one parking lot—Red's BBQ, according to supervisor Liam.

One thing that had changed by November 2014 was St. Louis County's social media presence. Prior to Brown's death, officer William explained, the police department planned to share with the public what is going on, "as soon as we comfortably know what the facts are." They were not pressed to urgency, which, he acknowledged, can create a vacuum of information. Prior to Brown's death, St. Louis County police had one public information officer to handle all media inquiries. However, by the grand jury verdict, the department had hired a dedicated social media coordinator to improve communication with the public. On the day of the grand jury verdict release, the department grew from having about 2,000 Twitter followers to about 55,000 followers in a matter of hours. By the next morning, officer Joseph told me, they had 10.2 million impressions, meaning 10.2 million people had viewed their tweets. They released about 40 tweets that night. From this experience, St. Louis County police fully realized the value of the social media platform. They began using it more efficiently. For example, supervisor Joseph described that when a reporter approached police, holding a brick and covered in blood, they took his photo and tweeted it. It was retweeted several hundred thousand times. It was a way to validate police claims that protestors were throwing projectiles. The same night, according to Joseph, police had seized a bunch of guns and those images too were tweeted to support claims that police were up against gunfire by protestors—a message that police felt was not conveyed by conventional media. Joseph told me, "Getting a good footprint on social media was huge." The potential of social media as a communication tool had been a massive oversight for the department and a lesson learned and tactic adopted after a few months of protest policing.

Shooting of Two Police Officers at Ferguson Police Station

Four months after the verdict, a small number of protestors gathered near the Ferguson Police Station on March 12, 2015, after Chief Tom Jackson of the Ferguson Police Department announced his resignation. Officer Sebastian said it was only about 30 protestors, a small crowd. However, at this event, two police were shot (not killed) by 22-year-old Jeffrey Williams (Williams was later convicted of first-degree assault). The reason this incident was impactful for officers is because they had been constantly concerned about being shot on a skirmish line, expecting officers to be shot and killed during the contentious and violence-ridden demonstrations, but seven months after Brown's fatal shooting, this was the first shooting of police by protestors—the first time officers had been injured by protestors' gunfire. Once again, the violence had not been anticipated by police. The night seemed calm, according to Sebastian. Police were back to working normal shifts, and he had been surprised he was asked to be available to work overtime if the announcement about Jackson's resignation led to problems. He had arrived there and initially thought, "I should be at home." Nothing was going on. That obviously changed with the shooting.

The Anniversary

While the initial protests and subsequent events like the verdict protests were unexpected and caught police off guard, public action during the anniversary of Brown's death was predicted. Officers expressed considerable trepidation as the anniversary of Brown's death approached. They wondered whether national media would come to cover the event and what people would do. Officer Henry had hoped that the anniversary would be different from the past year. He told me that he wished police could just "sit there and not do a thing but respect what happened and try to engage the community in a different way, you know, a barbecue or something that gets law enforcement and community members together, instead of watching TV [coverage] of fires and lootings and shots fired." But shots were fired on the anniversary. On August 9, 2015, news media were interviewing the interim Ferguson Police Chief Andre Anderson and during the live interview, shots were fired behind him.

Heterogeneity among protestors was pronounced for the one-year anniversary protests, Sebastian thought, and several others like supervisor Luke and officer Ryan agreed. The crowd seemed distinctly younger for the anniversary protests (teens and twenties) and appeared to have multiple factions or groups present within it. The disagreements within the crowd did relieve some pressure from police, said officer Levi, but officer Ryan still felt that even with their disagreements, the crowd presented a united front against police and the stance remained combative. Officer Owen vividly recalled that, at the anniversary protest, a mom with a small child, about age three, pointed at him and screamed repeatedly that the officer would rather kill her child than help her son. The child began screaming too, he said, and he remembered everyone taking pictures, "like she was doing some heroic thing."

The police response at the anniversary was decisive, according to officer Theo, who stated that police gave many warnings to the crowd standing in the street that they needed to move from the street or be arrested. When the crowd remained, police used OC spray (pepper spray) on individuals and arrested them, disbanding the crowd within about two hours. Unlike the protests one year prior, the anniversary protests lasted only a few days. By the fourth day, few people remained.

The Challenges of Protest Policing in Ferguson

Officers described facing challenges throughout the protests. Challenges took many forms, leading officers to feel as if they were facing them on all sides. Key challenges included the diversity of officers' training, policing styles, and experience; heterogeneity of the crowd; violence during nighttime demonstrations; cyberattack; officer fatigue; safety concerns; and problems the protest raised for them at home.

Heterogeneity of Officers: Policing Styles, Training, and Background

Complicating the situational context, officers from many different departments worked the Ferguson protests. I previously described the logistical challenges officers faced with communication, as a result of being on different radio frequencies and having a disorganized chain of command at the investigation scene. In addition, there were differences in policing styles, training, experience, and purpose. For example, the National Guard has a different mission and different requirements about how to interact with US citizens than do municipal police. Some of the municipalities working at the protests had the same standards as St. Louis County Police Department, and the agencies had a good relationship and worked well together. However, officer William told me, "There were times with some of the municipalities that you would have to kind of keep them back because their idea about what they were there for was different from ours."

Officers expressed that police from some agencies were less well prepared to handle the unrest than others. For example, officers explained that the Missouri State Police, who were in charge during a portion of the protests, under normal conditions typically drive the highways and handle traffic accidents and drunk drivers. Officer Henry lamented, "They don't go to domestics, they don't go to assaults, they don't go to homicides . . . They don't go to a lot of calls and interact with family members that hate each other or friends that are in a fight . . . they are not used to that." The consequence of their different daily policing experiences, he thought, was a different reaction to being personally confronted by people saying things like, "I'm gonna kill you and your family." As officer Henry pointed out, "It's gonna hit you a little bit different" than someone more accustomed to hearing that type of speech from the public. Henry thought it would be harder to remain calm, respectful, and professional in the face of it, while under extreme stress, if an officer was not used to that type of public reaction.

Being unfamiliar with the culture of the area and not having a relationship with the community disadvantaged officers as well. St. Louis County police do not have primary jurisdiction inside the city of Ferguson—nor did most officers working the protests. Supervisor Elijah explained the challenge, "We don't have relationships with any business owners. One thing that you try to do is have good community relationships going in [to a situation]. Well, the time to start that is not when they're all pissed off. It's not going to work . . . We tried as hard as we could. It wasn't going to work because they weren't familiar with us. Why would they trust us? That made it very difficult for us to do anything." Not having a foundation of trust and familiarity weakened the capacity of police to negotiate agreements about protest behavior.

During the protests, officers were paired with officers with whom they normally do not work (sometimes in vehicles with up to four officers). State Police troopers, being on a different radio frequency, tended to be paired with a municipality to help with communication. Officer Kathie described trying to get to know her assigned partner and what to expect on the first day that they worked together during the protests. They talked about their strengths and mannerisms when handling calls, how fast they can run, anything that might help them quickly know what to expect from the other partner. They were trying to minimize uncertainty and establish expectations quickly, so they felt comfortable relying on each other, minimizing the unpredictability of their circumstances.

Officer Henry said it is because of the diversity of officers' past experiences and backgrounds that he would have expected more knee-jerk, poor police reactions like that of a St. Ann Police lieutenant caught on video (and shared widely on social media) pointing an assault rifle at a Ferguson protestor after a verbal altercation. The officer was overwhelmed and unprepared and handled the situation incorrectly (but a St. Louis County police officer helped resolve the situation without further incident or use of force).

Department Systems Being Hacked

In addition to the demonstrations, St. Louis County Police Department also faced cyberattack. They were hacked by the group Anonymous during the first week of protests. This meant that their email systems and payroll did not function for a time, dispatchers could not send 911 call information to officers' mobile data computers, and officers could not run license plates or driver's licenses on computers in the field, hindering police effectiveness in providing services and adding to the issues police leaders faced. The group hacked 911 calls and posted them online. Individual officers received messages from Anonymous threatening to share their personal information publicly, and several police leaders and some officers did have their identities compromised. In response, officers scurried to subscribe to LifeLock™, an identity theft protection tool. It was an added strain to an already overwhelming situation.

Heterogeneity of the Crowd

Another challenge that about half of the officers (48 percent) spoke about was the heterogeneity of the protestors. Officer William said, "We looked at the crowds as one big body of people, but there were different people in there." At times, this generated tension; 47 percent of officers talked about fights between protestors due to different goals or tactics among them. It was not uncommon, according to officers, in fact somewhat routine after the first few days, said officer Thomas, for protestors to get shot by other protestors. Supervisor Gabe said that they had five shootings within five nights at one point; officer Henry had estimated that eight protestors were shot across seven nights of protest at another time. The officers were making it clear that shootings among protestors were common.

Officer Henry felt that the diversity of people at the protests differed every night. He saw residents from neighborhoods, people coming from outside the region to protest, and anarchists/agitators wearing bandanas on their faces, aiming to cause chaos. Supervisor Elijah described that there were groups committing criminal acts, assaulting officers or each other, damaging property, shooting, or throwing Molotov cocktails. Yet, in the midst of that were people expressing their First Amendment rights who were not committing violations. Another group were residents. They were coping with roadblocks and dense crowds that were impeding their ability to get to their homes, to go to work, to get groceries; their children could not safely go outside. During the unrest, supervisor Gabe told me that officers heard from residents in the area that they wanted the unrest to end, but that they were afraid to speak out in favor of ending the protests because they felt that they or their homes would be targeted. When officer Karen helped a resident who ran out of gas during the protests, the resident told her, "We're the people at home that are scared."

Perhaps because of the heterogeneity of goals in the crowd, officers saw an effort among some protestors to self-police, to calm people down and try to dispel anger and conflict, even trying to prevent looting and burning, according to officer Owen. Officers expressed appreciation for these efforts, seeing them as accommodations supporting social order. Supervisor Logan saw two key protestor groups, one being, "Your church leaders, they were kind of more, 'Hey, we understand why you guys are out here, but we shouldn't be getting violent.' Then you had your other factions out there that were, 'If you get an opportunity to shoot and kill one of these guys [police] then, you know, do it.'" Officer Theo thought the groups were generational, with the younger group causing trouble while the older group tried to intervene and focus on their social cause. Supervisor Connor noticed that in-fighting among the different protest groups became more pronounced as the grand jury verdict grew closer in November 2014, with more fistfights in the crowd, arguing about "What they wanted to do, how they wanted to do it, how they wanted to move."

The easiest solution for police would have been to ask the peaceful protestors to leave so that they could deal with the criminals without distraction, but that was not a reasonable or successful solution. This cannot work, supervisor Gabe emphasized, because one of the main reasons police were there in Ferguson was to protect the groups exercising their First Amendment rights, people who were not merely there to hurt police or others. Frustrated by the assumptions made about police at the protests, supervisor Connor said that police were not coming to work hoping to violate individuals' First Amendment rights. However, simultaneously addressing the problem behaviors and protecting peaceful protestors proved a challenging balance. To help maintain the balance, Chief Belmar's office prepared a handout for officers about the rights of protestors, according to supervisor Mason.

Daytime Protests and Nighttime Violence

Another challenging dichotomy that nearly three quarters of officers (72 percent) noted was the difference between protest behaviors during the daytime versus at night. Officers characterized daytime protests as "civilized." People, like church groups, even helped clean up the streets during the daytime. Supervisor Ben said of daytime protestors, "These people aren't going to go for that [violence]." During the daytime, police had manpower on standby at the Ferguson firehouse in case something happened, but often nothing did. Supervisor Wyatt, assigned to work the day shift, described seeing the officers coming off nights looking "beat down," and he felt guilty for not being there to help them, not having to face the same difficulties since he worked the day shift.

Officer Fred worked nights, and he described the first few hours of each shift as "waiting for the monster to wake up," which apparently happened at about 9:00 p.m. daily, according to supervisor Liam. Supervisor Ben shared, "Once it got dark, you know, you hear gunfire, you see people get more aggressive . . . people getting a little more courage, a little more angry and agitated." Officer William described it as sunset initiating the "changing of the guard" among protestors. Officers saw younger people arriving at night, wearing scarves over their faces, and carrying gas masks, goggles, and backpacks—symbols officers associated with trouble. Officer Andre thought that people viewed the nighttime as a chance to "get at police and smoke weed and do whatever you want and not get in trouble for it." Nighttime was "completely lawless," said officer Isaac. Some citizens told police officers, like officer Henry, that they did not go to protests at night because they didn't want to be in the midst of the type of persons who typically were there.

A frustration raised by one-third of police was children attending nighttime protests. Supervisor Wyatt described people pushing strollers and walking children at 10:00 at night. He questioned, "Why would you bring your kid into that crowd?" He explained his view that the children have no choice in whether to be there—their parents decide, but the children could easily be hurt, perhaps even shot. He felt that parents bringing children to the nighttime demonstrations were endangering their children's welfare. Officer Kathie echoed, "That was [like] war and for an innocent child to be down there, I mean, that's what burned me the most." As with the presence of children at nighttime protests, most of what the officers experienced during those times was interpreted through a lens of danger.

Crow Calls

Crow calls were a particular danger that posed a challenge during the protests. One in five officers (21 percent) mentioned this problem. Crow calls are fake 911 calls made to dispatch, reporting (erroneously) that someone needs medical attention (a "sick" call in police terms). However, there is no one in need of help; rather, the call is a means to draw officers into an area where members of the public wait to ambush and harm them. This issue was not limited to the protest period, as it also occurs under normal conditions, but officer Teresa claimed that crow calls were prevalent at the protests and happened several times during the first few weeks of protests. During the protests, any time police received a call for medical assistance in the apartment complex near where Brown was killed, they were concerned it was actually a crow call. Supervisor Jason described one such incident. He said,

> This crowd comes running down the hill, they're screaming "She's having a heart attack. Help her, help her. She's having a heart attack." And they are carrying this lady. So, I'm right there in the front and I'm screaming

put her down, put her down, because they're coming past the [skirmish] line . . . And as soon as they put her down, we go to pick her up. And we all bent down, there's four of us to grab her, and as soon as we did, they threw a rock, a brick through the window of one my K-9 unit cars and then tried to shoot a flare gun in there to set the inside of it on fire with the dog . . . This lady's supposedly having a heart attack, we grab her, run her into the fire department, put her inside, run back out there to the line. While we're dealing with that, she just got up inside, she goes, "Oh, I feel much better," and walked out. It was just a ruse.

In another instance, officer Teresa and several other police colleagues were shot at when responding to a request to assist an incapacitated person at the Canfield Green apartments. Officer Kathie described the fear of crow calls as exhausting—always scanning, always being on heightened alert was draining.

Safety

Nearly everyone we interviewed talked about safety during the protests, mostly about feeling unsafe, both at the protests and at home. Officers frequently reflected and expressed surprise that no officer was killed during the protests. Supervisor Elijah described this as a miracle. He said,

I can't tell you how many nights I was standing out there on the line. It's one thing when you hear gunshots from here to the businesses across the street, and they are behind corners and they are shooting rounds. But, when . . . you can hear the bullets passing your head, you are too close. With the number of people who were out there, with the number of officers that were out there, the fact that no one took a stray round, it's incredible.

Indicative of her state of safety, during the first week of the protests, officer Teresa wrote goodbye notes to her friends and family just in case something happened to her. She gave them to a friend to distribute in the event of her death. They were not needed, and officer Teresa did not tell her family that she had taken this precaution.

Many factors contributed to officers' feeling unsafe, including insufficient protective gear or being asked not to wear it, shooting and other violence from the protests, proximity and size of the protest crowds, crow calls, and general uncertainty (e.g., of their work schedules, work location, chain of command uncertainty, role confusion, duration of the protests). Officer Henry spoke of receiving intelligence during roll call about groups making threats against the police, that groups had stated their intention to shoot police. He felt especially vulnerable on the skirmish line. He said, "Some of those nights, we were sitting ducks . . . how easy it would've been for a drive-by shooting to happen." Supervisor Al said, "There was no place to take cover . . . there was no artificial barrier between the crowd and the skirmish line. It was just space. Again, no cover, no concealment, no way to protect yourself. You just had to stand there and hope that if they shot you, it was going to be in a non-vital area that was covered by protection."

Supervisor Ben said regretfully, "We kind of allowed the media to dictate us not being in riot gear, which, looking back, that was a mistake." He described standing next to a trooper on a skirmish line who got hit in the head with a beer bottle. After the attack, the trooper got up and put his sock hat back on and Ben told him, "Man, you need a helmet."

Officer William did not feel unsafe as a police officer, except for the night of the grand jury decision, when he gave himself about a 50/50 chance of making it through the shift. He described that the situation felt out of his control. "It was just complete chaos—there was no order whatsoever." Buildings were broken into, fires blazed, people drove around with masks on and guns in their hands. Supervisor Larry said that on the weekend of the grand jury verdict, his wife made him take a photo with his children before going to work just in case he did not come home.

Officers feared bringing harm to their homes and family. They described driving home from Ferguson at high speeds so that no one could follow them to their homes, where they had to leave spouses and children. Officer Anthony said that as a precaution, he slept with a rifle behind his door and a pistol on the nightstand and did not allow his child to sleep in the bedroom at the front of the house. Officers Karen and William and supervisor Larry all mentioned that during this time, they did not park their marked patrol cars in their driveways or on the street at their homes. Officer William started keeping a shotgun by the front door of his home and carrying a gun off duty. The feeling of danger officers described was persistent on the job and off.

Officer Fatigue

Given the suddenness, intensity, and longevity of the Ferguson protests, a clear challenge that police faced was fatigue, with no opportunity to recover. The challenge was pervasive, reported by 80 percent of police who worked the protests. Officers did not have days off and worked long days, perhaps 12-, to as much as 16-hour days, even 20–22 hours long a few times, in the first weeks of the protest. Officers spoke of getting only one to four hours of sleep each day. Supervisor Gabe likened it to playing sports, "This is like running gassers or sprints and your coach just keeps blowing the whistle. Do it again, do it again, do it again . . . And it's like, you're kidding me, more?" During August, the weather was hot and humid with temperatures approaching 100 degrees Fahrenheit during the day. They also had days of standing in the rain for hours and hours, getting soaked. There was "so much stimulus, all the time," explained supervisor Mason. As his simile above about running sprints suggests, Gabe felt there was no recovery time and "no end in sight for a while . . . I was fine and then you hit the wall. And again, we've never been through this before, we didn't know how long it was going to last." Every day, they kept thinking, this has to be the last day. Officer Henry and officer Levi both said that not knowing how long the protests would last was the most stressful part of policing the protests.

Wendy described going home one day, taking a shower, and passing out. She was able to get herself over the side of the bathtub onto the floor, but she just laid there for about an hour—not having enough strength to get up and go to bed. She was totally depleted. Wendy described, at the command post, watching officers leave the command post for their shift, "full, happy, cool, and they come back exhausted, dirty, some of them bleeding, red eyed from the mace."

Supervisor Dylan described officers on the line: "It [the strain] was definitely showing." Lucas, also a supervisor, stated, "They looked half dead." Exhaustion and stress turned to physical and emotional ailments. Burnout affected morale. Sixty percent of officers either lost or gained a significant amount of weight during the protests in August and early September 2014. Officers walked eight to ten miles daily in some cases, and ate fiber bars, McDonalds, White Castle, Gatorade, soda, and Monsters to keep going. It was not a healthy diet, just what was available to eat quickly. Despite feeling exhausted, more than a quarter of police (28 percent) talked about insomnia, feeling both exhausted and amped-up at the same time. Officer Fred said that every time he closed his eyes, he would hear gunshots, fires, screaming, and just noise, and he had vivid dreams when he finally could sleep. It was not restful. Officers spoke of having trouble with their backs, hearts, and blood pressure. Some officers spoke of drinking more to calm down, while others even started to smoke. Supervisor Oliver contracted pneumonia during the protests. It was not a healthy time for officers.

Challenges at Home

In addition to facing challenges while at the protests in Ferguson, officers spoke of the challenges the protests raised for their home lives. Officers with small children expressed some of the greatest difficulty of managing home life during the protests. Police told us that during the initial three weeks, because of the long days without time off, other family members had to take full responsibility for family tasks: caring for children, the home, the bills, even if they too worked full time. Officer Lisa was married to another county police officer (one of four couples she could recall who were both county officers at that time). Although both she and her husband had work responsibilities in Ferguson, she found herself following the gender stereotype and cleaning the house, buying groceries, doing laundry—getting much less sleep than her spouse.

Officers felt the emotional strain on and for their families. Supervisor Hugh warned, "You will never be able to explain what it took to get in your car and leave your family behind not knowing if tonight is going to be the night that someone drives up or walks up on you and blows you away." Family members felt this trepidation as well. Police officers' spouses, siblings, children, and other family members found themselves hooked on watching the news coverage and social media livestreams of the protests at length, trying to get information about their police officer while he or she was working at the protests. Officer Kathie said that her dad just could not stop watching CNN, even though he hated CNN, because of his worry for her—trying to catch a glimpse of her on the news. Supervisor Noah's wife had explained to him about her media fixation, "You have to understand, I am craving information." Supervisor Connor had a tech-savvy teen who downloaded an application to her phone so that she could listen to their radio channel. He described sitting in the back of an armored truck as bullets pinged off. On the radio they got on and said, "We're taking shots," and within about 30 seconds' time, his phone pinged with a text from his daughter asking if he was okay. Officer Anthony described taking a call at the precinct from the mother of a fellow officer who asked of him, "Can you keep my child safe?" Anthony said that this mother felt hopeless and was afraid of losing her only son. Officer Fred said that at first he just did not really appreciate the strain until his wife told him when he was leaving late in the first week of protests, "You have no idea do you? . . . Every day when you leave during this, . . . I'm saying goodbye to you for the last time." Fred told a story about when he was preparing to respond to a call about the officer shot near the Ferguson police station (March 2015). He called his wife to let her know that she would not be able to reach him for a while—so that she would not worry. However, in his haste, he did not hit the end button to the call. She later told him, "I couldn't hang up, but then I didn't wanna hear you get shot." When he heard this, he felt so awful for putting her through that stress. Officer Kathie avoided talking to family while on duty, not wanting to have a conversation interrupted by a call to handle something dangerous. Of course, that lack of contact during the shift plus no time to engage with family during the 10–12 hours off shift was difficult on officers and their families.

As chapter 3 discusses, Black officers often had a different experience with their families; they were not consistently supportive. Black supervisor Jacob understood that family members or friends viewed Brown's shooting through their personal experiences with racism, including racism from police, rather than as an isolated incident. But, Black supervisor Caleb felt disappointed with family members. He thought they would be supportive since he was a police officer, but the experience taught him that many family members did not like police. Supervisor Logan, also Black, described a family staunchly divided in support of police versus vehemence toward police during the protests. Supervisor Hugh said his sister and her daughters, who are proud of him being a police officer, walked in protest with their church in Ferguson. He questioned, "What are they marching for? Do they understand what's going on?" He described that it was difficult hearing the pastor of the Black church they attended praying for the protestors and saying that the police officers need to repent. He was frustrated by the judgment that the church expressed. Hugh felt as if in the course of the protests, the one thing that officers could turn to was their faith, and he was angry and hurt that the church had turned against police. While he retained his faith in God, supervisor Hugh did not go back to that same church after the protests. Supervisor Jason, who is White, also spoke about going to church during the protests. He described feeling terrified, sitting in the pew, being unclear about what the message would be and feeling like he could be condemned. Yet, there was not an anti-police narrative in the sermon. When the pastor prayed for the Brown family, he understood that, explaining, "It was a tragedy."

The children of the police had their own protest experiences. Supervisor Jason said that schools near Ferguson held Michael Brown events. Students at his son's school walked the halls and chanted during the entire last school period one day. Officer Kathie said her teenage daughter really had a difficult time with kids at school making nasty comments about police. Kathie's daughter was furious at the public, telling her, "How could they say these things about you . . . All you want to do is help people, and you're such good people, and they're lying and making up all these things." Officer Alexander told his teenage daughter to stay off social media and not to engage in discussion about the protests—not to say anything, but just to let people have their say. Supervisor Jason gave his middle- and high school-aged children the same advice.

Officers repeatedly expressed concern for their families' safety during the protests. Officer Fred told me of working with a state trooper, when the trooper's wife called him in a panic, yelling, "They're in our yard! They're in our yard!" referring to protestors. Fred stated, in awe, that state troopers are like robots, they do not get rattled, but in that moment, he saw a state trooper get rattled. Officer Levi worried when a protestor had stolen a backpack from his police car and it had a driver's license with his father's address on it, which led to concern for his dad's safety. Supervisor Wyatt described the discomfort he felt with people putting nasty things in his personal mailbox, rubbing things on the mailbox handle, and even dumping bags of leaves on his lawn and un-marked police vehicle.

In the midst and aftermath of the Ferguson protests, officers ad-opted numerous personal security measures to protect themselves and family members. These included suspending their Facebook accounts or using pseudonyms, adding cameras and locks to their homes, driv-ing excessively fast on the way home from work in an attempt to avoid being followed, parking patrol vehicles in garages instead of on the street or visible in the driveway, removing their name plates from their uniforms—eventually replacing them with numbers, carrying a gun off duty, changing out of uniform before going to the grocery store, even shopping in a different geographic area than normal, having children sleep in their parent's room or at the back of the house rather than in a front bedroom, and not allowing children to wear clothing that might associate them with police. In a move to protect officers' privacy, St. Louis County Police Department provided information and websites for officers to use to protect their identities, and the county removed officers' names from the real estate database searches. Officer Nathan said of the Ferguson protest experience, "There's a war on the police and if you're a police officer you have to realize that it's not just on duty, it's also off duty too."

Tactics to Handle the Unrest

Police tactics attempted to face the challenges they encountered. The choice of tactics was a process of learning, of trial and error. Chief Bel-mar said, "Certain things worked at certain times, but they didn't work at other times." Officer Henry felt that leadership in the department kept striving to improve their response. He said, "I think our command staff and police department did an amazing job of realizing what we needed to change all the way up to, even our anniversary weekend." However, one consequence of the changing tactics meant that officers did not know where they would be positioned or what they would face on the job. They did not know what to expect or how to mentally and physically prepare, according to supervisor Dylan. Officer Jack talked about the emotional challenge of the shifting approaches. He felt as if "the mission changed several times" and struggled with the uncertainty this created.

Officers' descriptions of their protest tactics incorporated use of skirmish lines, riot gear, surveillance and arrest teams, tear gas, working with the clergy, engaging with protestors, and working with the media. Reflecting on the tactics used, officer Caleb said, "The stuff that we did was not only to protect officers, but to also protect the public."

Skirmish Lines

Skirmish lines were adopted as a tactic from the beginning of the demonstrations, as early as the investigation into Brown's death. Officers described lines of as few as six to as many as 25–30 officers who stood on the line, hypervigilant about their surroundings—observing the crowd and passing any intelligence to the command post. At times, officers stood on a line for 1–5 hours, until being relieved, although as time passed, switching out became more frequent to protect officer well-being.

Skirmish lines were used to protect specific areas, such as the investigation area, businesses, or the Ferguson Police Department, or to move or contain crowds. Officers stood in between the protected space and the crowd. Officer Levi described how a skirmish line was used to help rescue a young girl from her car. He described the mindset of the girl, that she

> is slowly coming towards the protestors thinking, "There's a car coming, they're probably gonna move for me." I guess she didn't realize that they just don't move. So, she drives forward and has to eventually stop because no one is moving, and they end up surrounding the car, and they start beating on it. So, the point where it is surrounded, we can't see the car anymore, and she's calling 911 from inside the car. I could hear it on Ferguson's dispatch and they're saying, "She's terrified. She can't get out. They're beating on the car." So, we eventually go out there with a skirmish line and shove everyone back from the car.

In the beginning, some officers were unclear about their role on the skirmish line, saying, "We just knew that there was a bunch of angry people there and we're supposed to stand there, but we didn't know what the end game was or what the goal was." For much of the unrest, there was nothing in between the officers and the crowds, just space, and oftentimes, only inches. Supervisor Larry said it felt "like setting officers up in a shooting gallery."

Officers on the skirmish line were instructed not to interact with the crowd. Officer Caleb said that he wanted to "go unnoticed," because the crowd was yelling at officers "just trying to get officers to react in such a way that it would get captured on camera." Officers talked most about the challenge of standing on the line and not letting the protestors' insults and aggression get to them. Officer William said, "We were basically a wall for people to bounce their frustrations off of." Supervisor Jason heard people shouting about killing the officers and officers' families and tolerating hostile verbal abuse for hours at a time from two or three feet away. Supervisor Al said that often, vocal protestors would stand in front of a female police officer on the line and say vulgar and vile sexual things to them, that if those things had been said to his wife or daughter in a different context, "It'd be on. Fist city, but we couldn't do that."

Supervisor Oliver favored putting former military personnel on the skirmish line because he felt as if they were better equipped to handle it mentally, having been deployed to Iraq or Afghanistan. I was able to study this, having surveyed officers who conducted protest policing in Ferguson and also having asked them about their prior military experiences. Analyses showed that police who had previously served in the military (25 percent of police taking the survey reported prior military experience) were significantly less likely than officers without military experience (1) to agree that as stress compounded during the protests, they felt tired and had less energy; (2) to feel as if their stress slowed their reflexes and physical responses; and (3) to report problems with concentration. However, officers with prior military service were neither more nor less likely than those without military experience to feel capable of behaving professionally at all times, operating under the standard procedures of the department, of being impartial and fair in a variety of situations, or being able to show restraint and apply no more force than necessary during the protests. So, while officers with military experience appeared to feel less personally affected by stress in terms of their

TABLE 1.1 Mann-Whitney U Tests: Officers with Military Experience versus Officers Without

During the height of the protests in Ferguson . . .	Mann-Whitney U	Z
Capability of controlling yourself and acting professionally at all times	4788	0.050
Capability of upholding the qualities and standards of the St. Louis County Police Department	4735	0.211
Capability of being impartial and fair no matter what situation was presented	4712	0.251
Capability of restraining yourself from using no more force than the situation called for	4773	0.108
When I faced a stressful situation, I felt confident in my abilities	4426	1.097
After a prolonged stressful situation, I still felt confident in my capabilities	4568	0.678
During this time, as stress compounded, I felt tired and had less energy sooner than normal	3983	2.032*
During this time, as stress compounded, my reflexes and physical responses were slower than usual	3648	2.843**
I had poor levels of concentration	3838	2.337*

NOTE: $*p \leq .05$, $**p \leq .01$.

physical and mental capabilities, this did not translate into differences in their ability to act appropriately while on the skirmish lines relative to officers without military experience. The results of this analysis appear in table 1.1.

Restraint was how officers described their actions on the skirmish line (e.g., Fred), trying to be stoic and not react. Officer Owen said, "I am stronger than they are. They're not going to break me. That's not going to happen." Despite incidents like the one described by officer Fred, where a man stood six to eight inches from Fred's face and screamed into a bullhorn, "White devil. Racist White devil," officers explained that they realized the protestors were trying to win the public opinion battle and that their tone on the line had to be professional no matter what the protestors were doing, providing evidence of the value of procedural justice, or at least of not being unjust.

Officers and supervisors spoke at length about the mental challenge of being calm, professional, and passive on the skirmish line, and about being aware of the likelihood of being captured on cell phone footage. Officer Sebastian said it was the hardest thing about the protests. Officer

Theo explained, "It is mentally heavy on you, especially when you got people shining lights in your face and the big spotlights and everything, shining them in your face and yelling at you . . . That would give me a headache, no matter what." Officer Anthony told much the same story, describing, "You're just stuck out there, and these people were spitting on us and then here come the bottles of whatever, you know, and then the chants . . . and then the drum . . . the smells of the heat, you know, the screaming, car horns blowing, the shots, the radio traffic, all of it, and it was just bombarding you."

Supervisors kept a close watch over officers on the line, pulling them off the line and giving officers a break or replacing them if they appeared to be overwhelmed by the abuse. Eventually, police realized the value of placing more space between the protestors and the police on the skirmish lines and used barriers (e.g., bike racks, police vehicles, even police tape for a few days) to widen the reactionary gap to 10 or 15 feet. Supervisor Larry explained that both protestors and police needed the boundaries to ease the tensions.

Officer Levi expressed a view different from many of his police colleagues, questioning the use of skirmish lines. He pondered whether it gave protestors a target, saying, "If we weren't out there, there's no one to yell at." Levi said that in a few instances, the police set up barricades, stepped back, and were available in case something happened, rather than forming a skirmish line. He thought the response, at least a few times, was that the crowd was smaller. He said, "There would be some people who would go right up to the barricades and kind of test the waters and sit on there. And then someone would kind of step outside for a second, because they felt tough. So, they sat there for like another minute or two, but then eventually just got up and walked away or went back into the crowd." He took this as a sign that some police actions could provoke protestors or at least provide the necessary elements for civil disturbance, and therefore saw the value of soft tactics.

Riot Gear

Officer Anthony repeated a chant that Ferguson protestors used, "Why are you wearing the riot gear? Because I don't see a riot here." Officers, especially those on the skirmish lines, were cognizant of whether they were being permitted to use riot gear or had to stand there in the standard uniform. The Ferguson protests were the first time that supervisor Al recalls putting on riot gear to use in public. Riot gear included helmets with face masks, vests, batons, riot shields, and sometimes gas masks. Although unhappy about it, officer Ryan explained that the rationale favoring minimal use of riot gear is that officers wearing riot gear appear "geared up and looking for a fight" and this might "instigate" protestors into an aggressive response. For this reason, Chief Belmar opted against officers wearing riot gear at the outset of the protests. The idea was to wait until it was needed. Of course, officers, like Nathan, complained that "If it gets to that, then it's too late, because then they're already throwing the objects, which means they're already hitting you, and now we're going to have to run back and get the gear."

The struggle over riot gear use is a conflict between intention and interpretation (see figure 1.2). Police wore riot gear with the intent of proactively ensuring their safety, whereas protestors felt intimidated because they interpreted this action as aggression toward them, and they reacted to that perspective. This proved an important interactive dynamic in Ferguson, and police wearing riot gear featured prominently in the news coverage. A study by Arora and colleagues (2019) supports the idea that the way the media frames the police response to protest can influence the extent to which constituencies view the police response as legitimate, as well as the nature of subsequent legislation about policing—whether it facilitates police autonomy or tightens the regulations governing police conduct and oversight of police.

Although Chief Belmar was initially reluctant to deploy riot gear in Ferguson, officer Henry also recalled the chief expressing frustration with the media when they featured officers using riot shields and helmets, proclaiming the militarization of police, instead of featuring the shots fired by protestors that same evening. He recalled the chief commenting at a press conference, "When's the last time a riot helmet hurt anybody?" Officer Fred said, "Me putting on riot gear is the same as someone putting on a coat when it's snowing or cold. It's there to protect you. . . . Okay, it looks scary. That's the number one thing on the use of force spectrum is use of officer presence. If you have a bunch of scary looking dudes in badass uniforms it's gonna make some people be like 'Okay, we're gonna go home now.'" The sentiment behind "scary looking dudes in badass uniforms" reflects Muir's (1977) paradox of face. The paradox of face explains that the nastier the reputation of police, the less nasty police must behave to secure compliance. Applied here, police portray a violent and brutal appearance wearing their riot gear to instill the impression on protestors that police are tough and prepared to act violently. Their apparent bluster causes the protestors to choose not to act, so police in turn do not take any further action to instill peace and order.

When the Highway Patrol assumed command, Captain Ron Johnson asked that officers take off the riot equipment, believing it infuriated the crowd. When supervisor Noah was told to put away the riot gear because it "is too much and amping things up," his response was, "Really? I thought it was protecting me?" He felt frustrated saying, "It's like, do you realize, we are taking bricks and rock?" Sometimes, officers in the field felt as if the departmental image or police image received priority over their safety. Officer Leo told me that he felt that the public did not care about the officers, complaining that officers were "too military." His response to this view was, "Well, yeah, we have to, because they are using military grade weapons against us." Officer Nathan said, "I don't think command has any idea how close they were to having most people say, 'Well, I'm not going up there [to the protests in Ferguson],' because a lot of people were saying that 'If they're not going to give us gear, we're not going up there.' Officers felt they had a right to feel safe on the job."

Tear Gas

A protest tactic that received considerable focus in the media and among protestors as heavy-handed or militaristic was the use of CS gas, tear gas. Supervisor Al described their use of tear gas as the most aggressive approach that they used during the protests. By its nature, it is a diffuse approach—applied broadly rather than to targeted individuals. Even so, to some police, this response seemed insufficient given the situational context. Supervisor Gabe, exasperated, exclaimed, "For God sakes, we're shooting tear gas and they're shooting real bullets at us."

Responding to critiques in the media and by high-profile political figures, supervisors told us that the police tried to minimize their use of tear gas and maintain a low profile for their tactical unit (only the tactical unit deployed tear gas). Despite a prevalence of media photos depicting tear gas use, police said that they viewed tear gas as a last resort. When talking about using tear gas, supervisor Luke said, "The rule was, from day one, and always has been, we are not doing anything proactive or aggressive to this crowd until we are met with some sort of aggression." Officers described using tear gas for situations like the gunfire at Red's BBQ, to disperse that crowd. (Additional details about this incident, provided by officer Henry, appear in chapter 2, under the heading "Feeling Betrayed by the Media.")

Logistical challenges arose with tear gas use. Although officers in St. Louis County (but not necessarily all other departments assisting) had been issued gas masks, as officer Jack described it, they did not expect to use that equipment and so they "laid buried in a trunk in your basement." Officer Kathie's gas mask was missing a filter and did not work. As supervisor Jason explained, "When the tear gas goes into the crowd, we get it too." For him, he felt burning in his armpits. He also described that despite cleaning his gas mask with alcohol, when he put it on, he felt a burning sensation because the mask was contaminated. Yet, he and others we interviewed, like Ben, felt that CS gas was an important tactic to use because it was a way to disperse a hostile crowd or move it back without anybody getting seriously hurt. Without the gas, supervisor Jacob told us,

> The only things that we have left to utilize are the sandbag bullets, the less lethal shotgun, batons, pepper spray, and if it gets to that point, you know, lethal force. So, we really don't want to go there. So, if we can have a crowd disperse in a short period of time, [and] they experience some irritability, that is a whole lot better than someone having to shoot somebody, because once you [protestors] get to throwing Molotov cocktails, that's a deadly force situation.

That was an important point officers made repeatedly—that although frequently the situational conditions allowed for lethal force, police did not use it. Supervisor Elijah said so many people asked him how police were able to avoid using lethal force against demonstrators and he responded, "The only answer that we could come up with was by the grace of God."

Refrain from Action

Police in Ferguson described how they frequently alternated between hard and soft tactics, from enforcing the law to stepping back and allowing criminal acts to occur. Just over half of police (51 percent) brought this up during their interviews. Officer Karen said of responding to looting, we had to respond, and "either A, could take action, or B, we're not supposed to take action." In other words, their approach kept changing. Chief Constable Will Kerr of the Scottish Police, in a 2021 webinar for police about managing demonstrations, described the need for command staff to have "strategic patience," explaining that while policing unrest, the focus needs to be on the key priorities for the next 30 minutes—short term and focused (Police Executive Research Forum 2021), providing a rationale behind changing course. Much of the time, officers were instructed to show restraint, according to supervisor Ben. It was a difficult decision for the scene commanders, he said, whether to make arrests. When police elected to stand down, supervisor Al said that they had hoped the crowd would "burn themselves out." Intentionally doing nothing can be a valid response, and as mentioned at the beginning of this chapter, has been a common response by police at protests (della Porta and Reiter 1998; Earl, Soule, and McCarthy 2003). The strategy aligns with the paradox of detachment principle. Police tried to diminish the value to the protestors of looting by giving protestors the impression that police were not concerned about or did not prioritize protecting properties against this (Muir 1977). The principle, as applied to looting, assumes, however, that protestors viewed looting as a tactic applied against police or to bring attention to the social cause, rather than merely for personal gain (theft). Officer Owen appreciated that, "There's no right way to handle that," explaining that if looters are left alone, it could be empowering, and business owners and residents may become upset when their property is destroyed, but if police come down firmly on looters, people will complain of police brutality.

Officers felt highly conflicted when they were ordered not to enforce the law, and I discuss this further in chapter 2, in the section "Police Role as Crime Fighter." Officers wrestled with the challenge described by Egon Bittner (1970) and Carl Klockars (1985) of needing to use force to create order, but also needing to restrain the use of force in order to be perceived as legitimate by the public. Officer Anthony described that people came at police officers trying to attack them, but the motive was not necessarily to harm the police, but rather, "they were trying to ruin our reputation. They were trying to make us look bad," by instigating a forceful response. From this view, it seemed police felt that the protestors recognized the full value of police legitimacy and used its value as a tool to bring attention to their concerns about police discrimination and misbehavior. To preserve legitimacy and order, police needed to be fully prepared and willing to use force, and yet hesitate to do so.

Surveillance and Arrest Teams

After the first few days of protest, police began getting intelligence about the agitators, and they were able to organize enough to use arrest teams to go into the crowd and make targeted arrests, according to supervisor Connor. Officers went into the crowd or to protestor meetings in plain clothes, undercover, to gather real-time information. Once the undercover officers identified individuals who were causing the most problems and inciting violence, they relayed the information to arrest teams of five officers, who went into the crowd to arrest them. Initially the county command staff had considered only deploying two-person arrest teams, but they felt that they could not make targeted arrests safely in a large crowd with fewer than five officers. (Other safety concerns included whether to arm the undercover police officers and how to arrange an escape plan should they be identified as police.) This was a targeted approach. Officer Levi said they would arrest three to ten people in a group of 300 or 400 people. During the shutdown of a highway by protestors, they arrested many more, about 150 in total, but that high volume was atypical. Supervisor Hugh noted, "Once we started actually arresting people and they [protestors] saw that we were arresting people, we got a different response [from protestors]."

A targeted approach to managing a subset of violent individuals within the crowd and thus protecting the rights of the majority to demonstrate was a key theme discussed during a 2021 Police Executive Research Forum (PERF) webinar about policing demonstrations (Police Executive Research Forum 2021). Amnesty International's Senior Crisis Advisor, Brian Castner, a speaker at the event, described it as a "win" when police can prioritize maximizing the number of people permitted to exercise their protest rights in a safe way because police take a focused approach against those attempting to disrupt the protest and engage in violence and destruction. In the webinar, speakers advocated for tailored approaches like sending officers into the crowd to arrest violent individuals versus indiscriminate use of tear gas to disperse crowds.

A related challenge that police faced at the Ferguson protests, however, was how to charge arrestees, because the prosecutor repeatedly dropped the charges due to jurisdiction problems—with state, county, and city officers operating within Ferguson. Police struggled with trying to choose the correct charges to file (e.g., city ordinance, state law, county). After the initial intense period of unrest, to help address the problem, St. Louis County police created a card that had information for officers, including the charges they should use during an arrest.

Involving Clergy

Clergy engagement was another tactic used during the unrest. Not every example of clergy or church involvement was favorable toward police—one church reportedly catered to protestors, said supervisor Hugh. I talk more about this in chapter 2. However, largely, officers spoke about their positive involvement. The clergy showed up day after day with members of their churches, and they cleaned up trash and debris in the streets. They led vigils and marches. Supervisor Oliver said he proactively contacted clergy and other community leaders to share information about what was going on during the protests, hoping that accurate information would be shared with constituents.

Supervisor Dylan talked about how clergy, on their own initiative, came out and talked with the crowd and even prayed for the police. Dylan credits the presence of the clergy as delivering dual benefits: (1) helping members of the crowd to recognize violence was not the best approach, and (2) conveying to police that people still cared about them, a perspective that he felt police had lost in Ferguson. Dylan shared a story from the first weeks of unrest about when three or four clergy approached police and asked if they could pray for the police. He saw officers look at each other and knew that they were thinking, "Should we let them? Should we close our eyes?" His view, he said, was "When you're

God-fearing and you love Christ, you know, at that time, that God is not gonna let anything happen to you if you're praying to him. So, we were able to close our eyes and let these clergy people pray." While I cannot be sure it was the same instance, supervisor Joseph also described a time when four clergy approached a group of eight to ten police and offered to pray for them. With surprise, he told me that, "The next thing you know, we have people who are actually protesting come over, holding hands with police, holding hands with the clergy."

Speaking of the clergy, supervisor Dylan said,

> It made a difference to them [police], because it was like, it's a prayer of protection, and there were people out giving little St. Michaels medals and things like that, and you could see the officers take them, put them in their pocket. You saw some officers take the little medals and put them in their vest cover just for protection. You know, just, prayer was a good, a good solution for a lot of things when this was going on.

Supervisor Connor said that one important role that clergy voluntarily undertook was as liaison with protestors. He described that when officers stood on a skirmish line, a dozen or so clergy would stand together about 15 or 20 yards from that line, in between the crowd and the police. They served as a buffer. Sometimes police appealed to the clergy to convince people to leave, and that did happen, occasionally. Officer Nathan said of the clergy, "They would work with us to help the situation. Those were really the only people out there that were trying to keep everything peaceful and not violent."

St. Louis County Police Department has a chaplain program. During the protests, there were two chaplains available at the command post. According to supervisor Elijah, the chaplain prayed over the officers at each shift, before they deployed. This is not a standard practice, but Elijah told me he anticipated that if I asked every police officer who was there about that practice, 90 percent would say, "That was huge. It didn't matter if it was a rabbi or a Muslim or a Catholic, the fact that we all got together, bowed our heads for a minute and prayed for safety really is just huge." Supervisor Dylan agreed. He thought the chaplains' presence and prayers and discussions with officers diminished officer stress.

Chaplains remained on hand at the command post for officers to talk to. According to supervisor Elijah, many of them had backgrounds in mental health.

Engaging with the Protestors

A few police leaders spoke of engaging directly with protestors during the protests. This aspect of engagement was not an organized tactic deployed by the department, but rather something that a few leaders did in the hope of making an impact. Chief Belmar was proactive in walking among the crowd, trying to measure the pulse of the crowd and shaking hands—he estimated that he easily shook 10,000 hands in the first few weeks. He made it a routine to begin about 7:00 or 7:30 p.m., and he walked down West Florissant and Canfield Drive and back, talking to people, shaking hands, and having his picture taken with members of the public. He recalled talking with one older couple who said that they lived in the community. The wife said to him, "We all knew who you were when you first started doing this, your walking and talking, but you didn't know us. And now you know us too. That's really cool." When I asked the chief why he did this, he said he just thought it was the right thing to do, to go down and meet people. He said, "I thought that they were there for the right reasons, and I think they were owed an explanation from the police department, and I think I should make myself available to answer any questions that they had." It was during his time among the crowd that Chief Belmar had the opportunity to meet Sister Ebo (Sister Mary Antona Ebo, a Civil Rights activist who attended the Selma March in Alabama in 1965). He spoke reverently about her, likening meeting her to meeting Mother Theresa. Chief Belmar was pleased to have Sister Ebo tell him that she was praying for the police at the protests. He described the moment as "extraordinary." Of his experiences walking among the crowd, he said, "It taught us [him and other command staff with the department] how, in difficult positions, to put yourself out there."

Supervisor Larry said that while his officers stood on a skirmish line, he tended to approach the barricades and talk to protestors, giving them someone specific to hear their perspective. He first did this when he feared that an incident was about to happen. He interjected himself in an effort to defuse and prevent a problem. Then, he continued to do it. He managed to learn the names of many of the regular protestors and even forged some relationships. This approach appeared successful to him. He found that people wanted to talk with him. It is a good example of a shift from a confrontational to consensual communication approach, described at the beginning of this chapter.

It was through talking with a protestor on about the fourth or fifth night that supervisor Dylan said he came to better understand what led people to protest in Ferguson. The older man shared with Dylan his prior experiences with Ferguson Police, claiming that well before Brown was killed, Ferguson Police were verbally disrespectful to people and gave out many traffic tickets. He felt that Black residents were not treated well in Ferguson. The man told Dylan that he thought Brown's death would serve a higher purpose, "That this young man gave his life up for a reason." It helped Dylan to apply a rationale for why protestors had reacted so strongly to Brown's death. The discussion also foreshadowed things to come—that much more social action was to follow after that fourth or fifth night.

Some line officers spoke about initiating contact with protestors as well. Officer William said that he experienced a shift in mindset while policing the protests. He realized that he needed to "Put away the rifle, put everything back and go back to just talking to people, and even though they disagreed with what I was saying, using verbal skills and being calm. By being calm myself, I was able to calm groups down."

Supervisor Luke said he talked to people one-on-one to humanize police, to show people that he has a family, goes to church, goes to the grocery store, and cuts the grass. He hoped that people would see him as another person in the same society who also has a job as a police officer. His approach was to target talking to "the middle-ground" people—not the people who thought very highly of police or thought very poorly of police, rather those that fell in the middle and could lean either way.

After the first intense weeks of protest, beginning in September and October 2014, the US Department of Justice Community Relations Service organized meetings with local community leaders—like pastors of large churches, elected officials, and police leaders, trying to establish communication, address conflict, and build relationships. However, they did not achieve much, thought police leadership. Police leaders we talked to felt that some components in the meeting were just too divisive to overcome. Eventually, according to police leaders, attendance at the meetings became more focused and the meetings became more fruitful.

WORKING WITH THE MEDIA

St. Louis County police also engaged with the media, primarily trying to alter the media portrayal of police during the protests. Officer Jack thought that the department had not fully appreciated how important it was to stay on top of the media message and to quickly release information. Officer William agreed that they did not do a good job of "putting out our side of the story." That is a problem; Chief Belmar said, "If you're going to be good at anything, be good at how to deal with the media."

Two approaches that police we interviewed spoke about included holding press conferences to share information and allowing the media to accompany police. At times, the approaches that were meant to re-focus the optics in the media (e.g., show the violence police faced from demonstrators) created some tension among police. Since the media were unable to see every event as police do, police leadership attempted to visually depict the serious nature of some of the events, like an incident with armed men in a truck throwing a Molotov cocktail. Officer Henry said that police had been tipped about a truck or SUV at the protest that was purported to contain people with guns who had threatened to kill police officers. The truck believed to be involved was spotted, so a trained sniper sat on top of an armored vehicle to provide coverage against a potential attack. However, the media showed images of the sniper on top of the vehicle and this raised large-scale critiques about the militarization of police. An effort to counteract the bad press was to give the media visual access to evidence like the Molotov cocktail and guns (Given the interactional dynamic of protest policing, it would be enlightening to determine whether this is the same incident reported by the passenger of a truck in Cobbina and colleagues' [2019: 422] study interviewing Ferguson protestors. They quote a "revolutionary" Black activist who said he was "only peaceful protesting," saying that officers thought he and others in the truck had a Molotov cocktail and pulled an "AK-47," and put it to his head). On one hand, police leadership recognized how showing the evidence to the public via the media could shift the public perspective, but some line-level personnel felt pressured to protect the chain of evidence to be able to make a good case before the court. Lincoln complained that media people touched evidence, police tried to access incident scenes before they were fully processed, and leaders from other departments asked for crime scene photographs—all irregularities. Working with the media was challenging. Chapter 2 provides more in-depth coverage of officers' experiences with and opinions about the media.

Rationale for Protest Policing Tactics

Officer Malorie said that police changed tactics day to day. Her impression was consistent with the message I heard from Chief Belmar, that command staff were trying new approaches when what they had previously done had not worked. Officer Isaac astutely observed, "We couldn't come together on a balance to how we can let people protest and exercise their first amendment rights versus also keeping the peace and maintain the stability of the area." That was the essence of the police challenge. Almost 20 percent of officers proactively brought to my attention that police were in Ferguson to protect people's First Amendment rights. Supervisor Elijah said, "It didn't matter whether I agree with them or not, they had the right to be there and voice their opinions." The struggle was how police could ensure that right while also keeping officers and the public safe.

Apparent across numerous protest policing tactics, as told by officers, were efforts to inject procedural justice. Procedural justice tactics strive to give people the impression that they are treated fairly and with respect and that decisions that affect them have been made without bias, and based on facts. There is strong support in research showing an association between perceptions of procedural justice and individuals' willingness to cooperate with and support police, and even to obey the law (Kochel 2018a; Tyler 2006; Bradford et al. 2014; Sunshine and Tyler 2003; Murphy and Cherney 2012). Therefore, it was in the best interests of police to do all that they could to deliver procedurally just tactics in Ferguson.

Protestors view aggressive or punitive police tactics as unjust (Maguire et al. 2018). Protestors' accounts in Ferguson and Baltimore suggested that they were aggrieved by being surveilled, arrested, by "verbal assault," and by coercive action by police, and that these strategies undermined police legitimacy in the minds of activists (Cobbina et al. 2019). Research in Israel showed that police using tear gas, rubber bullets, and perceived military tactics (e.g., armored vehicles or uniforms) undermines procedural justice and alienates police from citizens (Perry, Jonathan-Zamir, and Weisburd 2017). Studies of the Occupy protests in the United States found that when protestors felt that police unjustly used force, they were more willing to engage in violence and to support the use of violence against police, as well as to support vandalism as a reasonable form of protest (Snipes, Maguire, and Tyler 2019; Maguire et al. 2020). Cobbina and colleagues' (2019: 422) interviews with Ferguson protestors led them to conclude that protestors viewed repressive police tactics as extreme and unacceptable, and they incited anger and animosity toward law enforcement. As one protestor ("Reuben") put it, "It made people want to basically attack them [the police]. That's what their reaction was when people was throwing tear gas back at them . . . For every action there is an equally or better, greater reaction."

Although police tactics in Ferguson included tear gas, bean bag bullets, armored vehicles, tactical uniforms, and riot gear, which research suggests invokes a sense of injustice, coupled with these strategies, police talked about engaging with citizens to let them air their views and concerns, about explaining police actions, minimizing untargeted aggressive responses, and holding press conferences and using social media to share information and be transparent with the public. Another way procedural justice appeared in police accounts in Ferguson was hearing immediate supervisors talk about how subordinates approached them and acknowledged when they could not go back on the skirmish line in Ferguson and treat people with respect and professionalism. Officers who had reached their personal limits acknowledged that, "You won't want me back up there, because I'll say or do something that will bring discredit to our department, so just let me sit this one out for awhile." Supervisor Lucas said numerous sergeants had this experience and accommodated the officers with the goal of professional police behavior in Ferguson.

Supervisor Gabe spoke at length about the importance of following policy, guidelines, the law, policing "the way we are supposed to," and treating citizens with respect. He said, "I did my job by the way that I believed it needed to be done, following those rules, and I didn't do anything wrong . . . It's going to work out," he thought. "They may not like the outcomes sometimes, but I think they'll understand." He relied on the idea grounded in procedural justice that proper treatment by police will earn respect for police authority, even if protestors or others do not like the outcomes that they receive.

Community Callout

Nearly all county residents (98 percent) surveyed during September and October 2014 were familiar with Brown's shooting, and 76 percent reported that the shooting and protests impacted them. Almost half of residents (43 percent) said that the shooting and protests impacted them in multiple ways, including positive, negative, and neutral impacts.

Several residents that we spoke to knew Michael Brown or members of his family, and so in that way there was a personal impact. Even people who did not personally know the family expressed feeling empathy and sympathy. One mother said, "As a mother of four sons, I am touched by it deeply. I can certainly feel for the mother of Michael Brown." Another resident also said, "I felt so bad for his mom. It could have been handled better."

However, the most common impact that residents talked about was feeling afraid and avoiding the protests, because of the looting and violence and tear gas. Residents described being afraid of what protestors were doing and what police were doing. Parents said that children were afraid to go outside and to go to sleep. One parent even took her daughter out of town away from the protests. An older woman shared, "My worst fear is that police have lost control in that area. The police can't do their job because they are too scared." This was not an isolated thought. A woman who had lived in her home for 30 years said that she felt like the police and local government were afraid of the protestors "and are letting them get away with far too much." A middle-aged Black woman described putting her sofa against the door at night, which she had never done before. This is important because when people perceive a protest situation as violent, and believe that their safety is threatened, they favor more punitive laws against protests and are less likely to view the protest as an important representation of democracy in action (Hsiao and Radnitz 2021; Metcalfe and Pickett 2021). Protests that interfere with routines (e.g., shutting down traffic) or committing violence and property damage, like destroying police cars, increase support for repressive police responses (Manekin and Mitts 2020).

Out of fear, but also aggravation, many residents avoided the protest area and stores (e.g., Target, Walmart, Schnucks) near the protests; some stopped visiting people in the area. One resident said that her grandpa moved out of his house in Ferguson and in with them because of the protests. A young female resident said that her church was near the shooting location, and she was afraid to go there with her children during the protests. One resident drove to Illinois to get groceries (across the Mississippi River from Ferguson). Another woman who went to her doctor's office in Ferguson days after Brown was shot found the door and windows of the office were broken, and said that they remained that way for about three weeks. A mother told us that they live close to the looting and riots and her child was afraid to leave the house. An adult told us the same thing, that "It's scary. I don't sleep and I'm afraid to leave the house." One middle-aged resident advised that while there was a small proportion of people starting trouble, about 15 percent she said, at the protests, are "troublemakers drawn to the area from other places," but most people "just wanted their community to be safe."

These fears likely are what motivated 27 percent of residents who told us that police did what they had to do under the extreme circumstances of the protests, and residents supported and appreciated their efforts. Some residents thought police could have done more, such as making more arrests or using store cameras to pursue accountability for the looters (which did happen later). One resident spoke out in support of police using plainclothes officers to control problem individuals in the crowd, although he credited this tactic to the Missouri Highway Patrol assuming command, not realizing that county officers had inserted the arrest teams.

Nearly equal in number, however, 24 percent of residents said that the police response was excessive. They spoke out against riot gear, helicopters, tear gas, and "tanks." Residents seemed to notice the shifts between tolerant and repressive approaches, commenting that police let the looting happen in the beginning of the protests, but then began applying aggressive tactics after the QuickTrip burned.

Confirming concerns expressed by Captain Johnson and Chief Belmar and others, 9 percent of residents said that aggressive police responses amped up protestors and made the situation worse. A middle-aged resident told us that he thought it "couldn't be peaceful after they had already harassed the protestors and younger crowd . . . Coming out in the tactical gear was just pouring gasoline on the fire, especially if they already had a bad relationship with the people of Ferguson." One woman claimed that she was peacefully protesting and "got gassed and shot at with rubber bullets. We were made to feel like animals. They [police] instigated the violence . . . How they reacted is what made us feel like screw this."

Four percent of residents—primarily Black—said that they were afraid of police. One Black father said, "It makes me cautious about my kids. Are they going to get picked on by the police? It makes me nervous." A Black female resident said, "I feel like they [police] are criminals. The only difference is the law protects them when they are wrong." The community callout in chapter 3 goes into detail about the differences in views about police by Black and non-Black residents during this time.

Tear gas tormented residents. Twelve percent of residents spoke out against police using tear gas. A 33-year-old Black woman described smelling the tear gas from her front porch. Another resident, a Black man who lived behind the protest area, said that tear gas seeped into his home—that there were times when he had to leave the house because the tear gas in the house was too much. It could take an entire hour to fully dissipate, he said. Still another resident talked about having to bring her dogs into the house from the yard, because they choked on tear gas. A 33-year-old resident whose friend and his wife were tear gassed while protesting said, "It was like Iraq out there."

Repeatedly, we heard residents tell us that the protests were noisy—the crowds were so loud. Residents who lived around the corner from the protests could hear them. Helicopters flew overhead. One resident, who had served in the military for eight years, said that the helicopters triggered her Post Traumatic Stress Disorder (PTSD). Several residents complained that noise from the helicopters kept them awake.

A few residents living in the area of the protests talked about crime increasing due to the protests. Stores were looted and burglarized. A 31-year-old man said that where he lives, vehicles were broken into, but even with all the police around, nothing was being done. A pattern of increased crime problems during Black Lives Matter protests was documented by Zhang and colleagues (2020).

Residents frequently described how their daily routines were disrupted by closures of streets, schools, and businesses, and by curfews. One woman had been worried about her sister being unable to get her medicine, because the stores were closed. A teacher at a local school said that the start of the school year was delayed because of the protests. Parents brought this up as well. A young woman said that on the Saturday of Brown's death, she could not get into her apartment complex behind the QuickTrip convenience store. A disabled resident reported that she could not get in and out of her apartment and so had to cancel appointments. People arrived at work late due to blocked traffic or had to leave work early because curfews closed the business, impacting wages. Several residents could not work because their place of employment completely shut down for several weeks. One resident who lived paycheck to paycheck said, "I couldn't pay my bills," and when we spoke to her several weeks later, she said, "I am still trying to catch up." One resident had worked at a store that protestors had burned down, and he subsequently had to commute about 15 miles to his new job. Another resident worked at one of the stores that was looted and was there at the time of the incident. She said that she was scared, it was traumatic, but she got out "in time" and was not hurt. An older Black woman talked about a family member's business that was damaged. A Black father described being at the McDonalds with his teenage son when police came in and asked everyone to leave. Police told customers that the McDonalds was unsafe and made customers walk from the area using a specific route, which for him was the opposite way to his home, walking around his neighborhood. The father told us that it made him nervous—being out in the protest area in the dark.

Despite the inconveniences and fear that the protests caused, some residents said that they were glad to see people acting in support of social issues, rather than being passive. Eleven percent of residents told us that they thought the protests had increased awareness and understanding about important issues like racial profiling, racial tension, crime, and policing.

Cobbina's (2019) study in Ferguson and Baltimore showed that people are more likely to participate in protests against police when they believe that the protest efforts will shape outcomes, when they have had negative experiences with police, and when they experience personal or group-based feelings of deprivation. Among Ferguson protestors, 63 percent of those interviewed by Cobbina had experienced a negative interaction with police prior to Brown's death; 76 percent said they were aware of others' negative experiences with police. Among Baltimore protestors, 51 percent reported personal negative encounters and 57 percent discussed vicarious negative encounters. About 20 percent of St. Louis County residents that I surveyed participated in peaceful protests (e.g., marches, holding signs)—23 percent of Black residents and 14 percent of non-Black residents. Two percent of residents had engaged in yelling angry comments at police, 2 percent said that they participated in obstructing traffic or other routines, and less than 1 percent engaged in aggressive or violent activities in Ferguson.

A strong minority of residents spoke out against looting (33 percent) and rioting (21 percent) as tools for gaining justice. They thought that rioters and looters were taking advantage of the circumstances, not pursuing social justice. As one 64-year-old Black resident put it, even though "Somebody has to voice out or speak out the frustration with police practices . . . Rioting and looting didn't have nothing to do with Michael Brown being shot." One middle-aged Black resident thought that while the events seemingly united the Black community, they also divided it into those seeking justice and those taking advantage of the chaos. Of the protestors, he said, "You have the people who want truth and justice, and you have people who want to tear stuff up."

Some residents, even Black residents, spoke about how the protests reminded them that racism exists. A 30-something White male said he feels that the protests have increased the distance between cultures and increased the racial divide. This feeling was most salient among but not limited to White residents. A White woman told us, "It has caused more hatred, Black against White and White against Black." Residents noticed increased racial tensions at mixed-race workplaces. One woman told us that as a Black nurse working with many White people, she felt she had to distance herself from conversations at work and humble herself for fear of losing her job over saying the wrong thing. An older White female talked about her church being affected by the racial divide. Another woman described an incident in September 2014, when she and her husband where driving and a Black man, two cars back, pulled alongside of them and "flipped them the bird," saying "I will blow your frickin' heads off!" She said it felt that the man was blaming her and her husband, being White, for "Ferguson."

Apart from providing insight into how the protests and protest policing were viewed by residents, the resident interviews also revealed insight about the etiology of the protests. Although it was seven months after the shooting before the Civil Rights Investigation report (US Department of Justice Civil Rights Division 2015) revealed that the city of Ferguson had been using criminal justice agencies as a revenue stream, one astute resident, a 45-year-old female, revealed this as the structural condition that provoked the collective grievance among Ferguson residents. She shared her view that,

> Much of what fueled the protesting was because preceding the shooting of Michael Brown, many people in that area were being racially profiled. Many people are economically depressed and then targeted consistently and cannot pay for their fines. This is happening, not just in Ferguson, but in other areas as well, where police are targeting people, specifically Blacks and Hispanics, for traffic offenses. . . . Even UMSL [University of Missouri St. Louis] students are being targeted for small violations. Many of us spend more time, gas, and wear and tear on our vehicles just to drive farther to bypass certain areas where police are racial profiling and writing tickets for everything . . . Much of this profiling is happening because they (police) are trying to build revenue.

She claimed her race as "other," but described a personal experience where she was pulled over by police and was told that she was being ticketed for following the vehicle in front of her too closely, and then she received a $125 ticket. She said, "I felt like I was being profiled not only by the officer, but also by the court system as well. I took this ticket to trial and I felt like it was a waste of time. The judge didn't really listen to what I had to say." Other residents also spoke about biased policing in Ferguson prior to the protests. We spoke to a resident who was an elected politician who reflected that Brown's death and the protests highlighted policing as problematic, long before Brown's death. It is interesting to question whether, if these interviews had revealed this pattern prior to Brown's death, the protests in Ferguson could have been prevented by acting against the use of criminal justice fines and fees to fund the Ferguson city budget.

The community surveys provided testimony that residents felt a sense of empathy and connection to Brown's death. It resonated with them and reinforced existing concerns about racism and frustrations over the inappropriate use of fines and fees to fund the city budget. One resident said, "If it wasn't Michael Brown, it would have been another young teen," recognizing that Brown's death was symbolic, but that if he had not been shot, another flash point would have led to similar results. In response, residents initiated collective action, with 20 percent of interviewees joining the protests. Their stories revealed how residents who protested interpreted the police actions, especially police using tear gas and wearing riot gear, as disrespectful and unjust. This shared view of police helped to unify the crowd against police, weakening their commitment to conform to social order, as the revised flashpoints model predicts.

2

Police Culture and Being on the Island

We felt like we were on an island by ourselves, fighting a battle that didn't have anything to do, I don't know, with us or
anything.
—Dylan, Black police supervisor

Everybody was against us. The media was against us, the
people were against us, it was us and everybody else.
—Noah, White police officer

The introduction of this book describes the paradox that society has
bestowed on police. We have assigned police the role of users of force,
something that the public simultaneously abhors but needs. Society
wants police to use force when it is necessary to ensure social order, and
by assigning police that role, police assume responsibility for all manner
of challenging social problems. However, society also wants police to
avoid using force whenever possible. Normally they do avoid the use of
force; police use of force is rare. About 1 percent of the US population
experiences police use of physical force such as grabbing, pushing, pepper spray, having a gun pointed at them, or being shot at (Harrell and
Davis 2020). The limited and often undetected nature of police coercion
facilitates police legitimacy. However, the context in Ferguson put the
threat of force and use of force by police in a spotlight. Placing police use
of force at the center of public attention removes the veil that normally
obscures this uncomfortable reality from public view and threatens
police legitimacy, trust in police, and police-community relations.

Police Culture as the Lens

Police culture has been described as a way for the police to cope with
the use of force paradox that underlies their role. Police culture provides

"a barrier of protection behind which they [police] hide so that they can do what we want them to do without at the same time incurring our chastisement" (Crank 2014: 97). Culture is a way of thinking about things, a sense-making tool for processing information, that lends itself to behaving in certain ways. Cultural knowledge and values emerge from repeatedly handling daily activities and problems. It is shared by those handling similar problems and conducting similar activities. The knowledge and values that the process produces are transmitted through socialization.

There are many ways to think about the police occupational culture. Police organizations have slightly different cultures, police officers ascribe to subcultures, and theory suggests that police management and line-level officers adopt different cultures. Acknowledging the many dimensions of culture (Paoline III and Gau 2018), this chapter focuses on a general, common police occupational culture. I have adopted John Crank's (2014: 59) "onioness of culture" as a lens through which to examine the Ferguson protests. Crank provides this analogy to describe the interconnected core elements of police occupational culture that shape how officers interpret the world and act. He depicts the culture as having a core with four basic layers around it that collectively explain how officers think and behave and, notably, why.

Crank describes the heart of the onion as the values that the officer brings to policing, the officer's altruistic belief that they can have a positive influence in society. This noble view is already formed when an officer begins a career in policing. Frequently, it is the motive officers give for becoming a police officer.

The layers around the heart of the onion describe officers' adaptations to their organizational and situational environments in policing. Layer one, the street environment or territory or beat, refers to the sense of responsibility officers adopt to control their assigned geographic area and the people within it. The officers' perceived purpose is to enforce normative standards of behavior and order—society's moral sentiments that have been adopted into law. This layer outlines the role of police in society, portraying policing as a morally righteous task—defending society against lawbreakers and jerks. This is what makes police "the good guys" defending society against "the bad guys." This layer outlines the reason for why police are the group assigned the authority to use force by society, because they are the guardians with the difficult job of handling criminals and securing social order.

Layer two emphasizes the situational uncertainty, unpredictability, and potential danger that threaten and challenge officers' ability to instill order and fulfill their role. The public wants police to handle the unknown, potentially dangerous situation, and police encounter tremendous variation in situational circumstances. Their task is to be able to view their environment suspiciously and distinguish from limited cues the likely behaviors and conditions that may produce harm and then minimize the threat to prevent it. Assessing risk and being prepared for danger consumes a large portion of officers' time, even if the time spent encountering danger day-to-day is much less. There is no sanctuary, and it is this consummate strain of scanning for danger that leads officers to adapt by assigning meaning to environmental cues about what is safe (e.g., wealthy neighborhood, well-manicured and landscaped park) versus dangerous (e.g., dilapidated area, low riding vehicle, gang colors) and to take steps to "maintain the edge," meaning to remain in charge and on top of all situations, to stay in control.

Layer three of the police culture is a feeling of solidarity and shared identity that develops among police officers. Two things about policing inspire solidarity. First, common experiences with the threat of danger at work inspires loyalty and camaraderie among those who mutually encounter it, much like in the military. Second, solidarity develops as a by-product of conflict, perceived antagonism by others such as threats to police authority or grievances from others. Shared conflict with others builds group unity. Feeling solidarity as police officers also can create isolation from other groups, kindling the sense of us versus them.

The final layer includes strategies adopted to deal with external oversight. For line-level officers, oversight includes management within the police organization or external oversight by courts, politicians, or the public. The policing context abounds with rules—administrative procedures, protocols, professional standards, chain of command, and laws—designed to constrain behavior and provide accountability. The rules and procedures emphasize personal accountability over implicating the organization (e.g., rotten apple, not rotten barrel). Under the weight of this oversight, coupled with their tremendous responsibility, officers develop a sense of mistrust, of feeling conspired against, that

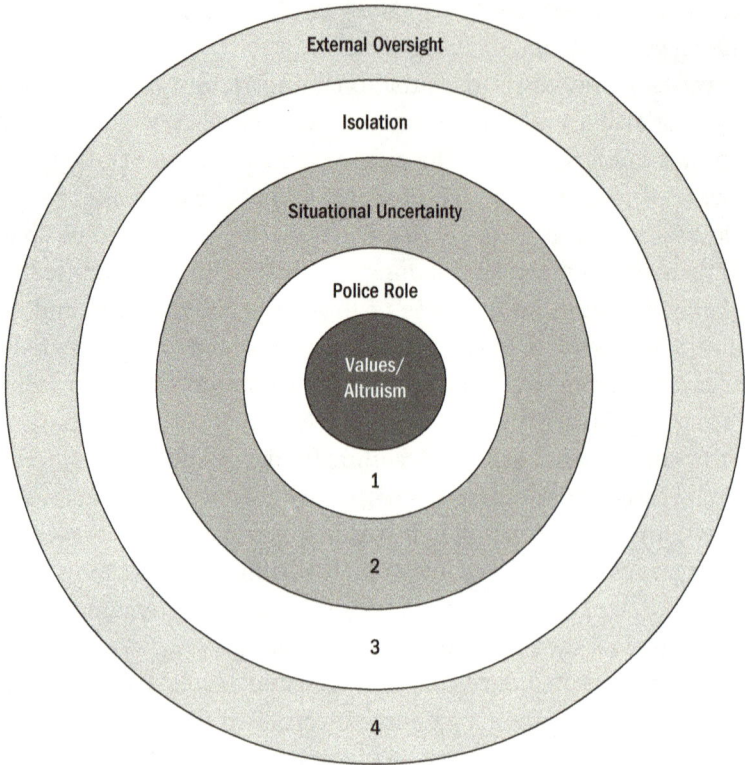

Figure 2.1 Conceptual Layers Facilitating the Police Occupational Culture.

often lead to an attitude of disdain that prompts officers to adapt to situations. They seek to become invisible by avoiding making mistakes, but also to do their part or pull their weight, help each other, not implicate one another, to keep secrets/CYA—they feel cynical. Within this layer, organizational justice is a tool to counter some of the potentially negative outcomes. Organizational justice entails creating a sense of fair treatment by the organization and supervisors toward officers (Nix and Wolfe 2016). Officers' beliefs that the police organization will make fair and neutral decisions and officers' trust in supervisors' support and fair treatment can mediate some of the cultural adaptations to oversight (e.g., secrecy) (Van Craen 2016).

Figure 2.1 presents the conceptual layers, the internal, operational, situational, organizational, and external influences upon police that are interconnected and interactive. Police interpret and adapt to these conditions through sense-making, which guides their decisions and behaviors. From these conditions and subsequent adaptations, police occupational culture—a shared way of thinking about issues and principles guiding conduct—emerges.

Applying the lens of a police occupational culture to officers' experiences in Ferguson helps to explain their interpretation of those experiences as well as to provide a rationale for their protest policing behaviors. Of course, this is not to suggest that all police think alike or are robots carrying out the police culture. However, there is empirical support that these concepts do operate in policing practices (Paoline III and Gau 2018).

Police Culture in Action

Applying this lens, the thread of police occupational culture throughout officers' accounts of their Ferguson experiences becomes apparent. Officers described their altruistic rationales for why they became police officers (the core). Building on that moral core, a prevalent theme in the officers' accounts was the importance of the role that police protect and defend society against agitators (layer one), despite the many imminent dangers they had to face in Ferguson (layer two). Chapter 1 outlined the tactics police applied to instill order and maintain control, and apparent in officers' stories is the cultural frustration they faced when unable to do so. Featured prominently in officers' descriptions was the frustration they felt in response to the vehemence of the media and public toward police and abandonment of police by government officials (see the discussion in chapter 4 about lack of reciprocity in the section titled "Applying the Job Demands-Resource Model to Policing Post-Ferguson"). Officers described their sense of isolation, loyalty, and solidarity inspired by threats to police authority (layer three). Finally, though, officers talked about how the support of their supervisors and police leadership (layer four), alongside supportive family and members of the public, helped to buffer the impact on them of the strains mentioned above. However, they also mentioned feeling a responsibility for each other, looking out for one another, and feeling guilty sometimes if they felt other officers faced more challenging circumstances than they did (an adaptation in layer four). Below, I provide the details from officers' accounts that gave rise to these impressions.

Noble Motives (The Core)

Just over one-third of police officers we interviewed told us their motivation for becoming a police officer, even though we did not ask them for this information. Officer Henry described the feeling as a calling. He mentioned how in the Bible, there are examples of protectors and that is how he sees the role of police. Supervisor Luke said, "That's what we signed up for, to protect the people that can't protect themselves." Supervisor Ben told me that,

> A lot of us that got into this profession, you do it for, what I believe are the right reasons. You want to serve the community, you want to give back to the community, and in my case, especially early on as a young officer, I wanted to lock up all the drug dealers and the troublemakers to make the community better. So that's actually giving back. I look at giving back to the community as you give outstanding neighborhood policing to the good citizens and you lock the bad people, the criminals up. I couldn't think of a better way to give back to the community.

Several officers told us that the basis for their desire to give back and improve society stemmed from growing up in difficult circumstances like living with poverty and crime or even having negative experiences with police. Supervisor Hugh said he became a police officer because he saw racist policing as a child. Police would chase him and other young Black children and even shoot at them, and he said, "I always thought to myself, that can't be how police work is. It can't be that way." Officer Anthony said that he had not really applied himself at school, but a health teacher in high school encouraged him, saying, "You can be better." Anthony felt inspired by her words. In that class, they learned about health professions, and he realized that he wanted to help people. He had compassion for people, but thought policing was a better career fit for him than the health field, because of his athleticism. However, he said, "If I wouldn't be doing this [policing], I'd probably be in nursing."

Several officers talked about coming from a family of police. For example, supervisor Jason told us that everyone in his family were police officers, "both grandfathers, three uncles, my father, and now me." Officer Kathie said that many of her family members were military, police officers, or worked in probation and parole, and so she was raised with values that respected God, family, and giving back to her community. By way of explanation, she offered, "Giving back is embedded into who I am." Because it is common for police officers to come from families of police officers, this cultural value, this noble notion of making society better, feels inherent in their identities.

Officer Caleb said that protest policing in Ferguson made him reflect on why he became a police officer—to help people. Supervisor Dylan said about the purpose of police, "We're here to provide solutions, resources, [to] provide safety. Safeguard is what we are here for, we're not here to do anything else other than provide a safeguard for the community."

"The Good Guys" Defending Society's Norms and Laws

Three themes from the officer interviews exemplify Crank's layer one of culture, the notion that policing is a morally righteous task involving police defending society against criminals and jerks. The first theme is adoption of the crime fighter role. Many officers struggled when ordered not to act in response to crimes. The second theme is that public vehemence against police during the protests besmirched officers' view of themselves as the "good guys." The third theme is that the prevalence of violence among protestors provided a challenge for police to distinguish the "bad guys" from the society that they vowed to protect.

POLICE ROLE AS CRIME FIGHTER

Police culture specifies a role for police to defend society against the "bad guys," to handle emergency situations that may require the use of force to protect society from harmful criminals. A core strategy police apply toward this end is crime fighting/crime prevention. The organization, structure, and traditions of policing encourage officers' actions such as preventative patrol, investigation, and arrest in pursuit of this goal.

Consistent with this value, police civilian, Pamela, explained that normally, "crime is crime" and officers work to prevent and address those who are committing crime. However, as chapter 1 describes, there were many times during the Ferguson unrest that police were advised to refrain from arresting looters and people committing arson and were instructed to take no action. Supervisor Ben explained that officers struggled emotionally with this tolerant approach, because they could not act on criminal violations, which is central to the police crime fighting mission. Officers could not conceive how refraining from coercive action against the "bad guys" promoted the safety and security of the protestors and officers. Inaction created a sense of anxiety among officers being asked to operate opposite their training and cultural values—to refrain from arresting looters.

Officer Fred described hearing on the radio, "They're starting to loot the Family Dollar. They're starting to loot the Beauty Brands. They're starting to loot the Ferguson liquor mart [he forgot the name]." Fred described being ready to go stop the looting, but then being told, "Stand down. Retreat to the command post." He described,

> We're standing on the line, watching people violate the law. They're taking people's livelihoods, they're ruining people's businesses, and to be told to stand down and not intervene in that, why even show up to work the next day? That was probably one of the lowest points for me, when we're all out there to stop bad people from doing bad things, and when you have us ready to stop this, a plan in place to stop this, but "Stand down, it's just businesses."

Officer Karen shared the same view. She explained,

> My instinct and my duty is telling me that I have to go here, prevent or stop whatever crime's happening, take those guys into custody, put them in jail. And we'd get right there, and they'd say, "Lay off, disregard, don't go there." And we'd have to sit there and watch these guys loot the store. And they'd see us sitting there not doing anything. So that was probably the hardest part, blatantly conducting dereliction of duty, but by command.

This sentiment was shared repeatedly by officers. Officer Sebastian said he heard windows breaking and saw about 20 people looting the

Midas shop. Police had nearly 50 officers right there. He thought that police finally had a chance to do something, because they had sufficient resources available. However, he was told, "No, we are just going to hold right here." He thought, "What are we even doing here? You could train apes to stand here in the middle of the street and get verbally abused and get rocks thrown at them." Officer Teresa grappled with going back out to police the protests in Ferguson after being required to stand by and do nothing while people were ransacking Sam's Meat Market in Ferguson. She said, "What's the point if we can't do our job and help people or protect people." She described feeling "useless" after this incident.

Officer Anthony said he felt "let down" by the need to limit the police response, to allow rioting to happen, citing the role expectation and capacity to be the protectors, that, "We've always trained how to use riot gear, how to do certain formations, and how to move, you know, how to make arrests during civil unrest. And now here we are on stage in the longest active riot in US history, and we weren't allowed to do anything." Anthony similarly described feeling disenchanted by having to show restraint in the face of verbal and physical attacks on police and even while shots were ringing out. It was a clear violation of the police culture. Supervisor Noah explained, "That's just like letting the dog out of the cage and then shocking him and putting him back in the cage, and then, you know, at some point that dog has to come out of that cage again. Instead of the dog running out and biting on command like he's taught to, the dog is second guessing the command. The dog is a little slower. Should I do this, should I not do this?" Officers did not understand the reasons for the restraint, nor did they agree with any reason that could be offered, said supervisor Luke. He found himself trying to explain to subordinates why they did or did not do things, but thought, "I should not have to do that." He felt like adherence to orders should be sufficient justification to officers and did not fully appreciate the significant challenge that showing restraint and ignoring crimes provided the police culture.

CROWD VEHEMENCE AND PERSONAL ATTACK DISTORTED THE "GOOD GUYS" PERSPECTIVE

During the protests, at least for a little while, officer Henry wondered whether police were doing the right thing. He said that for a time,

.I kind of thought of myself and our police departments up there as the bad people [not White knights], you know. We're doing something bad for the community because, you know, this officer shot and killed someone, and all these protests are happening nationally . . . I think that's just a human nature feeling, when everyone is against you, or you feel like everyone is against you, you start doubting yourself, and you doubt what you are doing there.

The public's response to Brown's killing, widespread protest against police, threatened the image of police as "the good guys." During the Ferguson protests, protestors held signs and chanted things like "F*** the police," "Hands Up Don't Shoot," "No justice! No peace! No racist police!" and "Injustice anywhere is a threat to justice everywhere" (e.g., Nashrulla 2014; Young 2019). Officer Kathie, who had worked in North County before the protests, was stunned and hurt by the public response. She said, "To try and help a community and take care of them and protect them, and then for that to happen, it was, that was painful. Very painful." She felt like it was not just the badge people were attacking, rather she felt they were saying, "You're not a good person." It felt to officer Anthony that there was no defense, that he was not able to defend himself against the vicious claims against his occupation, and if he did try to defend himself, "Then I'm the bad guy."

On the third night, officer Teresa described the surreal feeling of looking around her and seeing people throwing bricks, buildings going up in flames, wearing a gas mask and riot gear, and not seeing her hand in front of her face. She said, "It was nothing like I could imagine." The anger of the crowd was palpable. She struggled with the situation because, "They didn't know me, I didn't do anything to them. But . . . I wear a badge, so I'm automatically hated because I've been grouped in with, I'm a horrible cop, and I'm a baby killer, just because I wear a badge. They lump us all together." Forty percent of the police we interviewed felt overwhelmed by hate, animosity, and anger projected at them as police during the protests. Black supervisor Dylan said, "I was just hurt that the community looked at us [police] as people with no heart." Much like the public felt that police discriminated against Black suspects as a group, police felt condemned as a group by the public, even while experiencing personal insults and threats to themselves and their families. As Teresa explained, "They were picking us out. They were saying 'you' then they read our nametags, and they'd say something." Supervisor Jason described that people pointed their fingers like guns, looked at the nametag and would say, "I got you Kochel [pseudonym]" and "I'm gonna kill you. I am gonna kill your whole family. I can't wait to watch you die." Of standing on the skirmish line, officer Fred told me, "Never in my life have I felt so alone." The Ferguson experience vigorously challenged the cultural image police had of being the "good guys."

DISTINGUISHING THE "BAD GUYS" FROM SOCIETY

Before the protests, identifying the bad guys and who police protected the bad guys from was an easy task. Officer Kathie told me, "I liked working midnight because I thought it was kind of cool that all these people were peacefully sleeping at night, and I am out patrolling, protecting them. I'm like their guardian angel while they sleep, that's what I, that's my mindset."

Ferguson provided a challenge for officers trying to make the symbolic distinction between the bad guys and the society that they were protecting. "Those first couple of days, it was pretty much everybody against us," said officer Henry. This was why officers had initially questioned whether they might actually be the bad guys. However, the narrative shifted among officers whereby the bad guys were clearly groups and individuals, agitators, committing violence at the protests. As Officer William framed it, "There's 500 people there [at the protests] and there's 100,000 in North County. That 500 were not representative of the overall views of the population. They were much more radical or antipolice than the average population . . . I think people are much more reasonable than the groups of people that we dealt with after dark up there [in Ferguson]." Police determined that they were tasked with protecting the residents and businesses in the area. Also, officers articulated that peaceful, daytime protestors deserved and needed protection to facilitate peaceful protest activities, up until the point at which protests become violent, such as at night. Officer Isaac described that at night, "all the thugs and idiots [bad guys] came out, and they used the cover of peaceful protestors [those needing protection] to do whatever the f*** they wanted to do."

Supervisor Luke responded to family and friends who asked why he kept going back to Ferguson: "It's the good people of Ferguson that we're doing this for," and he was relieved when he heard other officers saying this as well. The good people to him included "a lot of older people . . . and . . . if you look in the city of Ferguson, I'm sure I could account that 99.9 percent of them are on our side of peace . . . That's what we signed up for, to protect the people that can't protect themselves." He contrasted the good Ferguson residents with "all the protesters and the thugs and the criminals that are mad at us." He believed that the remaining "0.1 percent" at the protests were people coming into St. Louis from out of state to take advantage of the chaos inherent in the unrest.

Officer Karen also viewed residents as victims in need of protection from violent protestors. She described stopping to help a resident who had run out of gas in an area near the protests. The resident told her, while the officer and resident were driving to get gas, that although she supported her community, "We don't support this community [meaning the protestors] . . . We love, we protect ours, and we're the people at home that are scared . . . We're scared that this Ferguson thing is gonna filter out into our neighborhoods and we're gonna be the victim of a home invasion or a robbery." But the moment that officer Karen figured it out, she said, was after working in Ferguson for several weeks. She and all the officers were "just so tired," and "everyone didn't want to be there. Nobody wanted to help the people in the community." However, she went into a QuikTrip convenience store for a drink one day before work, in her uniform. Someone came up and shook her hand and told her, "Thank you so much for being here. I know you guys are going through a rough time out there, but just know there's people in our community that really need you and really care about you guys." At that moment, she thought to herself, "Okay, this is the community that we're working for. It's not the knuckleheads that are out there rioting and looting, people that don't even live here. These are the people that we wanna be here for." Being clear on the roles in society is important to the occupational culture. To retain the image of noble protectors, there must clearly be someone whom police are protecting.

In his classic book chapter titled "The Asshole," Van Maanen (1978: 307) quoted a veteran police officer saying, "What our job really boils down to is not letting the assholes take over the city . . . They're the ones who make it tough on the decent people out there." His chapter provides an explanation for how specific people are labeled by police as lawbreakers/criminals versus troublemakers ("assholes") versus everyone else. His process aptly applies to how police distinguished groups of people in Ferguson. Lawbreakers, people who need to be arrested, included extremely violent protestors shooting guns and throwing Molotov cocktails. As just described, the group that police felt the need to protect (everyone else) included residents and some daytime protestors and church groups who peacefully marched. The largest group would qualify as Van Maanen's "assholes," deviants who police viewed as disrespectful, who affront police authority, offend police, and behave irrationally and outrageously and thus threaten order. Many of the nighttime protestors (see "Nighttime Signaled Danger" below), whom police described as yelling vile and threatening things to police and throwing dog poop bags, water bottles, and urine at police, fit this category. Van Maanen's thesis is that this is the group to whom coercion is likely to be applied by police in the form of street justice. Certainly, in Ferguson, the troublemakers experienced the effects of tear gas, the Long Range Acoustic Device (LRAD), and bean bag bullets—diffuse and coercive responses to large gatherings of troublemakers who seemed threatening to police. However, many times, officers described merely standing on skirmish lines and taking it from "the assholes."

Officer Henry synthesized the police adaptation and response to different categories of people.

I think our command staff and police department did an amazing job of, of realizing what we needed to change all the way up to, you know, even our anniversary weekend, you know, on how we, how we dealt with protests, and our relaxed approach and having gear on standby just in case, and I mean we had shootings up there, we, we had to deal with, we had things that, um, still had that criminal element, but then we were still engaged in community at the same time, and recognizing the fact that there's a couple different types of people that were at these events. There were people that wanted that community engagement with law enforcement and wanted to protest. We had day protests with parades that went peacefully. We even had night protests that went peacefully, but it was a certain criminal aspect that brought guns to these events, that caused problems, and I think our department did an excellent job of recognizing the difference and not throwing everyone into one group, of saying, "You can't protest here because you're doing this," when it was just one or two bad eggs that we had to get in custody.

Situational Uncertainty and Danger

A key adaptation within police culture is meant to help police to cope with uncertainty and danger. It provides a basis to quickly interpret environmental cues and attribute risk to officers' and others' safety. Officers' past experiences give meaning to environmental cues. For example, when an officer is hurt or threatened while handling a domestic disturbance, a bar brawl at 2:00 a.m., or a large group of teenage males gathered on a street corner, qualities about those situations are assigned a signal of danger (e.g., extremely drunk individuals holding glass bottles, bulge under the t-shirt of a young man wearing what are perceived to be gang colors, screaming angry person with blood and scrapes on his knuckles) such that being called to future scenes with similar characteristics puts officers on notice of the potential danger. Environmental cues are defined and iteratively redefined as signaling danger or safety as officers accumulate experiences and talk with other officers about their experiences. Being able to draw on stereotypes about the symptoms of danger and safety helps officers to react quickly to potential threats, even with limited time and information to assess a situation. This tool is a shortcut to cope with the uncertainty, danger, and fast pace of officers' work environments.

Officers described a great deal of uncertainty and danger at the Ferguson protests. Learned suspicion is why officers applied extra caution during medical calls near the protests—they learned through experience that they were often fake calls designed to target and harm police. Recall also from chapter 1 that officers described reminding one another about suspicious characteristics that symbolized danger at protests, like people with backpacks, baggy clothes, or bandanas. Officers stressed the need to focus on people's hands at the protests, to anticipate thrown projectiles. Two major signals of danger to officers in Ferguson appeared to be darkness and the shift in command from Chief Belmar, St. Louis County Police, to Captain Johnson, Missouri Highway Patrol.

NIGHTTIME SIGNALED DANGER

One of the most dangerous signals in Ferguson was darkness; 69 percent of police we interviewed articulated an important distinction between daytime and nighttime protests. Supervisor Gabe explained that "Under the cloak of darkness, we were easy targets." This time period lasted from about 8:30 p.m. to 3:30 a.m., according to officer Anthony. "It was a totally different landscape," said supervisor Wyatt. Police identified some "legitimate protestors" at night, but the people who attended the Ferguson protests at night chiefly were younger and were agitators and criminal opportunists, "more vicious toward law enforcement," according to supervisor Logan. A visual distinction made by police is that the daytime protestors held signs, whereas nighttime protestors held rocks, bricks, frozen water bottles, and Molotov cocktails, projectiles to be thrown at police or through storefronts. Other frequent nighttime symbols of danger were fights and guns. Approximately 40 percent of officers talked about guns at the protests. Supervisor Hugh said that they could sit at a nighttime protest for five minutes and point out five or six cars with guns. Officers saw people walking with guns in their pants. A seasoned, experienced, Black police officer, supervisor Dylan said, "It was scary. It was scary."

Nighttime protestors fit Muir's (1977) paradox of irrationality. The paradox is that the more extremely irrational the behavior used by the threatening group, the more serious that threat feels to police. This was evident in Ferguson. When the protest violence seemed absurd, extreme, and without explanation to officers, police felt highly threatened. Supervisor Noah described the nighttime crowd behavior as "out of control." Supervisor Alexander said people were "caught up in the moment . . . mob mentality." He believed that people who came to protest at night thought to themselves, "There are no laws. I can steal and do stupid stuff that I will not normally do, but I can get away with it now." The actions of many nighttime protestors did not appear motivated by social justice, they seemed opportunistic and irrational to police.

At night, officers operated "on the edge"—a point when danger feels imminent, at the threshold of chaos and violence. Crank (2014) suggests that on the edge, officers are conditioned by police culture to minimize the danger. Officer William, who had served in the military, explained how threats to officer safety contributed to a mindset among officers that allowed them to see members of the public as "the enemy." He explained that repeatedly facing large crowds who yelled at police and threw things at them, even if it was only isolated members of the crowd who were responsible, contributed to officers being hyperfocused on their safety, on the potential threat. The consequence, he said, is that officers could not deal with people because they began looking at everyone as being a threat against police. Officer Henry said that they were always wondering, "What officer is it going to be?" who gets shot and killed. At night, the threat was always on officers' minds, it always felt imminent.

CHANGING COMMAND SIGNALED UNCERTAINTY AND DANGER

The other factor that officers talked a great deal about, which they believed increased the level of uncertainty at the protests and contributed to dangerous conditions, was the change in command. Governor Nixon announced less than one week into the protests that Captain Ron Johnson of the Missouri Highway Patrol was to take control of commanding Ferguson protest policing from Chief Belmar of St. Louis County Police Department. More than half (56 percent) of the St. Louis County police personnel talked about how impactful this change in leadership was for them and for how the protests were handled. Officers did not feel as if anyone else prioritized officer safety as highly as Chief Belmar, and they were very skeptical of other police leaders. They also were skeptical of politicians who became involved in dictating the response to the unrest. Officer Henry said that officers he knew "honestly thought politicians wanted a police officer to get shot." With the change in command, officers felt sacrificed. Supervisor Logan, a Black officer, felt that motivating the decision to put Johnson in charge was putting a Black officer in a position of leadership, hoping to "breach the gap," between protestors and police, but officers felt that their safety had been deprioritized in favor of altering the police image and appeasing the protestors.

Officer Henry provided an example of when officers called for help from the scene of the McDonalds, but the tactical unit was not dispatched by the Missouri State Police to help the officers. Members of the county tactical unit said that they heard the cries for help over the radio and decided to self-dispatch and went in to assist. Officer Henry said that a member of the tactical team said, "Go. We're not waiting for a police officer to get shot in order to do something." Then, supervisor Connor said, "We got beat up pretty bad pulling out because they [State Police], they told us to pull out. As soon as we pulled out, we pulled up on the side of the hill, we parked there, we stood there, and watched a whole lot of looting going on."

Officer Anthony said,

> We felt like we had, we were fighting with one arm behind our back, and we just had to stand up there and endure. So, we were taking it in the rear from the public and then we were taking it from the rear from the leadership here . . . And I'm thinking, if you had the same aggressive approach to these people throwing at us as you do us . . . This would have been over with like a Tyson fight, in about 30 seconds.

Officer Luke agreed with Anthony that the state police applied too much restraint. Officer Fred went so far as to suggest that "If the governor wouldn't have intervened, we wouldn't have had any further problems [with the protestors]. By the end of the week, we would have been done." He saw efforts to minimize the police response as "retreat" and thought that the protestors consequently were emboldened and became more aggressive.

Officer Fred told me that the day after the State Police took charge, officers were told, "We will not gas these people." And that was the day when a protest crowd charged the command post. On the radio, he heard a series of progressive descriptions, first that a crowd of 200–300 was moving toward the command post. Then, he heard an estimate of 300–400 people blocking Canfield Drive. Then, he heard, "Be advised, they're coming to the command post." He described that the Target parking lot, where the command post was located, looked like a military base due to all the police, and the crowd brought the fight to the police, he saw "a lot of people fighting us," "a lot of people taken into custody."

County police described the change in command as demoralizing and insulting. Supervisor Logan said, "It gave the sense the department didn't really know what they were doing or how to handle it, so they needed to bring someone from the outside to handle it." Supervisor Hugh emphasized that St. Louis County knew their standard procedures and knew what needed to be done to get the situation resolved, but instead, people who were not even there (the governor) determined that they had a better solution. Supervisor Jason said, "When we showed up for work, it was just, all of a sudden, it was changed and we were basically given a timeout, so we're sitting in the parking lot geared up, and they're like 'The highway patrol's gonna handle it from here. Just stand by and sit down.'" Supervisor Elijah thought that the change in command "Took us back, I think any progress we made, it actually backed us up a little bit." Supervisor Jason told us that the Highway Patrol officers were embarrassed by the governor's decision. Jason said that "They felt that we did everything correct." State police troopers approached him and told him that.

Supervisor Mason said that Chief Belmar told officers to support Captain Johnson, but Mason thought that the change in leadership was disruptive to all of the agencies involved in the protest response. Supervisor Hugh explained that state officers do not have experience working the street or even urban contexts. Troopers spend much of their careers in unincorporated rural areas and handling traffic. Ron Johnson and those who worked for him were not coming from a position of experience and expertise, officers explained. Officer Karen said, "Once the patrol, Highway Patrol took over, it was really hard to take orders from someone who was not familiar with the area, not familiar with the community [although Johnson had lived in the general area previously], not familiar with our department, and was basically telling us to not do our job."

St. Louis County police felt betrayed by Johnson. He was a Black police officer, and numerous officers felt as Jason did, "I felt bad for him, because I knew why they put him in charge of everything, and he was not gonna win on any side, if there was sides. The police department, he was not gonna have their support and he wasn't gonna have the citizens' support." Police leadership spoke about how about four days after the official transfer of command to Johnson, there was a quiet shift back to St. Louis County police. Supervisor Logan thought that "They probably would've been better off just using somebody local with St. Louis County or City that had already built relationships in those communities."

Officer Solidarity in the Face of Grievance

Police culture explains police solidarity and unity as a by-product of a shared threat or grievance against police. Ferguson demonstrated a clear grievance against police. Police we interviewed felt attacked and accused by numerous groups. Supervisor Connor said, "It just seems like everybody jumped on the opposite side of the battle, right, so fast before the narrative even had a chance to get out there." Accusations and betrayal by the media and the government featured prominently to police in Ferguson.

FEELING BETRAYED BY THE MEDIA

Civil unrest began in earnest within a day of Brown's death. Officer Henry attributed this swift public response to the media and their portrayal of the shooting as racist and unjust. The media portrayed their impressions of the incident in the absence of facts about the investigation and what happened. He described the media's early role as "feeding the fire" and pointed out that, especially the first week of protests, no one in the media was saying, "Well, we just got to wait for the detail to come out." Police civilian Wendy added, "They found the angriest activist they could find to put on the news. They never found the moderates. They never found the police supporters." This perspective, feeling like the media is biased against one's position or group, is common when deeply involved with the topic (Nix and Pickett 2017; Hansen and Kim 2011). Case in point, in her book, Cobbina (2019) quoted a Ferguson protestor who also perceived that media coverage misrepresented the protests, but took the opposite view of the police officers that I surveyed. The protestor felt that the media had portrayed the protests as unruly and rowdy, when his view was that the protests were peaceful.

Officer Henry blamed commercialism for the perceived media bias. He said, "The actions [riots, looting] that happened on Sunday, that sells for media . . . That's their business . . . They don't want a reporter just standing there saying, 'We gotta wait for facts,' because no one is gonna watch that station. They gotta watch the SWAT team throw tear gas and flashbangs, and the interactions of the negativeness between, you know, police and community." In other words, the media chose to portray the events from an angle that would draw more viewers and airtime, that are action-based—"that is what keeps them in business," he said. Officer Owen said that while he understands that the media is trying to get ratings, "I don't think that justifies basically sacrificing good people that are trying to do good things [police]." Supervisor Oliver felt that the mission of the media affected how the public viewed police during the crisis. He offered, "I think we all learned that sometimes the media wasn't reporting stuff that was truly accurate and it really hurt us with what we were doing up there."

Officer Owen shared that eight people had been shot (not by police) over the course of seven nights at the protests (Other officers provided higher estimates of the number of shootings at this time), and yet, these shootings did not make the news, because they did not fit the intended narrative of the media. Rescues by police of the protestors who needed to be extracted from the crowd because they had been shot were not covered in the news, noted supervisor Dylan. Supervisor Jason said he was involved with four rescues of reporters, media crews that were "getting beat up by the crowd, robbed, shot at." About the media's failure to report these incidents, Owen commented, "That is not the story they are looking to tell. Police overreaction, brutality . . . was what they were looking to sell." Supervisor Noah described that the media presented pictures of the daytime protestors, then put those images right next to images of police handling nighttime unrest, when they were using tear gas. The implication was that police used tear gas against peaceful protestors. He said, "All that does is inflame, and that's what it was designed to do." Officer Kathie, who worked at night, said, "Everybody's talking about peaceful protests and there was nothing peaceful about anything I saw." She bemoaned not personally videorecording the public in action to give the public a better idea of what officers experienced during the nights of protests. Supervisor Dylan provided an important perspective about the media coverage, telling me, "It's always three sides to the story, their side, your side, and then the real truth."

Supervisor Noah described his experience with the media while deployed overseas in the military, and his description mirrors stories told by officers handling the Ferguson protests. He recounted that,

> They came in, they tried to be your friend, and they buddied up to you. They'd get the interviews, they'd get this footage, and they'd be like,

"You're doing a great thing here. We appreciate your service to the country. What you're doing here is excellent." And then, you know, a week later it would hit the *New York Times* and it was all bad things, and it was all the inadequacies, and it was nothing about anything good . . . I guess that's news. The good and normal doesn't sell. But it was all the bad stuff.

Officer Henry provided the perfect example to support Noah's claims. It was the night that Red's BBQ restaurant was set on fire. Shots had been fired and someone had thrown something into the restaurant that caused the fire to catch. Police responded by setting off tear gas to move everyone away from the area. Then, they divided into two teams to make sure everyone was gone. One team went in front and inside the building, while Henry's team went behind the restaurant. Just as he and his supervisor were leaving, they heard a faint cry for help, a female voice. She said, "I'm over in the brush . . . I'm a reporter; I got stuck back here." Henry said that they quickly took her to a secured area where they talked to her about what had happened. He described the incident:

She is frightened as all hell. She actually saw one protester shoot another protester because that happened that night. And she was telling us about that, and she didn't know what to do because she didn't want to make a big deal of it because then she actually saw the person that shot the other protester. So, if she started getting her notebook pad out . . . criminals would see that and so she just acted like she was part of the group. And I totally understand that, that's fine, that's safety, right. So, we're sitting there and, and I mean she is crying, you know, she was nervous as hell, she was a *New York Times* reporter, we found out. And I go, well, I go, "So this makes it easy for us, you know exactly what happened here, you know. You saw another protester shoot someone, you were involved in the shots fired, you saw them just put Red's BBQ [on fire]." So, I go, "I'll be looking forward to your article tonight," thinking that's all gonna be in there. Not one of that was in her article. Not one paragraph about her getting trapped, about her seeing one protester shoot another protester, about her seeing guns in the crowd, about any of that in her article that night. And that, it just put us over the edge of like, I mean if no one is gonna report this, you know. But the first time we shoot a canister of tear gas we're everywhere, you know.

He said that it felt like a conspiracy.

> It felt like no matter what we did, it was wrong. And no matter what happened at the scenes, they weren't reported correctly, you know. The only thing that was recorded was us shooting tear gas, which we did, we had, we had to sometimes, but it [the news] never said, you know, shots were being fired at the police, or bottles were getting shattered in front of the police, or bricks, bricks or rocks were getting thrown. Yeah, I mean that was, that was probably one of the most frustrating of that night, and we still talk about that.

Officer Sebastian also felt bitter toward the media. He described seeing a picture in the media of a man that police arrested. The picture portrayed the man with numerous tactical officers drawing down on him (pointing their guns at him). Sebastian said that the photo looked like an infantry squad going after one man. What preceded that event was numerous efforts to arrest the man who had thrown rocks at police throughout the day, but the picture did not incorporate that part of the events. Media coverage emphasized police militarization. As officer Henry commented,

> They made us seem like we're just arriving on scene and just shooting tear gas left and right, you know? . . . It made it seem like people were just having a peaceful rally inside of, in a street not saying anything to a police officer, then all of a sudden, the big bad military shows up, and we're just sniping people with tear gas, you know. That's what the coverage seemed like on Twitter and on national TV, some local stations.

He felt that the media did not recognize that helmets and plastic shields are not used to hurt people, rather they protect officers from getting hit in the head with a brick or in the face with a rock. The media's hostile portrayal of police propelled officers' sense of isolation from others and unification with one another (Feldman et al. 2017).

There were several types of media represented at the protests, including news media and livestreamers/bloggers. Officer Henry said he noticed that anytime a fight broke out between protestors, or protestors created a disturbance, livestreamers would turn away, because the images would not fit the narrative that the social media influencer wanted to portray. One example of creating an anti-police narrative came when a shots-fired call went out and later, on Twitter, someone posted a picture of a female who was shot with the message, "Look what police did to this protestor." That was not what happened, but there is no fact check on social media, no consequences for lying or misrepresenting facts.

Officer Henry said that after the first couple of nights, all of his fellow officers were on Twitter, looking to see what the public said about the police response at the protests and whether they reported things that happened, like shots fired, that paint a more negative view about the protestors. He said it was like a bad dream and he was waiting to wake up. The challenge with social media is that it presents a high-profile platform for a small portion of the population. It is not representative of any group or the whole, but it is what is accessible.

Eventually, in November 2014, the department hired a social media specialist to help with the communication challenges they faced. The social media specialist had days, like the day of the grand jury verdict, where she constantly tweeted and posted on Facebook. Her overall vision was "to make sure that people knew that we understood that this was a pivotal time in the department, in St. Louis County, what was going on as far as race relations." Pamela, a police civilian, told me that the department wanted the public to know that "Everybody has a right to protest, but if people are going to use it as an excuse to commit criminal behavior, we're not going to tolerate that . . . We were concerned about the people who were not protestors, they were criminals. They were literally using the protestors as a front to go and commit crimes, whether it's burning down buildings, looting, and so just to put that message out there."

After months of feeling condemned in the media, officers did perceive a shift in media coverage. Officers thought that at least the local media began to cover two sides of the story. Also, social media posts began to show a negative side to protestors, including protestors standing very close to and spitting on police. People in the public began to realize what police were going through. Officers thought the shift began around the time of the grand jury verdict, which coincided with when St. Louis County Police Department hired the social media specialist.

The social media specialist released surveillance videos of looting incidents (e.g., people breaking into stores, breaking things, stealing things) from inside a business, one each week, to the local news media. Officer Henry said that these media-assisted efforts led to 50–60 arrests. Henry wondered if the media were thinking at that point, "Man, maybe we shouldn't have covered this the way we did during the first couple of weeks on what happened, because we didn't have the facts."

FEELING BETRAYED BY GOVERNMENT OFFICIALS

Police also felt betrayed and abandoned by all levels of politicians during the protests, from aldermen to the US president. Police believed the politicians did little to encourage discussion, mend fences, or repair police-community relations. For example, officer Jack pointed out that when US Attorney General Eric Holder came to St. Louis, he met with the protestors, but he did not come to the command post. In his speech on August 21, 2014, after this visit, Holder said that he met with the family of Michael Brown and spoke to them "as a father of a teenage son myself" ("Attorney General Eric Holder's Statement on Developments in Ferguson, MO," 2014). Supervisor Connor said, "It was hard sometimes because you would listen to the Attorney General talk and you knew that there was an agenda being pushed, and that was frustrating, but . . . I'm just a guy who lives in St. Louis County, that works for St. Louis County, right? I'm not going to be able to take on the Attorney General of the United States and make him understand my viewpoint." Holder's remarks focused on his personal understanding and appreciation for mistrust in police, the underlying tensions motivating the mistrust, and the importance of the "appropriate use of force" (ibid.).

Officer Thomas commented that the public "look at elected officials as the leaders of the community, or the leaders of state or country, and so on. And when somebody in that position comes out and directly makes a remark, 'The police screwed up, they did this completely wrong,'" it makes an impression on the public. Older officers who worked for the county for 30 years and who built the organization especially felt the experience was "a personal attack on what they've built," said supervisor Mason. Officer Thomas questioned Governor Nixon's role in deciding who should lead the protest policing response, what tactics should be used, and when the National Guard should be engaged in protest policing. He said of politicians, "You have no background in this. I don't tell you how to run your something." By way of example, he continued, "I don't tell the CEO of QuickTrip how to run that business, because I have no idea how . . . I don't know what Governor Nixon does, I have no clue. But I don't go on TV and say, 'Nixon you are screwing up. You're doing all this completely wrong.' However, he can get on TV and tell me I'm doing my job completely wrong."

Not only were politicians unhelpful, thought officers, but sometimes officers believed politicians being vocal incited problems with the public. Supervisor Elijah remarked that it felt like a political game for politicians. On the day that Michael Brown was killed, Supervisor Jason said that he watched while police command staff briefed Missouri State Senator Maria Chappelle-Nadal, whose district 14 includes Ferguson. He explained,

> Being naive, I thought she was going to go out there and get everybody to calm down, "Let's let this investigation unfold before we decide . . ." And as soon as the commanders gave her a briefing on what was going on, she marched out into the street and started the F*** the police narrative and the chant. I was just beyond disbelief. I was like, this is an elected leader that is going out there doing that? And she's getting them more agitated.

Of the militarization of police, officer Anthony spoke of feeling angry about remarks made by then US Senator Claire McCaskill, Missouri, whom he felt blamed the police and commented publicly about how the camouflage uniforms and armored trucks were intimidating to the public. And he thought, "You know what? We've had a SWAT team for God, over 30 years. And this equipment that we had, you would of thought that we just ordered it from e-Bay and just we're reading directions and we're opening it up as we're reading."

Officer Henry spoke of the impact of one of Governor Jay Nixon's first press conferences about the Ferguson protests on August 19, 2014, during which he called for a "vigorous prosecution" of officer Wilson, "who shot and killed Michael Brown in broad daylight" in order to "achieve justice for this family" (Kraske 2014). Officer Henry said of that public stance, "That hurt us, because that was so quick after, where he didn't know any facts either." Henry felt that Nixon's message conveyed to the public that the "officer did something wrong and we're gonna fix it." The lieutenant governor at the time, Peter Kinder, agreed with Henry. He told Fox News that the governor was wrong to have said that and that instead the governor should be seeking justice for all the parties. In response to this discussion, president of the Missouri Fraternal Order of Police expressed that, "Darren's been vilified in the press and by politicians with minimal facts being made public" ("Missouri Gov Calls for 'Vigorous Prosecution' of Ferguson Shooting Case" 2015).

When three White House officials (Assistant to the President and White House Cabinet Secretary Broderick Johnson, Deputy Director of the White House Office of Public Engagement Marlon Marshall, and Advisor to the Public Engagement Officer Heather Foster) attended the funeral for Michael Brown on August 25, 2014, it fostered a similar feeling among officers. Officer Henry said that the White House did not send officials to the local military funerals of veterans killed in the line of duty, yet officials attended Brown's funeral—with no knowledge of the specific circumstances of his death at that time. Henry said, "That's kind of a slap in the face to our country, I think . . . What does that show your nation of who you are backing?" He felt that President Obama, acting without actual knowledge about what happened, like Governor Nixon, was "picking sides" and should have remained neutral and waited for the facts to be known rather than repeatedly expressing concern for Brown's family and failing to support law enforcement. President Obama's initial statement on August 12, 2014 and follow-up comments on August 18, 2014 did not directly condemn police actions, they were just as Henry said—Obama's remarks were very sympathetic to the family and community and spoke about the ways that the federal government would be investigating and involved in Ferguson. There was no reference to supporting law enforcement. Obama spoke about "a community in Ferguson that is rightfully hurting and looking for answers," "a gulf of mistrust that exists between local residents and law enforcement," and being "personally committed to changing both perception and reality" (Hudson 2014; "The President Speaks on Iraq and Ferguson" 2014).

Officer Henry wished that the investigation had been completed before federal officials appeared to condemn officer Wilson. Officer Jack agreed, "All they had to do was come out and say, 'You know what? The rioting is wrong. We're gonna let the investigation unfold.'" Supervisor

Dylan said that it was important to officers what the president thought. "Everyone pays attention to the president of the United States whenever he talks," said officer Henry.

Officers did not feel supported by the president, the US attorney general, senators, or the governor. Supervisor Dylan thought it would have made a big difference to have their support. According to supervisor Elijah, "It felt like we were going to be made the sacrificial lambs . . . we had no control over the offense leading up to it, and we had no control over fixing the issues that were at hand. The people that were responsible, the legislators, the ones that could make the changes, seemed like they turned their back on us too. And we were left out at the abyss by ourselves. That was a little disheartening to see that." Officer Anthony described police as "expendable" to politicians, while officer Ryan compared the experience to the feeling he had when getting a blatantly terrible call from a referee in high school, that, "The ref makes a bad call, and you turn around like, 'Come on ref.' I was like, didn't you see the other guy do that? You know? I'm just, it's that same kind of like, seriously?" Officer Anthony mused that the issue of race was just too big for politicians to address and so they focused on something seemingly more manageable—the police. Focusing on police allowed politicians to deflect from the larger issue to which they contribute.

Although Captain Ron Johnson was law enforcement, a state trooper, his assignment to command the police response to the Ferguson protest was made by Governor Nixon and thus was viewed as an extension of politics. The decision was poorly received among officers. Supervisor Jacob noted that policing is the only profession that politicians (e.g., mayors, senators, governors), who never have been police officers, would feel like they know the best way to do the job. He commented that politicians and others do not go "to the president of the hospital . . . to tell a surgeon how to operate." The governor's decision to assign Captain Johnson to lead the police response made the same impression in the minds of officers.

Already troubled by that action, officers also cited disappointment in Captain Johnson's remarks about "being ashamed to wear the police uniform." In a speech that Johnson made on August 18, 2014 at a Michael Brown rally, Johnson said that he apologized to Brown's family as a "person wearing this uniform," and he spoke about his "Black son," concluding that he will "Stand tall with you and I'll see ya out there" (CBS This Morning 2014). Johnson's comments made officers feel betrayed, as did his marching with protestors while wearing his police uniform. Officer Anthony stressed, "As police officers, we can't have political signs in our yards." He felt that Johnson should not have adopted a political position, especially while in uniform. Supervisor Alexander said, "I just feel that when you become a policeman, you lose the Black card, you lose the White card. You got the blue card, basically. Everybody's equal, everybody's the same."

Officers also felt wronged by Johnson's comments on the news on his first night in charge, when Supervisor Connor told me that Johnson stated, "We had a quiet night. We had a good night." Yet, Connor noted, that night they had several incidents, including a shooting, including officers being trapped by the crowd and needing rescue, officers being hit with rocks and bottles and being injured. During the next day at roll call, supervisor Connor said Johnson was asked, "why did you lie on TV last night?"' Johnson reportedly defended himself, denying that he lied on television, but the officer pressed back saying, "No, no, you did." And Connor said you could see heads in the crowd nodding confirmation, that people were frustrated. But, also according to Connor, Chief Belmar squashed these reactions by his officers and put things in perspective to command staff, which Connor then relayed to his subordinates. The perspective underscored the importance of police solidarity and unity. Connor relayed to his subordinates:

> The whole world wants us to fail. Nothing would make the politicians happier than if we fall flat on our face. That crap that just happened [calling out Johnson] can't happen, because what's gonna happen is if you continue to go down that road, you're gonna reaffirm everything they already think about us. You're gonna cost the chief his job, you're gonna cost me my job, you're gonna cost you your job. That's the only thing that's gonna happen. The only thing we could do is keep our heads up, do our jobs, and do right.

He felt that his subordinates were able to take this critique to heart because they also realized that if something "got bad down there in that corridor [in Ferguson], I wasn't going to get on the phone and ask for

Ron Johnson's permission to do something to keep my people safe." Connor felt that officers under his supervision had confidence that he would look out for them and their safety and prioritize their well-being over politics. It further helped that officers believed that Chief Belmar also had their safety as a top priority over politics.

FEELING BETRAYED BY THE CHURCH

Although chapter 1 discusses the fact that at least one-third of police spoke about how the clergy played a positive role in helping to improve safety and the environment at the protests, police also spoke about feeling betrayed by the church. Supervisors Jacob and Hugh, both Black, talked about how their personal churches accused or condemned police in their sermons at the time, and that they found this judgment to be particularly hurtful and difficult to take. Supervisor Hugh said that during the day, the clergy talked about God and hope, but at night, they chanted with the protestors, "You must repent, you're going to hell. God doesn't love you." Hugh said, "That was one of the things that for me, bothered me the most. Seeing those people, clergy people who we call leadership, who we believe have faith in God and shouldn't have judgment, becoming that same thing that we were trying to stop." Several officers also spoke with frustration about a specific church in Ferguson that provided for the needs of the protestors (e.g., shelter, food, changes of clothes), appearing to support their message and indulge their methods. Supervisor Luke said, "They would clean them up and dust them off and pat them [protestors] out the door and say, okay, there's more protesting to do. Get on up there." For him, it was frustrating. He felt that the church should have focused their support on people with a "legitimate agenda." He saw that church as supporting chaos and causing problems. He struggled to distinguish the hostility, the looting, rioting, and throwing things at police from a worthy social cause. Luke explained that the police were there for the public, to protect the public, but that specific church was working to cycle troublemakers back onto the streets.

SOLIDARITY AMONG OFFICERS

Solidarity among officers constituted a defense mechanism in response to police feeling assailed by negativity and grievances. Officer Fred described what it felt like, that no one was on his side. He said,

The only people that I had in my life that actually gave a f*** about anything was my wife and the guys and the girls to my right and left at work. I thought the world was against us and I never thought I would ever experience something like that. We were standing alone together on the thin blue line. The only people that understood and knew what we were going through were us. You know, I mean I think my belief in the brotherhood and the comradery on the thin blue line solidified.

Police civilians were able to see officers' solidarity clearly. Pamela said that at the command post she heard officers talk "very protective" of each other, "as they should be." Also, Wendy observed that normally, police interact with each other like an older and younger brother, "They're constantly picking at each other, but as soon as somebody from the outside comes in and tries to hurt one of them, they're thick as thieves, you're not gonna touch him. That's exactly what happened. I have never, in the [first] three weeks, I've never seen more cohesion among people who normally would be kind of picking at each other." A robust aspect of police culture, the solidarity among police became even more robust during the Ferguson protests. Supervisor Noah saw the us-against-them mentality increase at this time, although several officers spoke out against that view. Supervisor Jason said that although most officers feel that residents in North County have a "dim" view of police, "we can't have an us-versus-them mentality." He talked about working hard to engage residents in dialogue, offering, "That's the only way. We gotta quit looking at them like they're the enemy and they gotta quit looking at us like we're the enemy."

Individual Accountability and Strategies to Cope with Oversight

The final layer of police culture outlined by Crank (2014) (see figure 2.1) describes the strategies police use to cope with external oversight, the constraints and accountability imposed on them while they navigate their challenging role. Police culture outlines several forms these adaptations take, but central in officers' descriptions of Ferguson were the value and importance of acknowledging individual accountability (versus organizational accountability) and pulling their own weight.

INDIVIDUAL ACCOUNTABILITY (ROTTEN APPLE, NOT ROTTEN BARREL)

Police culture emphasizes individual officer accountability as a way to deflect critique of the organization. In the Ferguson context, police coped with external oversight on the profession of policing by focusing on the behaviors of officer Wilson and on whether he behaved appropriately during the encounter with Brown—the flash point that initiated the protests. Although supervisors and officers could distinguish between the shooting incident and the societal issues imbued into the protests, much of their discourse focused on the initial incident and whether the shooting was justified.

Before the grand jury verdict, both the police working the protests and the public protesting lacked the facts about the shooting—they did not know whether officer Wilson's actions were justified. However, the signs, chants, and protestors' behavior toward police at the protests showed officers, they told us, that the public had condemned all police. In response, officer Anthony said, "First of all, not every cop in America was on Canfield [Drive] shooting Mike Brown." Anthony felt that the public and the government wrongfully set about crucifying an entire profession based upon a single incident involving one police officer. Similarly, officer Leo said, "I didn't shoot Mike Brown." Leo was angry with the media attention and condemnation, saying, "I don't give a f*** about Mike Brown or Darren Wilson." He bemoaned, "We're getting pulled in and put into the spotlight . . . because we neighbor them [Ferguson]." But, supervisor Ben told us, "We're all different," meaning that police are individuals and act individually.

Perceived public condemnation of all police following the assumed improper actions by officer Wilson, without evidence, created a sense of injustice among police handling the Ferguson protests. Officer Ryan explained that because of the news coverage, the public adopted the misconception that police misconduct is "rampant." Police, however, were looking through the lens of individual accountability, deflecting blame from the organization or profession and not understanding why the public would "lump all of us into one category," looking at police as a whole, that "everybody is corrupt," according to supervisor Logan. For example, officer Henry explained,

I just want the, the recognition of, you know, for the most part, law enforcement is good for a community. It's not a negative thing. There's bad officers out there just like there's bad everything else, um, but 99.9 percent of the time police officers do the right thing. And, the times that they do mess up or if the times that we do find a bad police officer, I want that taken care of, you know . . . Just because he is a police officer doesn't mean now I just backed him because he is a police officer. I wanted to wait to see what the facts were too.

In defense of individual accountability, several officers emphasized their support of the prosecution and accountability of police officers who misbehave. Supervisor Luke described telling a protestor, before the grand jury verdict, that if the investigation shows that officer Wilson's actions were not justified, "There's nobody down there [in Ferguson] that's going to be more upset with him than us [police] . . . It makes us all look bad." Officer Fred pointed out that "There are idiot cops out there," they—idiots—are in every occupation, but they are "shuffled out" and not given "the responsibilities that other guys got." In other words, there are a few bad officers, but they are small in number and dealt with, as in any occupation. Officer Anthony agreed, saying, "I have issues with, and a lot of good police officers have issues with police officers who are doing the wrong thing out there, because it endangers everybody. It really does. We [police], you know, we really don't like them [police who do wrong]." Supervisor Jason summed it up, explaining, "Most officers . . . they would like to believe that officers are always in the right, but if you are in this job or read any papers, you can see things go, officers make bad decisions. And we all agreed [that] if Wilson made a, if this was a bad shoot, then hold him accountable." By emphasizing holding the individual officer accountable, the organization and the profession avert blame. As Black supervisor Dylan said, "There are some bad seeds in everything . . . whether it be police work, whether it be politicians, firemen, whoever, you know, you're not going to have a perfect tree of people."

PULL THEIR WEIGHT AND HELP EACH OTHER

A second common cultural adaptation among police that we heard from officers working Ferguson is placing high value on individual officers doing their part. As mentioned above, officers felt a tenacious commitment to each other during the protests in response to being aggrieved by the public, politicians, and the media. Forty percent of officers brought up the need to "help my people [police]." Supervisor Gabe stressed that Ferguson was a time when "team mentality was king . . . You had to support each other, you had to." He recalled that whatever the department needed from people, that is what they did, "because they wanted to help." That extended to Ferguson Police as well. Supervisor Gabe said that as a member of the St. Louis County Police Department he realized that Ferguson police needed their help and that they had to do their part. He saw this same mentality among officers from all of the departments responding to mutual aid and protest policing, saying, "If they came in, they were in our huddle. They were our guys, you know, our gals. Immediate interlocking of arms, so to speak, in order to accomplish that task, whatever that task may be."

Officer Nathan said, "Everybody depended on everybody else to do their job and if somebody didn't do their job, someone would get hurt." Although working the protests in Ferguson was challenging and exhausting, officers kept going to Ferguson because that is where they were needed, officer Anthony told me. Supervisor Larry explained, "I didn't go into Ferguson to promote my career or to get notoriety. I went to support my fellow officers." At roll call, officer Anthony told his colleagues, "Let's back each other up." An example of this support was provided by officer Karen, a newer officer, who told a story about feeling terrified while working the night of the grand jury verdict. Despite the fear and uncertainty that night brought, she felt supported and reassured because a more experienced officer "stuck by me all that night." She felt protected by his presence and experience. His actions provided the support she required to get through that shift.

Many officers described feeling guilty when they were off work, because they were not in Ferguson helping their police colleagues, their "brothers and sisters," as Supervisor Larry called them. Officer Fred said, "When I was off duty I wanted to be on duty." This sentiment was not motivated by being a workaholic or an adrenaline junky. Police described listening to the news or getting on social media when they were off so that they could stay on top of events and help the officers working the protests, even when they were off duty. Fred explained,

I'm worried about the guys out there, you know, I'd fire up the livestreams, I'd send sergeant texts saying "Hey, this guy's doing this with this. This guy's doing this with that." And it would get heated and stuff in front of the PD. I'm like F***, I wanna be there for them, with them, but, you know, instead, I'm at home. And I felt guilt about that, but, you know, when you're off duty, you're off duty, no big deal. I mean it was just, just, Ferguson just consumed your life.

Supervisor Wyatt said the same thing. He worked days, so he went home at night, but he watched the news when he got home. In doing so, he would "find myself driving back up there" to try to help. An officer whose wife gave birth during the protests described to his supervisor, Elijah, that it was a difficult decision about whether to be gone from the Ferguson protests the day of the birth, that he felt like he was "letting down his fellow officers by not showing up that night or the next night." Elijah even described that although two county officers had arranged to leave the department to accept jobs with other departments during the protests (they had resigned), both officers delayed their departures from the county to "stay and help their fellow officers." Officer Kathie described being put on leave during the protests because she had been part of an officer-involved shooting. Yet even though she could not work at the protests, during the period of her leave, she brought meals to the officers working the protests and tried to be a support to them. She felt that she needed to do something to help.

Police in Ferguson embraced the idea that they were "all in this together. It doesn't matter if you're a captain or patrolman," said Chief Belmar. Even police civilians working the unrest described feeling that they must pull their own weight and help. Wendy said, "As long as they [officers] were standing there every night on that line, I would be there in the morning with hot coffee, breakfast, Band-Aids, Kleenex, whatever they needed. And I would be there until they all left in the evening to go out to stand their lines." At the command post, Wendy asked herself, "Am I doing enough? What else can I do?"

I heard from supervisors that for them, pulling their weight meant doing what they could to help, support, and protect subordinates from harm. Supervisor Alexander explained that while officers were on the skirmish line, he stood in front of them, between them and the public.

His mindset was, "Hey, you can stand behind me and I'll deal with this . . . Taking care of my guys." Supervisors' protection of officers was especially zealous for Black officers on the skirmish line being berated by the public. Supervisors' efforts to look out for those officers are described in chapter 3. It came down to what supervisor Larry told his officers, "I don't expect you to fight by yourselves or to resolve this problem. We are all in this together."

Conversely, officers and supervisors spoke against police whom they perceived did not pull their weight. Largely, they were talking about police leaders whom they believed were not engaged with officers—they did not attend roll call and did not go out on the line with the officers under their supervision. Supervisor Alexander thought that perhaps some police leaders "saw their own mortality, and it affected them," an empathic perspective on why some supervisors may have failed to lead in the field, but for Alexander, "It pissed me off." He questioned, "How are you more special than everyone else?" Officer Karen said that not all supervisors were skilled leaders. Officer Anthony explained that some supervisors just stopped supervising during the protests. This failure to perform on the part of specific supervisors did not go unnoticed and was widely condemned by police.

Moderating Influences

Several factors helped to moderate officers' cultural responses to feeling betrayed and isolated. Three themes gleaned from officers' accounts included (1) being treated well by supervisors and the police organization—organizational justice; (2) support from family, friends, or even from the public; and (3) feeling assured that police were doing the right thing. These factors helped buffer the influence of the grievances and feelings of isolation on officers' morale and ability to provide protest policing.

ORGANIZATIONAL JUSTICE AND SUPPORT FROM LEADERS

Officer Fred told me, "I would follow Chief Belmar through the gates of hell." He felt supported by the chief and believed that the chief was proud of his officers. This support inspired loyalty, hard work, and compliance. I repeatedly heard line-level police expressing confidence in Chief Belmar, in his leadership throughout the protest experience and the just approach with which he led the officers. Chief Belmar said he recognized that his presence and that of other senior commanders at the protests was important to and appreciated by officers, and he made being in the field and visible a priority. A high-ranking supervisor, Wyatt, also affirmed how important it was for Chief Belmar and other command staff to leave the command post and be "on the front line" alongside officers. He said, "The guys saw that, the other officers from the other agencies saw that, and that went a long way." Affirming his impression, officer Karen said, "I give Chief Belmar a lot of credit because every night that I was out there, he was out there. If we couldn't wear a vest, he didn't wear a vest. And he was out there actually being a leader . . . I do have to give him credit because he was out there fighting with us." The confidence line-level personnel felt for Chief Belmar's leadership was the reason changing the command to Captain Johnson during the protests was so devastating to them.

Supervisors spoke of their efforts to support and protect their subordinates during the protests. Supervisor Dylan spent a great deal of time standing in between the skirmish line and the protestors. He felt, "That's my job. That's what God gave me the ability to do, was to be out front, be a leader, and make sure that your troops are protected and that they can see that you care about them." In Ferguson, he said that he asked his officers each day if they were okay. Officer Joshua thought talking with supervisors and using their support was important, "because they're the ones that are gonna back you." Supervisor Logan felt the same way. He said that supervisors must constantly communicate with officers because then the officers will feel more connected and that "you got them." It builds trust. Failing to communicate with them will cause officers to wonder whether the supervisor would support them if they got into trouble—not "covering up for corruption," he said, but rather supporting the officer despite pressure, much like the public and political pressure against officer Wilson.

There were some questions about organizational justice during the protests. County officers newer to policing (less than five years), relative to more experienced officers, appeared to have a more tenuous sense of organizational justice, for example, questioning whether the department would support them if they had a questionable use of force situation like Darren Wilson. They felt like a number, expendable to the department—if an officer messes up, they are done because the department will look out for the department. Officer Sebastian first formed this opinion because he said the department was hesitant to send in officers in response to their requests for aid, out of concern for the optics, putting officers at risk in order to avoid looking bad on the news. Officer Owen echoed the same view, asking himself "Am I more important to them than public relations?" Officers with this view were few in number but suggest an area with room for improvement. The pattern of newer versus older officers feeling more skeptical of organizational justice and support does raise an interesting question about the nature and duration of the process needed to instill a sense of organizational justice among officers new to policing.

SUPPORT FROM FAMILY AND FRIENDS

Most police spoke about experiencing their families' and friends' support (88 percent) and how that support helped them endure the experience of protest policing. Much of the support was in the nature of taking care of routine tasks since the officers worked long shifts without days off—neighbors bringing food, handling chores, letting the dogs out, or driving children to practice and events. Supervisor Elijah said that during the protests in August, he never had to cut his grass—neighbors supported his wife and helped with chores, gift cards, and food. In winter, officer Sebastian did not have to shovel his driveway. Officer Andre said a neighbor offered to wash his laundry. Police were often receiving texts from family and friends to ask how they were doing and to provide encouragement. Several officers' parents reportedly drove in from out of town to be an emotional and physical resource. Supervisor Oliver spoke about how some teachers asked his son how his dad was doing, and that was very positive for his son. Officer Henry shared that his baby had a double ear infection that first week of protests, and although his wife worked full time, he could not help them, she handled it all. Officer Alexander came home one night to a living room filled with water, Gatorade, protein bars, peanuts, etc. His teenage daughter had overheard him telling her mom that officers in Ferguson were having difficulty making time to eat. She took it upon herself to conduct a Facebook campaign, which was so successful that Alexander had to share the snacks across multiple precincts. Officers repeatedly expressed extreme gratitude for extended family and neighbors that helped sustain their well-being and even helped counteract some of the negativity from the protest experience. Officer Henry said that he would get 20–30 voicemail and text messages daily from family and friends reaching out to him and encouraging him. For him, he said, "That kind of counteracted some of the marching and nastiness" of the protest experience. However, chapter 3 discusses that among Black officers, some family members were not supportive.

SUPPORT FROM THE PUBLIC DURING THE PROTESTS

Although it seemed to officers that no one publicly supported police during the Ferguson unrest, officers provided many examples that showed otherwise. Officer Henry said that before going on shift in Ferguson, he went to a local convenience store (not one in North County), and he said that each day, five or six citizens would shake his hand in that store and say, "Thank you for your service." Officer Karen said, "That was always something to kind of keep us going." Recognizing this, when people asked supervisor Oliver what they could do to help police, he told them, "When you are at a gas station or at the store and you see a policeman, just tell them thanks. That is all I need you to do. That goes a long way."

Support also came in the form of prayer. Officer Kathie said that one day when she was in a convenience store, a small Black woman came up and grabbed her arm and prayed for her. She said that officers texted each other when things like that happened, because hearing about it would "lift our spirts." Supervisor Dylan described going to a store and having a woman stop him. The woman's daughter had prepared an art project and she wanted to give it to a police officer. On the art project, which he still had when I spoke to him more than a year later, it said, "You're my hero" and "God loves you and so do I." Dylan said, "That melted me right there . . . I got a little teary eyed." Supervisor Wyatt said that cards from elementary students saying "thank you" were hung on the walls at the precinct and he felt that having evidence of support from the community was vital to enabling officers to get through the experience of protest policing. Officers spent so much of their time at the protests being berated and called names, that small acts of kindness or appreciation were impactful. Supervisor Joseph said that people saying hello or saying that they are praying for police began to make him feel as if maybe the entire world was not against police.

Members of the public, local restaurants, companies, clubs, Citizen's Academy attendees, and church groups donated snacks, drinks, supplies (e.g., lip balm, sunscreen, hand sanitizer, hand-warming packets in winter), and money (which they processed through their 501c3 welfare association). One company dropped off about $25,000 in water and sports drinks. Police agencies from across the country sent gift cards.

Police had to be selective about what food (e.g., homemade items) was given to officers. Officer Sebastian said that although most people seemed genuine, "You don't want to be the one to eat a cookie with laxatives in it or something." Wendy was responsible for coordinating the food donations and assured me,

If you handed me food and it was homemade, not wrapped, and I didn't know you, I was gonna thank you, maybe even give you a hug if you were a little old lady, but as soon as you drove away it's going in the garbage because I don't know who you are. So the guys knew if it was on the table, even if it looked homemade, if it was on the table I knew where it came from so it was okay to eat.

Out of this same caution, officers working the Ferguson protests (after those first few weeks and things slowed down) were selective about where they dined while working. Officers mentioned three restaurants that they frequented. At one of those restaurants, officer Jack recounted that the server told him that someone had paid for the meal and 'It's gonna be free for awhile.' The person had anonymously purchased a $5,000 gift card and asked the restaurant to use it to pay for officers' meals when they ate there. The generosity of people helped make officers feel that not everyone was against them.

Some public interventions were highly symbolic. Officer Teresa, who felt so berated and betrayed by the public during the protests, also told me about an incident that helped her cope, stating, "No matter how often you hear the negatives, there is always someone standing up for you. In the public, there was a girl who stood in front of us [her name was Lexi, 19 years, a St Louis University student, another officer told us, and she was featured in a St. Louis *Post- Dispatch* story (Moore 2015)], saying she'd rather [she] get hit with a brick than the police officers." Officer Luke said that "We think of her as a hero." Of Lexi's courage, officer Teresa commented, "For every hundred people who say bad things to us, that one positive just brightens up our day. As much as I wish we could all get along, I know that's not going to happen any time soon. So . . . I'm grateful for the people who support us." Similarly, officer Fred had not realized that people from the public went and stood in front of businesses, lining up, trying to protect the businesses from being looted or set on fire. His nonpolice friend called him one night during the protests and said he was going out there to stand in front of businesses, and Fred said that he was touched by the show of support.

ASSURANCE OF DOING THE RIGHT THING

These examples of public support may have contributed to the third moderator officers spoke a great deal about. It was the perspective that police behaved righteously during the protests. Officer Henry said that during the tired and tough times of the protests, he and other officers reminded themselves, "We're doing the right thing, you know. We're keeping people that want us out there safe . . . and that is what kind of made you show up each day." Supervisor Larry explained that people get into policing because they want to better society, and that one thing that helped make protest policing in Ferguson bearable was "Knowing what I was doing was right, knowing what law enforcement represents is correct." Officer Fred spoke proudly about handling the protests with professionalism, despite the media coverage of police and public and politicians' treatment of police. It was important to police to feel that, "I didn't do anything wrong . . . I did my job the way that I believed it needed to be done," said supervisor Gabe.

Conclusions

I was struck by how completely officers' accounts of their protest policing experiences reflected the police occupational culture. Looking at Ferguson through this lens can give nonpolice some perspective about how police viewed protestors, residents, the media, and politicians.

Adopting this view shows why police felt that they were on an island, separated from everyone else, how they struggled to maintain the edge in the face of perceived and persistent danger, and improves understanding about the coping tools police adopted to navigate the experience, including factors that helped to moderate the more extreme aspects of the experience.

Community Callout

Much like officers described feeling a sense of unity with fellow officers, but set distinctly apart from all others, because the world appeared to be against them, a clear division was apparent in the community surveys. There were distinct patterns along racial lines—motivated by prior experiences with police and group position/social identity. Prior research supports that people view the protest goals of minority groups through their group position (Drakulich et al. 2021).

The differences by race were about how residents viewed police and protestors. Black residents expressed a unified opposition to and mistrust of police built on a history of accumulated negative experiences, perceived as shared among Black residents as a group. Black residents were vocal that Brown's death symbolized that shared experience. This is consistent with what Cobbina (2019) found among Black protestors in Ferguson, as well as in Baltimore, and she too concludes that Blacks in her sample viewed police with suspicion and believed police acted in a biased manner due to their own prior experiences receiving differential treatment by police. Black residents in my surveys were most likely to praise the public's contentious response to Brown's death. Conversely, as a group, non-Black residents did not convey a strong negative response to policing following Brown's death nor during the protests, and they advocated for the public to rely on the criminal justice system to investigate and properly administer justice rather than protest and riot.

The 2014 community survey of residents showed that in the two months following Michael Brown's death, Black residents' trust in police declined by 26 percent and perceived police legitimacy declined 8 percent (see table A.4 in the appendix for a description of these measures). Black residents' comments showed that many believed that officer Wilson had been wrong in his handling of Michael Brown (note that the grand jury decision came a month after the surveys were concluded). Black residents expressed certainty about Wilson's guilt and a desire to punish Wilson and police more broadly, saying things like, "The police officer murdered that boy," calling Wilson a "bully, not a professional police officer, and he needs to be jailed," saying "He did it, he should be charged," beseeching that "Police deserved what they got" and "The officer should be punished."

Black residents' comments suggest that some believed initial witness reports and claims made in speeches by Reverend Al Sharpton that Brown had his hands in the air when he was shot (Anonymous 2014a). Sharpton claimed, "A White cop kills a Black man who had his hands in the air, by shooting him nine times, and then he laid there for three hours before any response came." Several Black residents referenced Brown as being an "unarmed child" and referred to his shooting as "uncalled for." A 30-year-old Black man told us, "His hands were up, he should not have been shot." An 18-year-old Black woman said, "I was mad, because they didn't have the right to shoot him!" Numerous residents bemoaned that an alternative response to shooting Brown would have been more appropriate (e.g., shoot him in the arm or leg, use a taser).

A few Black residents also appeared to connect the shooting to Brown's presumed robbery of the store earlier in the day rather than his interaction with Wilson on the street, saying things like "He should not have died for stealing" and "Michael was in the wrong, but he shouldn't have been killed. The police response was a little too much." These remarks appeared to speculate on the deservedness of Brown being shot for the crime of robbery rather than on the threat Brown may have posed or did not pose to Wilson during their encounter. The idea of the shooting as punishment appeared several times.

Mistrust of police was prevalent, particularly of Ferguson police. Numerous residents distinguished between Ferguson police and St. Louis County police. A 46-year-old Black woman said, "Some police are good, and some are bad. County police are good." Likewise, a 36-year-old Black man told us, "The county police are good, and the Ferguson Police are bad," that Ferguson police had a "bad reputation for being prejudiced." County officers we interviewed did not share this view. The officers who commented believed that Ferguson Police Department had a good reputation, that they were professional.

Black residents talked about "crooked cops" and "bad apples" and their view that police band together in solidarity to protect each other. One Black woman believed that, "Police take matters into their own hands and manufacture evidence." A 27-year-old Black man said, "Police just made a mistake (shooting Michael), and they were standing up for each other like a family only to protect their own." An older Black woman remarked, "No matter what happened, the other cops will defend the one who shot him." A Black woman said that she thought, "The shooting may have been justified, but I think it is a cover-up to make the police look better." Concerns about a police cover-up were threaded across numerous Black residents' remarks, suggesting residents' thought police protected officer Wilson from accountability. Black residents did not trust the evidence. One Black male said, "They released footage of Michael Brown at the market—that didn't happen." He questioned the integrity of the video evidence. However, a 70-year-old Black woman did concur with what one of the police interviewees, supervisor Dylan, told us. She said that there are "three sides to every story: yours, mine and the truth," practically quoting Dylan's sentiment, inferring that the circumstances were not as simple as some people viewed them.

During the protests, alongside mistrusting police, Black residents reported seeing aggressive policing tactics more frequently than they had reported in the 2013 survey, an increase of 21 percent. However, further statistical modeling (described in Kochel [2015a]) showed that the difference is explained by the closer proximity of Black residents to the location of Brown's shooting and the protests. When adjusting for how far away residents lived from the location on Canfield Drive where Brown was killed, racial differences about aggressive policing tactics were not significantly different by race. Residents living near the protests were more likely to personally see police on skirmish lines, wearing riot gear, deploying tear gas, and tangling with aggressive or violent protestors, and that factored into their assessments about policing tactics.

Seventy-six percent of Black residents disagreed with the police response to the protests, 48 percent strongly disagreed. Black residents viewed the police response to the protestors as too extreme, too aggressive, and too militaristic. A 27-year-old Black man talked about police tear gassing "women and kids." A 38-year-old Black man talked about police using force against "unarmed protestors," "unarmed kids," and "a peaceful civilian population." It is not clear from his comments whether he got this impression from watching news media accounts about the protests or from personal accounts of witnessing or participating in the protests. An interesting trend in the surveys is that egregious comments about the police response at the protests were prevalent among Black males, but only a few Black women, about 14 percent, commented about the police tactics at the protests. Comments from the Black women we surveyed focused on the validity of Brown's shooting and whether police would cover up for officer Wilson.

For non-Black residents surveyed, assessments of trust and police legitimacy immediately following Brown's fatal shooting remained stable (showing a nonsignificant 2 percent improvement during September and October 2014 over prior surveys). The stability of their opinions appeared to be motivated by diffuse support and respect for police. As a group, non-Black residents had previously trusted and respected police and continued to do so after Brown's shooting, whereas Black residents had less favorable views of police prior to the shooting and those opinions worsened consequent to Brown's death (see also Kochel [2019]).

Although residents expressed a full range of opinions about police tactics at the protest, from not enough being done to address looting and rioting to feeling like police waged war on the protestors, residents' opinions about the protest policing tactics also fell along racial lines. Nearly two-thirds (62 percent) of non-Black residents were supportive of the police tactics used at the protests, feeling as if police responded to violence and public disorder, doing what they needed to restore social order (about 20 percent felt the police response was not enough). This is consistent with research showing that Americans value law and order, and when people are fearful of protest tactics, they are more supportive of police interventions such as wearing riot gear, making arrests, and applying nonlethal force at protests (Metcalfe and Pickett 2021). Conversely, three-quarters of Black residents (76 percent) disagreed with police tactics. Half of Black residents (49 percent) said that the amount of force police used to handle the protests, riots, and looting was "way too much," and an additional 31 percent said the amount of force was "a little too much." In contrast, 41 percent of non-Black residents thought the amount of force police used at the protests was "about right." Just over one-third of non-Black residents (36.5 percent)

Amount of Force Police Used to Handle Protests, Riots and
Looting in Weeks Following Brown Shooting

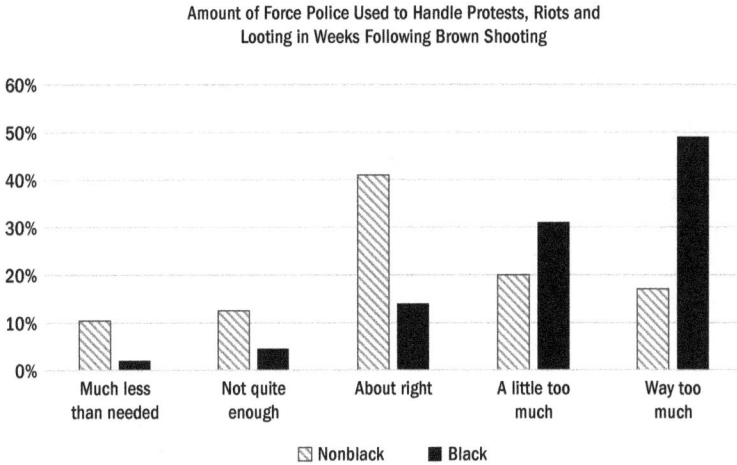

Figure 2.2 Racial Differences in Views about the Level of Police Force Used.

thought the amount of force was more than necessary. Figure 2.2 shows the breakdown by race regarding perceived police use of force at the protests.

Racial divisions persisted when examining residents' opinions about the protestors. More than two-thirds of non-Black residents (69 percent) condemned the protestors' tactics. Research supports that when protestors are predominantly Black, majority group members perceive a greater degree of violence (Manekin and Mitts 2020). Non-Black residents described protestors' behaviors as inappropriate, condemning behaviors like looting and shutting down the highway (these activities are also associated with higher assessments of violence), and lauded the cogency of the criminal justice system and due process as the better solution. They viewed pursing a resolution within the system as the best way to handle officer Wilson's shooting of Michael Brown (versus civil unrest). Non-Black residents felt that the public should trust the system to properly investigate the shooting and to produce a just and appropriate response. One resident explained, "Civil people don't act that way, they use the courts." Another resident agreed, offering, "It goes against everything that I was taught as a child, which is to respect the police. If the policeman was wrong in shooting Michael Brown, the court should settle it, not the people."

Conversely, Black residents felt highly skeptical of the system's ability to achieve change, saying things like "The system is set up for failure" and "The system doesn't care about people." One Black resident insinuated that, "you take the sheets off of the KKK and dress them in suits and uniforms . . . that's why we got these problems going on . . . There is no doubt racism exists." An older Black woman said she felt that the government and its representatives in policing were inherently racist. One Black woman explained the racial divide this way, "Whites sympathize with justification of the shooting. Blacks agree with the abuse of power." She meant that White residents focused their attention on Brown's behavior during the encounter and whether it meant police were justified in shooting him, while Black residents drew from the encounter that police routinely abuse their power.

Brown's shooting by police resonated with Black residents. They described an accumulation of negative experiences with police that built a well of mistrust. Several said that they or their sons could easily have been Michael Brown. One Black woman told us, "There are so many Michael Browns out there . . . Racism happens all the time. I am not sure why it had to take the Michael Brown incident for people to understand. This kind of thing happens so frequently." Residents told stories about their discriminatory and violent past encounters with police, involving unjustified stops and shootings. A Black male described that it was impactful to him when he had returned to St. Louis from Vietnam in February 1971 that a White police officer shoved him against a wall and had no empathy that he had just returned from Vietnam. A mother provided a more recent example. She said, "There are good police and bad police. I once saw police beat up someone. My own son walks home from work and oftentimes gets off work at night. He has been stopped numerous times by the police and is asked, 'What are you doing out walking so late?' and 'What is in your backpack?' Just consistently harassing him when he leaves work. This has happened so many times that it has changed his view of the police." The problems Black residents have with police have been enduring, according to comments like that made by a 58-year-old Black female who said, "The police have always treated us this way . . . It makes me sick. Nothing ever changes." Another Black woman exclaimed, "The police have been bothering me my whole life . . . My cousin got shot ten times when he was 15 years old. This happens all the time."

Two-thirds of Black residents supported protestors' actions, although quite a few Black residents spoke against rioting, looting, and vandalism of property, isolating their support to peaceful protests. Black residents felt empathy for Brown's family and viewed the protests as a necessary forum to draw public attention to a long history of negative treatment of Black Americans by police, with hope of inspiring change. Black residents applauded the fact that the radical approaches used by Ferguson protestors achieved results by raising public awareness about racial discrimination in policing. as one resident jubilantly pointed out, "Ferguson is on the cover of *TIME* magazine!"

Because of the value placed upon bringing attention to the cause, some Black residents downplayed the impact of the civil disobedience. For instance, a Black man told the interviewer, "The riots don't affect me because they are not happening. The looting, it's a convenience store. They have insurance and payroll damages, so that doesn't affect me. But every Black male in America feels intimidated when they're stopped or pulled over by police. They're just seen as a threat by their mere presence." He seemed to weigh the cost versus benefit of civil disobedience and seeing the benefits, even the violence at the protests seemed worth it to try to overcome discriminatory policing practices.

Drastic differences in opinions and discourse among residents by race provide a discernable example of the political and cultural components of the revised flashpoints model. Black residents, feeling powerless and subjected to structural injustices, were amenable to protest in response to Brown's death, whereas non-Black residents were less estranged from police and were not primed for collective action at that time. Furthermore, although Black residents tended to denounce protestors' use of violent tactics, the opportunity for recourse and change was sufficiently culturally valuable to prioritize support for civil disobedience above that concern.

3

Being Black in Blue

Law enforcement does not know how to deal with certain
people. Black people . . . It is a culture thing.
—30-year-old Black resident of St. Louis County

This past DOJ report . . . there's always ways for a police
department to get better . . . and the worst thing that they
could find was we needed to do a better job of minority recruitment. That problem is everywhere. That's a national
problem.
—Henry, White police officer

The call for more minority officers in policing can be traced back to
the Civil Rights Movement and the 1967 US President's Commission on
Law Enforcement and Administration of Justice. The President's Task
Force on 21st Century Policing (2015) renews the call (recommenda-
tion number 1.8). The rationale is that hiring more minority officers
will improve police-community relations that have been strained by
racial discrimination. Aiming to employ a police force representative
of the community it serves is a principle of community policing and
is promoted by the Commission on Accreditation for Law Enforcement (CALEA) in their Standards for Law Enforcement Agencies. Early
studies showed that in US cities with higher numbers of Black police
officers, residents held more favorable views of police, and the differences between opinions of Black and White residents toward police were
smaller than in municipalities where Black representation in policing
was lower (Decker and Smith 1980; Skogan 1978). The potential benefits
of increasing minority representation among police include improving
residents' views of police, improving police-community relations, reducing conflict between the police and the public, increasing impartiality,
reducing disproportionate impacts, and increasing police accountability

in minority communities (Cobbina 2019). Indeed, as Cobbina (56) points out, "Many communities of color have called for police departments to recruit more people of color to reduce police violence against them."

Increasing diversity and hiring minority officers continues to be a challenge for police agencies. While the share of minority officers nationally has nearly doubled during the last 30 years, growing from 14.6 percent to 27.3 percent since 1987, it still does not equal the share of minorities in the United States, at 37.2 percent (Reaves 2015). Black residents are underrepresented in policing by approximately 6.4 percent (Governing 2015). The incongruity is most apparent in high crime communities, which often contain high proportions of Black residents. About a year before Brown's death, I had conversations with the St. Louis County police recruitment officer about the challenges of recruiting minority officers. He bemoaned that even when minorities are hired, they are often lured away from the department by higher salaries that other agencies can offer. Only about 9 percent of St. Louis County police officers were Black in 2013, versus 12 percent nationwide at that time (Reaves 2015), and compared to 25.7 percent of the population in St. Louis County. However, 71 percent of St. Louis County Black officers were assigned to North County, where the civil unrest following Brown's death occurred and where 75 percent of residents are Black. About one-third of command staff within the department were Black at the time of the protests.

Community Callout

Michael Brown was Black. He was killed in a predominantly Black neighborhood. Much of the social outcry following Brown's death drew attention to race, with a strong presence of "Black Lives Matter" messages and emphasis on racial tension and discrimination by police against Black residents. Several Black residents described the sense of "us against them" between residents and police. A 32-year-old Black woman said, "We don't trust police at all." As reported in chapter 2, Black residents' trust and confidence in police declined drastically following Brown's death. Black residents felt wronged by the criminal justice system and they claimed to want improved relations between the police and the Black community.

Therefore, during the first two months after the shooting, I asked St. Louis County residents to what extent they believed that hiring more minority officers would help to improve confidence and trust in police. The majority of both Black and non-Black residents reported that increasing the proportion of officers who are minority race would improve their confidence and trust, although more Black than non-Black residents were optimistic about this mechanism of change (75 percent of Black residents and 55 percent of non-Black residents). Almost no residents thought increasing the proportion of officers that are a minority race would be a detriment to confidence and trust in police (2 percent of Black residents and no White residents).

This sentiment was echoed among Cobbina's (2019) protestor interviews in Ferguson and Baltimore. Protestors said that Black officers enforced the law more fairly, were better able to understand the Black community, Black culture, and situations involving Black males, they know more about the neighborhood, and were more polite and respectful than White officers. Cobbina (2019: 58–59) quoted a Black Ferguson resident who said of the Black officer, "He identifies with us," and a White Baltimore resident who believed, "When you've never walked a mile in someone else's shoes you can't truly understand."

Yet, underrepresentation of minority officers has been a difficult shortcoming to overcome in policing for a long time, and poor race relations can further negatively impact minority recruitment (Holdaway 1991). A man attending a rally during the week of Michael Brown's funeral reportedly asked one Black officer, "Where's the Black officers at? I don't see that many Black officers." And the officer, Anthony, responded, "Probably the same place where the Black baseball players are." By way of explanation, Anthony told me, "it's just not a coveted job by a lot of African Americans, I would imagine."

To move toward greater representation in policing, it is important to ask why policing as a profession may not hold wide appeal among minorities. Like supervisor Elijah questioned, "If you grew up in a family where there is a negative impression of the police, why would you want to be one?" This skepticism motivated Black police supervisor Ben's questioning about what might draw Black recruits to policing, especially following the terrible treatment of Black officers in Ferguson. He said, "There is no way I would have wanted to do this job . . . looking at all this stuff that has transpired."

Theories Supporting Recruitment and Hiring Minority Officers

Several theories provide justification for why more minority officers may improve police-community relations and reduce feelings of marginality within minority communities. The social identity theory/group value model (Bradford et al. 2014; Blumer 1958) explains that when officers reflect residents' racial groups, this sends a symbolic message about status and social standing to members of that racial group in the public, conveying to them that they are part of the "in" or governing group in the area rather than part of the "out" or marginalized group. Identification with the social group that the police represent can help to generate pride in the group and help to promote a view that police authority and structures are legitimate (Bradford et al. 2014). This was reflected in a study by Marschall and Ruhil (2007), who found that across 52 US cities and 53 school districts, Black residents were more satisfied with their neighborhoods, public schools, and police services when they were represented by Blacks in city hall, on school boards, and when the proportion of police officers who were Black was higher. While racial parity is not the only way to promote feelings of inclusion and support for the police institution, social identity theory suggests that it may be one avenue. This perspective does not assume that Black officers behave differently from their White counterparts, but rather, that their existence itself has meaning for Black citizens.

In contrast, representative bureaucracy theory suggests a more active role, that members of racial minority groups in power will share similar values and beliefs with others from their racial group and as they increase in number and influence in the police organization, they will act on behalf of the interests of that group, including acting to address discriminatory practices against the group. The theory advocates that as representation of minorities in the police workforce increases and the proportion of minority officers begins to approximate those in the population, this should improve the services that these officers deliver to members of their own race (Lasley et al. 2011; Selden 1997) and may even change the culture of the department (Weitzer, Tuch, and Skogan 2008). The assumption is that the officers' cultural background, being "Black," will influence their behavior in favor of active representation.

For instance, a few studies have supported that Black officers are more favorably disposed to community policing and less supportive of selective enforcement approaches, which can disproportionately impact Black communities (Gau and Paoline III 2017; Paoline III, Myers, and Worden 2000; Paoline III, Terrill, and Rossler 2015).

Culture May Counter

Some scholars are less optimistic about the role that minority representation can have in policing, due to strong organizational and occupational cultures. Departments formally socialize officers to be loyal to the organization and to place operational policies and procedures above personal perspectives and values (Barlow and Barlow 2018). Furthermore, the police occupational culture is strong and is reinforced daily by working in a dangerous and unpredictable occupational environment. Although the current thinking about police culture allows for multiple subcultures and values rather than a singular monolithic police culture, the question is whether, when individuals become police officers, they become "blue," favoring their identity or perspective as a police officer more heavily than their racial identity in making decisions, viewing situations, and in directing their behaviors (Paoline III and Terrill 2013). Some scholars expect that as the proportion of minority officers increases, the cycle of socialization to traditional aspects of the police occupational culture will break (Sun and Payne 2004).

Available Evidence on the Effects of Officer Race and Police Culture

Numerous studies support that officers' identification with the police occupational culture and socialization to the culture has a strong effect on officer behaviors. Wilkins and Williams (2008) even found that, in a highly socialized police department, as the percentage of Black officers increased, there were *more* racial disparities in police stops. Their findings may represent efforts by minority officers to demonstrate their allegiance to the profession over their race. Protestors in Cobbina's (2019) study in Baltimore and Ferguson felt that is what happens among Black officers. Nicholson-Crotty, Nicholson-Crotty, and Fernandez's

(2017) review of available research suggests that the proportion of Black officers in a department must be sufficiently large to see positive effects on outcomes such as racial profiling, searches, arrests, or police killings of Blacks, and up until that critical volume is reached, employing Black officers can operate as a backfire effect. Sun and Payne (2004) found that Black officers are more coercive than White officers when handling disputes. Yet they also found that Black officers are more supportive than White officers in predominantly Black neighborhoods. Sun and Payne conclude that police socialization may affect some of Black officers' behaviors, whereas other factors, including their racial and cultural background, may affect other behaviors. A recent study by Gau and Paoline III (2017) found that Black officers are less cynical toward citizens than White officers. Black officers are less likely to believe that people who call the police for help bring their problems on themselves. Of course, some prior literature suggests that when factors other than race are accounted for, there are few differences in Black versus White officers' behaviors (Terrill and Mastrofski 2002; Worden 1995). Thus, the research is mixed on the role that officer race can play in changing the behaviors of officers toward citizens.

Research supports that residents may *view* their experiences with police differently based on officer race. Theobald and Haider-Markel (2008) found that Black Americans assess police motives and treatment during encounters more negatively when the officer is White than when the officer is Black. Black drivers stopped by Black officers were more likely to indicate that the stop was legitimate. Research also finds that Whites do not experience dissimilar views based on the race of the officer (Cochran and Warren 2012). This too would support the notion that increasing minority representation can help minimize negative assessments during encounters with Black citizens, while not harming the views of police held by non-Black citizens.

Prior research has given little attention to the public's treatment of police officers and whether there are differences depending on the race of the officer. My interviews with officers suggest that during the civil unrest in Ferguson, citizens treated Black officers differently than their White colleagues. Below, I describe those experiences as told by the officers and relate them back to the notion that hiring more minority officers can promote better police-community relations with minority communities.

Experiences of Black Officers During the Unrest

Reflecting on past research and theoretical rationales for increasing minority hiring and improving representation among police raises questions about Black officers' experiences in Ferguson. Did Black officers empathize with Black residents and their plight? Did Black residents see themselves reflected in government when they saw minority officers and feel validated and accepted into the "in" group, as social identity theory would suggest? Did Black officers cope better with the stressors of the civil unrest?

One goal of the police officer interviews was to try to understand the experiences of Black officers, and so Black officers are overrepresented among those we interviewed, providing rich details about their experiences. One-quarter of police we interviewed were Black, relative to 9 percent of St. Louis County police officers working in communities. Among police who completed the survey, 8 percent were Black, 82 percent were not, and 10 percent did not report their race. These ratios are similar to the department's proportion of officers by race. The survey responses provide a representative sample from which I systematically assessed differences in officers' attitudes by race. The appendix provides details about the study methods.

Four major themes were gleaned from these data. (1) Black officers were especially poorly treated by the public during the civil unrest. (2) Black officers, more so than their White peers, felt the conflict extend into their families. (3) Black officers reported feeling empathetic toward the plight of the public. (4) Black officers reported being better prepared and experiencing fewer negative effects from the civil unrest in Ferguson.

Black Officers Were Especially Poorly Treated by the Public

It is clear from interviews with officers who worked on the front lines during the Ferguson unrest that they believed Black officers were more poorly treated by protestors. Nearly all of the Black officers I spoke to raised this issue (91 percent) and almost half (44 percent) of the White officers brought this up. Sebastian, a White officer, remarked, "Everything to the protesters was about color." However, under these circumstances race did not matter in the way that representative bureau-cracy theory, social identity theory, and community policing principles predict. Caleb, a Black officer, explained, "It was bad being a police officer, but it was even worse being an African American officer." Al, a White supervisor, agreed that he had never witnessed verbal abuse so extreme and that Black officers received the brunt of it. To police, Black residents did not appear to value having their racial group represented on the police force at this time.

Officers told only one story that was the exception. Officer Anthony, who is Black, had been part of a line of police vehicles responding to an officer aid call on West Florissant Avenue (see figure 1.3). They were from various police departments. When the cars stopped, protestors surrounded the vehicles. Behind Anthony he saw a Florissant officer, who was White, in a new Charger, along with about three other police vehicles. The only other Black officer had jumped from his vehicle to try to rescue the officer in need of aid. Anthony said that he saw the protestors break the window to the Charger, punch the White officer in the face and spit on him, and they were throwing rocks at the windows of the remaining vehicles. Anthony told the dispatcher to "Be advised, we are in a hornets' nest" and suggested that the vehicles make a U-turn and leave the area. Anthony said all the vehicles except for his were damaged—that "it was unbelievable what those people did with their hands, and just, you know with bricks." He believed it was because he was Black that protestors left him and his vehicle alone. He said that he had locked eyes with a Black protestor, but he saw Anthony and left him alone. He found himself comparing the Charger, the body of which was destroyed, totaled, to his vehicle without a scratch.

The animosity was apparent at the skirmish lines in a resounding and personal way. While officers of all races on the skirmish lines experi-enced considerable animus from the public, as described in chapter 1, officers were consistent in their view that Black officers were targeted by protestors for harsher treatment. By way of example, supervisor Elijah mentioned that at one point, he had 15 Missouri State Highway Patrol officers on a skirmish line and only one of them was a Black trooper. "He took more abuse in the crowd than any White officers, and he just stood there, and he took it, and he didn't react to it. He just remained calm." Supervisor Noah described the difference by officer race as "100 times worse, the nastiness they were spewing at them [Black officers] versus what they were spewing at us [White officers]."

Nearly half of Black officers (45 percent) and 29 percent of White personnel talked about the protestors being up close and in their faces. Black officers endured heckling and insults and pointing fingers within inches from their faces. They were often called "Uncle Tom," "Sell-Out," and "Traitor." Noah, a White supervisor explained, "When they got right up on us, that was the worst that ever could happen because that's when the individual face-to-face, racial, it was one-on-one at that point. The officers are supposed to stand there stoic and not return, and they're just going to go for hours. . . . that was the hardest and it was harder for the African American officers than it was for us." Noah was trying to explain that in close quarters, it was difficult not to take the insults personally, and so it felt more challenging to maintain a professional demeanor. Repeatedly and for hours, officers heard words that felt like a personal attack; yet, officers had to respond impassively and professionally to these circumstances—an emotionally exhausting experience, they told us.

Supervisors spoke about having to be cognizant of this pressure and tension focused on Black officers, and several supervisors reported checking in individually and frequently with Black officers or even pulling an entire skirmish line to give relief to a Black officer who was repeatedly being singled out and harassed by protestors. Officer Andre said that his supervisor told him that "you can always just, you know, get swapped out just to get a breather, to cool off, or something like that." However, he never chose to do that. He said, "I was actually afraid to do that because I think if I did that, the protestors would see that and think that I'm, like they're actually getting to me. And I didn't want them to think they were getting to me at all. So, I actually just stood there and took it the whole time."

Despite protestors' name calling that suggested Black police officers were traitorous or had acted against the Black public, across the 45 police we interviewed, officers referred to only one protestor's remark that specifically conveyed having a negative experience with Black police officers. Supervisor Ben talked with a Black protestor from just west of St. Louis, and the protestor told him that he never had a problem with a White police officer, that the only negative encounter he had was with Black officers. This is consistent with past research that found Black officers could be more aggressive in handling conflict, but as mentioned, it was the only remark officers shared to support that pattern.

Why did protestors target Black officers and not all officers equally? It would seem to be motivated by a perceived conflict of social identity. Malorie, a Black officer, explained, "Because I am Black, I was seen as on the wrong side or otherwise I would share their perspective. . . . Because I am Black, people assume I should feel the same way." Supervisor Ben heard people yell at him, "Eventually you are going to have to choose sides." He said that while he did not feel torn about his identity or his role, which was "to do what's right, make sure none of my officers get hurt, [and] make sure none of these innocent citizens get hurt," he did say that some of the younger Black officers felt pulled in different directions. According to Ben, "African American officers get it worse than anybody out there because on one hand they want more African American officers, at least that's what they say, but on the other hand you're a traitor, you're a sellout and all that stuff." Protestors shamed Black officers. Black officer Andre said protestors yelled at him, "You, you supposed to be one of us. You a nigger. You supposed to be one of us." At one point he was standing on a skirmish line next to two other Black officers, just by chance, and he said that a man with a megaphone stood right in front of the three of them and yelled into the megaphone, "They [police] don't respect you. They made you all stand together." He too said he did not feel conflicted, "because I know I am doing the right thing." Karen, a White officer, reported hearing protestors say to Black officers, "Man, how can you do this to your own community? How can you be on their side?"

These racially motivated insults directly raised the issue of social identity for Black officers, posing the question of whether they belong to their racial group or their professional group. Sebastian, a White officer, expressed frustration about it, saying, "Like what the f*** is he supposed to do, he's a Black dude doing a job." Essentially, he advocated that a person should not and does not have to choose one social identity—he or she can be part of multiple groups, including being Black and being a police officer. Anthony, a Black officer, agreed. He did not feel that he should have to trade one identity for another. He said, "I was angry with the Black community, even my own family, you know . . . I mean, I'm just as Black as you are, you know."

Yet, numerous comments did show Black officers choosing their occupational identity as their dominant identity. Karen, a White officer, mentioned how a Black officer that she rode patrols with for a couple of weeks during the protests made clear that the Black officer's identity was as a police officer, recalling the officer proclaiming to her about the protestors that, "These aren't my people. Like yeah, I'm the same skin color as they are, but do you correlate with the people that live in the bayou because they are White? These aren't my people. These aren't my family. These aren't my friends. They are not my community. That's what's most frustrating is because I'm Black they automatically think that I'm on the bad side. This is my side. This—you guys—are my community." The officer proclaimed clear allegiance to his professional identity, diminishing his identity as a racial group member. Similarly, Black officer Malorie said that she was embarrassed by the way the Black community behaved and asserted, "I had to do my job first." She wished to be clear in her priority for doing the job over priority for personal or group concerns about racial tensions with police.

Of feeling caught in the middle, Pamela, also Black, described how as a Black female, she has known people who were mistreated by police, but also people who were treated well by police. She said, "it's frustrating to sit in the middle and have to try to explain, you know, they [the Black community] feel this way because of this, but the officers also feel a certain way because they are out there trying to do their jobs." At the same time, she said that she felt "grateful to be in a position where I could kind of see everyone's point and just be able to remind people that it's a human experience." In this advocacy role, she did perform the functions outlined by representative bureaucracy theory.

In general, protestors' targeting of Black officers for insults seemed to further unite and promote solidarity among officers—reinforcing an us-versus-them divide with the public. Isaac, a Black officer, stated, "When we were standing on the riot line and they [other police] saw that the African American officers were being targeted—These are our brothers and sisters, we gonna come to each other's aid." Overall, police viewed Black officers through their professional identity and the public seemed to resent Black officers for it.

As touched upon in chapter 2, police felt betrayed by Captain Johnson when he appeared to align more with his racial identity than his identity as a police officer. During his speech at a Michael Brown rally on the Sunday after Brown's death, Johnson stood in his police uniform before a large, predominantly Black crowd and said that he empathized with the Brown family, he apologized, as a police officer, for his death, and referred to his own Black son whom he said wears pants sagging, his hat cocked to the side, and has tattoos on his arm. He concluded with "I love you, I'll stand tall with you, and I'll see ya out there" (CBS This Morning 2014). Of that speech, White supervisor Alexander said, "He's not one of them. He's one of us." Alexander knew that Captain Johnson was trying to strike up a relationship with the crowd, but, he said, "Every policeman that rides up there [North County] sees that kid all over the place [Black, with sagging pants, tattoos and a crooked hat] and . . . that does not stick out up there. The police see it every day, so that's just, that's nothing. That doesn't set off any of my bells." He called Johnson's comments "pandering" and was clearly offended by this perceived intention and abandonment of the police identity.

Black Officers Felt Empathy and Understanding

Despite having their loyalty and identity challenged, several Black officers were able to rationalize why they were the recipients of demeaning remarks from Black protestors. Although it was challenging not to take the insults thrown at them personally because of their race, Black officers were able to distance themselves to a degree. Hugh, a Black supervisor, explained, "They're not really angry with me, they're angry with the uniform or they're angry with what the uniform represents . . . But, there were some very distinct moments where being an African American in this uniform and being an African American itself, was very difficult. Very difficult to identify with one or the other because the lines were so clearly drawn, that split."

Sixty percent of Black officers (versus 9 percent of non-Black officers) expressed their empathy for the frustrations underlying the protests. White officer Karen said that she could empathize with people who lived where people experience policing daily, where it is common to experience being arrested and locked up. Similarly, White officer Mason lamented the amount of poverty, unemployment, crime, and very little opportunity that existed in North County. He felt that people could not live in those conditions and not feel resentful or angry. He said, "The anger gets directed towards the police, but in a lot of ways, I think it's just anger towards, resentment towards their place in society at large." Supervisor Gabe, also White, actively sought to understand by asking a college professor for a reading list that would help him better understand race relations.

Black supervisors Logan and Elijah grew up in North County. Logan told us that when he was young, he was harassed by police quite often and "so I can understand some of the feelings on the other side of it . . . I understand what a number of residents are thinking—like some of these guys would get pulled over for just say a taillight violation but end up walking away with like ten different tickets." He said that his children (both under 25 years) have been stopped and harassed by police too, most recently for having an air freshener hanging from the rearview mirror (Logan described using air fresheners in the car as a Black cultural thing, but something police associate with an attempt to mask drugs). Where he lives in the St. Louis area, there are few Black families. Logan acknowledged that he knew that racial profiling exists, that protestors felt as if police were abusing their kids, but he also had the feeling the protests could have happened anywhere. "It just happened to happen at Ferguson," he said, meaning that problems with racial profiling, racial tensions, and cultural misunderstandings are not isolated to Ferguson. He acknowledged his conditional support, "I understand the protesting. I understand the people wanted change . . . I totally disagree with a lot of the tactics." His children were torn as well. They understood the problems being raised, but also worried about Logan being at the protests. He said that his children believe that he is "out there doing the right thing," but also feel a sense of distrust for other officers. Black supervisor Elijah appreciated that some of the protestors "really feel like they're changing the world. Some of them are like, hey, some things are not right—the legislation of the drug laws or racial profiling or whatever—and they are reasonable."

A quarter of officers raised the point that they had grown up in North County or currently reside and/or have family (e.g., spouse, parents) living in the area where Ferguson is located. Of those officers who shared this information, 27 percent were Black. In some cases, officers recalled growing up feeling harassed by police while living in North County or another predominantly Black community, and so they understood the basis of the attacks. Hugh relayed, "I grew up in the inner city of St. Louis . . . [and] I remember when the police used to shoot at us when we were in the city as kids—standing in an alleyway and a police officer pulls up and shoots at us." These prior personal experiences provided a source of empathy and understanding for the frustration felt by residents and expressed by protestors.

Officers living in the North County area during the unrest faced the social identity tension both while working and off duty. Thus, it was difficult for these officers in particular not to experience the scorn and rejection as personal attacks waged by members of their own community. Dylan shared his experience going to his barber in that area during the unrest. His routine previously had been that he would walk into the shop, and customers and barbers alike greeted him personally and asked him how he was doing. He often had customers thank him for his service as a police officer or offer that they were praying for him. During the civil unrest in Ferguson, he described walking into the barber shop to be greeted by silence and leaving the same way. As the unrest extended to months, Dylan used his barber shop trips to try to engage the customers—to explain the process of the grand jury and ask for their patience before making judgments about the circumstances of Brown's death and about police more generally. He referred to this effort as "gathering my friends back." Another Black supervisor reported receiving a similar cold shoulder during his barber visits during the unrest, but in his case, he changed barbers; "I found myself feeling like I was under attack every time I went to the barber shop, so I had to change barbers," said Jacob.

Community policing principles advocate that officers live in the community where they work, to encourage the very process that Dylan described. The idea is that even during off-duty hours, officers would engage with residents on a personal level (e.g., in the barber shop). Such interactions provide the officer with an understanding and appreciation for community norms, concerns, and culture beyond anything that could be learned during a fairly anonymous police-citizen encounter, such as when police stop someone in a car or on the street. A White officer named Lucas, who grew up in North County and who also worked in that area as a police officer for 15 years, explained the potential benefit to knowing the community culture and expectations. He said, "I knew the streets, I knew the people and I ran into people that I'd gone to high school with, and I don't know, for me it was easy. I had that relationship with the Black population up there. But you have to know how to relate to the people that you are serving and protecting. And when you don't have that I think that leads to a lot of problems."

During the unrest, being from North County or having lived in similarly disadvantaged, high crime, and predominantly Black neighborhoods created empathy. Several officers mentioned being from nearby East St. Louis, Illinois, which struggles with similar crime and economic challenges as North County. The population is 98 percent Black. Among officers who reported having an appreciation that protestors were acting the way they did because of their personal life experiences, 64 percent of these officers had lived in North County, had family from North County, or grew up in another nearby disadvantaged, high crime, predominantly Black area. As a result, they drew from these experiences and background to gain perspective and understanding. In a few cases, this shared understanding was the basis of one-on-one conversations between police officers and members of the public gathered in and around Ferguson. Empathy and understanding are the outcomes expected by community policing advocates who push for officers to live in the communities they serve. Yet, this familiarity with the community also had the effect on many of the same officers of making the scorn and frustration expressed by the public during the civil unrest feel very personal and particularly painful. Dylan explained, "I really think they looked at us as people with no heart."

The Publics' Claims Were Antithetical to Officers' Motives

Chapter 2 described the noble motives that prompt officers to become police officers. Nearly half (45 percent) of the Black officers I interviewed (and 24 percent of White officers) volunteered that their motives for becoming a police officer and/or the way that they see their role as a police officer were and are to give back to the community and to help people. While officers of different races share this altruistic motive (Raganella and White 2004; Reiss 1967), it is especially salient among minority officers. Hunt and Cohen (1971) found that 45 percent of Black survey respondents were attracted to policing because they wanted to help people, versus 30 percent for Whites. The same community orientation and the desire to make a difference were echoed more recently in Bolton and Feagin's (2004) interviews with Black officers, and this motive continues to be ranked more important among Black officers than White officers in a more recent survey of New York City Police Department officers (White et al. 2010).

Black officers who worked the unrest in Ferguson reported about how difficult it was to hear insults about being a traitor, especially in light of their altruistic motives for becoming a police officer. Bottoms and Tankebe (2012) explain the reason that this was so difficult to hear is because an officer's concept of themselves as a police officer is shaped and reshaped through interactions with the public. A police officer enters into the policing occupation with one self-concept, perhaps as described here—noble intercessor, saving good people from bad things—but, how the public interacts with and engages with the officer and their efforts to exert authority continuously reshapes that self-concept. When the feedback the officer receives from the public contests the officer's self-concept, this is distressing and uncomfortable. Bottoms and Tankebe refer to the process as the dialogic model of officer self-legitimacy, also discussed in chapter 4.

Isaac, a Black officer who was told by a Ferguson protestor, "You're an Uncle Tom," commented, "it kinda hurt me because I took this job to help people, that's the reason why I wanted to be a police officer." Anthony, a fellow Black officer, struggled with the same disconnect to his self-concept. Anthony said, "My four best friends in this police department grew up in the city and not so nice neighborhoods . . . And we wanted to give back to the community. So we are all out here doing a job and people are like, hey, Uncle Tom this, and so on and so forth." Hugh, an officer who talked about being shot at and chased by police as a young Black kid, explained, "There was only one reason I became a police officer. It is because I didn't want my people to ever see that again." He became a police officer because he knew that biased, aggressive policing is not how policing is supposed to work. Supervisor Jacob, who is Black, actively sought to be interviewed as part of the study, telling us,

"Not often enough are we in positions to affect policy that will actually benefit the community." His hope was that this book would help bring perspective and change. Black officers described a strong desire to make an impact. They adopted a role orientation reflective of the "problem-solver" officer (Muir 1977). Worden (1995: 59) explains that problem-solver officers "regard their clientele as people who endure tragedies not of their own making," and view themselves as a positive resource to help residents address their problems.

Although altruistic motives encourage people to pursue policing as a profession, fear of being viewed by Black communities as a traitor continues to be an impediment to minority recruitment (Bolton and Feagin 2004), and the fear was actualized in Ferguson. Black officers' feelings of rejection despite their altruistic motives emulate what Alex (1969) reported, that Black officers face double marginality—neither embraced by Black citizens nor fully accepted by White officers, nor are they well-integrated into the police organization. Based on interviews with Black officers in New York City, Alex found that residents looked on the Black officer, who was (and still is) generally assigned to work in high minority communities, as a source of potential oppression and even as a tool of a predominantly White police institution. However, Black officers were not readily accepted by White officers and experienced organizational discrimination. This may continue to be especially salient for Black female officers, who also struggle with gender bias in policing. Nearly a year after the protests, Malorie, a Black female officer, noted, "In the store, people will ask you why do you do that job [police officer]? People come up to me, perhaps because I am Black or female. . . . Everybody has a question *still*!"

What kept Black officers returning to the streets of Ferguson in the face of this rejection? Anthony explained why he went back out into Ferguson even after being mistreated, "because I'm needed, you know, I'm needed." The rationale appears to be the same altruistic reason that Black officers provided for getting into policing in the first place. This bears out findings reported by Lasley et al. (2011), who learned that Black officers, more than White officers, thought that officers interacting with the public would allow them to be more sensitive to community members and their needs. At least in Anthony's case, he recognized that he was needed.

The Conflict Extended to Family Members

In addition to taking criticism from protestors, some Black officers reported that family members questioned and even berated them, in some cases, about being a police officer. More than half of the Black police personnel that I spoke to (6 of 11) described that at least some family members were unsupportive of them during the civil unrest. Particularly frustrating to two Black officers with whom we spoke was that family members listened to the media accounts and drew negative judgments about police without hearing from the officer or being willing to hear any other information that could present an alternative account. Supervisor Ben said that his younger brother argued with him about what happened at the protests based on news accounts. When Ben tried to explain that he was there, "literally right there when that happened," still his brother would argue, "That's not accurate." Another of those officers, Isaac, venting his frustration, told his family, "Don't make your opinion off one side, listen to both sides, and then you as a person, as an adult, can make your own decision after that." Supervisor Jacob was not on speaking terms with his cousins because they were forming opinions based on little information.

Caleb, another Black officer, had expected more support from his family, but instead he was disappointed that the events divided his extended family. Similarly, in Logan's case, he described how his mom staunchly defended him in the face of vicious criticism about law enforcement from his aunt, about whom he said, "I mean if you listen to her, police were the worst people in the whole world." Logan said, "It caused a rift in the family." Officer Malorie's family "pulled back and kept their opinions to themselves."

Much of the questioning and antagonism toward Black officers by family, friends, and acquaintances was revealed through Facebook. Hugh, a Black supervisor, asserted:

> I probably had 800 friends on there [Facebook]. I probably have about 400 now. . . . One of my fraternity brothers was so aggressive with repeatedly showing me every day: "See this is proof. This is what you're doing. This is what you stand for." . . . I completely had to cut him off and a lot of my other friends had to cut him out. . . . That's how vicious

that aspect of being African American and having to deal with that side of the community that was very angry. They were forcing that down our throats. They would send me videos and ask, "What do you think about this? Why would they do this? Would you do this as a police officer?" You could never turn it off.

Andre, another Black officer, said that while he was arresting someone for looting, the arrestee said to him, "Man, I bet all your f***ing cousins, all your f***ing family, I bet they hate you." The officer reflected, "there's a lot of people in my family who actually do hate me, but those are the people I really don't care about." Andre later mentioned, "A lot of my family members, they would like call or text me, you know, I can't believe you're a cop, aw, why are you doing this? . . . Why are you involved in all of this tear gassing and stuff."

According to my conversations with Black officers, families sometimes coped with the social identity crisis (profession versus race) by treating the family member who is a police officer as an exception among officers. Ben explained, "it's funny how all of our families think that we're an exception. Like oh no, you're good, but the rest of them . . . and it's funny and I go, that's how ignorant that whole thing really is. You think I'm special but everybody else is bad, but I'm not." And not all Black officers viewed relatives who were critical of police or engaged in protesting as problematic or in the wrong. Andre mentioned that his uncle led a march one day and Andre reported feeling positively about his uncle's efforts. Malorie, another Black officer, said that her best friend protested and Malorie told her friend, "As long as you don't get in my way, I am okay with that." This view goes back to the empathy that some Black officers felt for the cause behind the protests.

In contrast, none of the White police personnel (n=34) raised concerns about their families not supporting them in their profession during the Ferguson unrest. However, several White officers (18 percent) did report, like their Black colleagues, that some friends expressed views or raised questions that led the officer to reduce contact with them or unfriend them on Facebook. Joshua said, "I unfriended lots of people on Facebook who were negative toward law enforcement." Social isolation is often blamed for the perpetuation of a police occupational culture and reinforcement of the distance between "us" and "them"—the police and the public. The experiences officers had during the Ferguson unrest, especially Black officers, with their families and friends may have widened the gap.

Perceived Preparedness and Impact Among
Black versus White Officers

This raises the question—what is the consequence of protestors', family members', and friends' insults and aggression directed especially toward Black officers during the civil unrest? Did Black officers feel less satisfied with their jobs following Ferguson? What were the mental and emotional effects of handling the events in Ferguson on Black versus White officers? Did officers of different races feel differently prepared to handle the unrest or feel more or less effective at doing so?

Past research suggests that compared to White officers, Black officers may be better positioned to cope with negative treatment from the public. Hawkins (2001) found that minority officers were less likely to be depressed or feel negatively about their job when encountering poor treatment by the public. So, if Black officers are less cynical, less impacted by these experiences, or better positioned to cope with poor treatment, this provides another reason to redouble efforts to employ more Black officers.

The St. Louis County officer survey showed that there was no difference in Black versus non-Black officers' satisfaction with the job following the events in Ferguson. Both groups reported being somewhat satisfied and showed a slight drop in satisfaction following the Ferguson protests. Despite the negative behaviors aimed at Black officers during the unrest, on nearly all other measures, Black officers reported more positive assessments than their White peers. Black officers reported fewer mental and emotional effects during the height of the unrest—less anxiety, stress, and problems with concentration, fewer slowed responses, and less difficulty sleeping. Black officers also reported fewer long-term Post Traumatic Stress Disorder (PTSD)–like symptoms, such as feeling panic without reason, avoiding situations that remind them of stressful past experiences, and having physical and emotional reactions to encounters that remind them of Ferguson. Black officers reported fewer negative attitudes toward policing following Ferguson than non-Black officers. Specifically, non-Black officers were more likely than Black officers to report that negative publicity about law enforcement since Ferguson made it difficult to be motivated at work, caused apprehension about using force, made them less proactive, and made law enforcement as a career less enjoyable. The appendix includes details about these outcomes, including summary statistics (see table A.1).

It is not immediately apparent what may have positioned Black officers to better cope with the strains of protest policing in Ferguson. Some possible explanations include that Black officers were more accustomed to working with residents in the impoverished, predominantly Black North County neighborhoods and had prior experience with the animosities and frustrations expressed by residents during the unrest. Nearly two-thirds (62 percent) of the Black officers interviewed had worked in North County prior to Ferguson, versus 31.5 percent of non-Black officers. Prior cultural experiences and struggles with double marginality may have buffered the impact of the criticisms raised during the Ferguson unrest against Black officers. This rationale parallels available research on stigma for convicted criminals, which found that Black offenders are less impacted by the stigma of conviction given their prior stigmatic cultural experiences. One Black supervisor seemed to validate this perspective, although at the time he was speaking about officers with military experience. Ben suggested that officers who had prior experience with conflict and negative reactions from the public may have "thick skin" and be better situated tactically and emotionally to cope with the public behaviors during the Ferguson unrest. Compared to officers who are "used to citizens by and large loving them, complementing them, thanking them for their service, and this [Ferguson] was a totally different situation."

A second possible explanation is that the empathetic attitudes expressed by some of the Black officers during their interviews provided them with the perspective needed to not internalize the verbal attacks too personally. It is possible that being able to rationalize reasons for the mistreatment of police neutralized lingering emotional and mental strains. Indeed, Hawkins (2001) found that in general, Black officers suffer less emotional exhaustion than White officers.

Still a third alternative is that Black officers felt better trained and prepared on the skills needed to address the unrest (e.g., leadership skills,

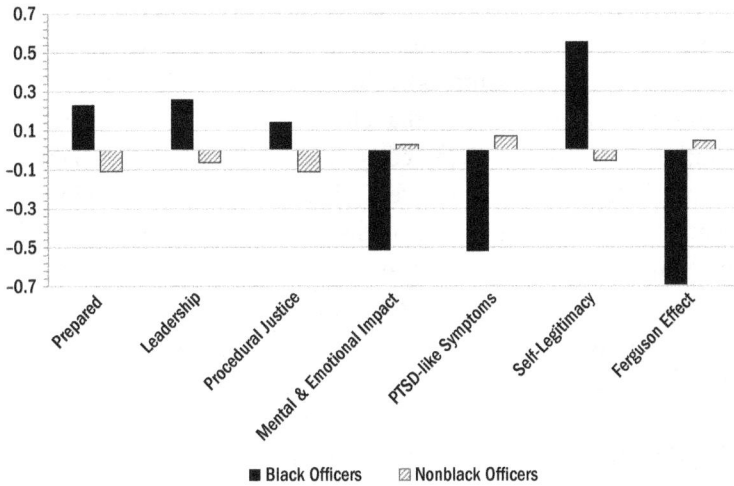

Figure 3.1 Black versus White Officers' Self-Assessments of Preparedness and Impact.

endurance, training in procedural justice that facilitated the ability to listen and respond professionally), despite the stress and emotion the circumstances caused. In the officer survey, I asked officers to retrospectively assess themselves on a number of qualities leading up to and during the civil unrest. As a group, Black officers reported significantly better assessments on two of three measures. Black officers felt better prepared, prior to Ferguson, to handle uncertainty, difficult situations, and confrontation, while keeping their cool and maintaining sensitivity to people and their surroundings. Black officers also felt more effective as leaders—making decisions, setting priorities, motivating and guiding others, and resolving problems. What was only marginally different by race was officers' perceived effectiveness at delivering procedurally just treatment during Ferguson—being professional, impartial, and fair, restraining their use of force, and upholding departmental standards of conduct. On this score, Black and White officers were more similarly effective—Black officers had a higher score, but it was not significantly higher. This could be due to the professional nature of the department (focused on proper procedure, committed to training, striving to be effective), coupled with the media spotlight on officers' behaviors at this time, helping to minimize differences across officers. Figure 3.1 shows the comparison by officer race across all these dimensions. Table A.6 in the appendix provides the corresponding t-test results. Higher positive scores show higher assessments of that quality, whereas negative scores show lower self-assessments of that characteristic.

Another outcome receiving considerable attention post-Ferguson has been labeled the Ferguson effect. This refers to officers feeling cynical, wanting to withdraw, and decreases in productivity that can arise from feeling poorly treated by the public and unappreciated in the profession. Chapter 4 examines this issue further, however, it is worth mentioning here that Black officers in the county experienced the Ferguson effect less and expressed more efficacy than non-Black officers on one of the protective factors against the Ferguson effect—the concept of self-legitimacy. Self-legitimacy is a valuation that officers make about the extent that their authority as a police officer is viewed by inhabitants of a community as legal, morally proper, and deserving of respect and adherence.

A White supervisor, Lucas, shared a story about policing post-Ferguson. He described a scene in St. Louis County post-Ferguson in which a White officer used force on a Black suspect. The on-scene supervisor identified a Black witness who had videotaped the use of force event, so the supervisor asked to view the video. The witness refused to allow access to the supervisor. However, subsequently, when a Black officer arrived on scene and asked the witness for permission to view the video, the Black officer was permitted to watch it. In viewing the video, the Black officer told the supervisor, "It's all good. Everything was legit; everything was fine." But, as Lucas explained, the actions were indicative of the witness's trust in the Black officer and mistrust for the White supervisor. For these two police, we would expect that the Black officer viewed himself as having higher levels of self-legitimacy, but the White officer probably did not believe that community members respected his authority.

As shown in figure 3.2, Black officers that we surveyed post-Ferguson had more confidence in their self-legitimacy than did their White peers following Ferguson. Yet, this difference in self-legitimacy by race also existed prior to Ferguson, according to officer surveys I conducted in 2012 and 2013. Black officers, more than non-Black officers, historically have believed that the public viewed their authority as a police officer with respect, thought residents trusted them to make right decisions for the

Self Legitimacy

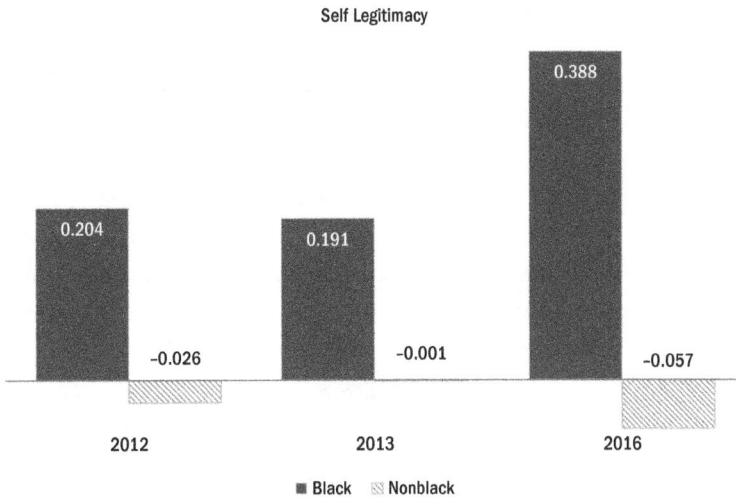

Figure 3.2 Black versus White Officers' Assessments about Self-Legitimacy.

people in their assigned community, and that residents would obey their authority and accept and adhere to their decisions as a police officer.

I am not aware of any study that has previously reported this association between race and self-legitimacy, and it is not clear whether it would be replicated in other geographic areas and conditions. It is compelling that the trend is consistent across three different years of officer surveys, both before and after Ferguson. An important question is why officers differ by race in their confidence that the public respects their authority as right and lawful. Since most Black officers in the county are assigned to work in predominantly Black precincts, I speculate, consistent with social identity theory, that many Black officers may perceive that residents where they work value seeing themselves reflected in policing, despite the protestors' behaviors in Ferguson.

It is interesting to also consider whether Black officers with elevated levels of self-legitimacy may, even without a high proportion of them in the organization, advocate for services or provide good services to Black communities. It may be useful for future studies to examine whether officers are more likely to act in the interests of their racial group in the community when they perceive that people in that racial group respect the position they are in and perceive their authority as police officers as valid.

Conclusions

These officers' experiences in Ferguson, despite the especially difficult ordeals of Black police officers during the unrest, seem to support the long-held call for more minority officers. It would seem from Black officers' experiences that not only do perceptions of police by residents stand to gain, but Black officers working in minority neighborhoods may also be better positioned to cope with experiences like those in Ferguson and come through them with less cynicism, fewer emotional scars, and a more positive outlook on their jobs.

Of course, this is not meant to suggest that resolving poor police and minority community relations is as simple as hiring more Black officers. Studies in minority communities with predominantly minority police departments have shown that poor relations go beyond race and are inherent in social structural problems associated with disadvantage and opportunity (Weitzer, Tuch, and Skogan 2008). On this issue, Cobbina (2019) and I agree that minority hiring in itself is not going to resolve the racial tensions in policing.

4

Policing in the Aftermath of Protests

I think there's going to have to be a significant change in the
way that we do things.
—Hugh, Supervisor

The Ferguson protests highlighted racial tensions between police and
Black communities and desolated the historically favorable public
image of police. The protests provided a critical juncture that called
for and produced changes in policing. In this chapter, I describe the
challenges and changes in policing that St. Louis County officers experienced within the first year after the protests. St. Louis County police
officers talked extensively about how the protests damaged the police-
community relationship. Initially, Brown's death, the demonstrations,
and media coverage of police during the protests devastated public trust
in police, but also altered the posture of police toward the community.
The officers we interviewed recounted these experiences and how they
worked to recover.

The need to understand how public protest against police impacts
policing has remained remarkably relevant since the Ferguson protests.
A report released at the end of 2020 by the 2019 President's Commission
on Law Enforcement and Administration of Justice makes clear that civil
unrest against law enforcement continues to be prevalent in the United
States, for essentially the same reasons that gave rise to the Ferguson
protests. These demonstrations, such as the many protests nationwide
following George Floyd's death at the hands of Minneapolis Police officers on May 25, 2020, continue to present challenges for policing, to
police authority, and for public trust and relations (Executive Office of
the President of the United States 2020). Government-sponsored ad-
visory groups from both ends of the political spectrum, like former
President Trump's Commission on Law Enforcement and Administration of Justice and former President Obama's Task Force on 21st Century

Policing stress the necessity of police agencies in the post-Ferguson era to adopt policies and practices that promote positive police-community relationships and police legitimacy, alongside effective crime reduction. However, as I discuss in the final chapter, other activists have called for abolishment of policing as an institution (Vitale 2018).

After the Ferguson protests and following other protests since Ferguson, the immense challenges faced by police officers, such as public mistrust, exhaustion, and cynicism, have threatened the capacity of policing to deliver these outcomes. One specific hurdle that has received considerable scholarly attention post-Ferguson is derived, at least in part, from the mutual suspicion and frustrations of police and community members. The *Ferguson effect* describes the notion that officers experiencing public demonstrations against police or even observing them remotely in the media will interpret the messaging in those experiences and feel unappreciated by the public, stressed, and emotionally depleted, will become more distrustful and less caring about the plight of Black citizens and others living in high crime neighborhoods, and withdraw. Prior research supports that police officers who experience stressful situations followed by emotional exhaustion or burnout, especially if or when the officer also feels that the police organization has mistreated them, can become cynical toward citizens and view them as deserving of their troubles (Hawkins 2001; Ryan 2010; Trinkner, Tyler, and Goff 2016). Being emotionally exhausted promotes officers developing an increasingly more negative view of "clients" and wanting to leave the job (Hawkins 2001; Maslach and Jackson 1984).

During the first year or so following the Ferguson protests, scholars and practitioners feared that reduced officer proactivity and interaction with residents, motivated by emotional exhaustion and cynicism, or by officers' fears that even appropriate and justified uses of force could trigger widespread negative media coverage, would worsen police-community relationships and elicit increases in crime. Police-community relations have become a focal concern in modern calls for police reform. Although anticipated crime increases stemming from the Ferguson effect did not materialize (see Pyrooz et al. 2016), concerns about the impact of reduced engagement and proactivity on police-community relationships have not abated. A study by Wolfe and

Nix (2016) showed that officers reacting to negative publicity about police were less willing to engage in partnerships with the community.

Studies examining experiences with and outcomes of the Ferguson effect, summarized below, have been limited to investigating how police in general react to perverse media coverage of police. These studies do not show the impact when the negative news stories are about the officer's own police agency. St. Louis County Police Department is a large agency with more than 900 commissioned officers interacting with the public. The mere size of the force provides potential for a significant community impact in that jurisdiction. Furthermore, numerous other police agencies across the nation have, since Ferguson, had similar experiences with extensive negative media coverage and highly volatile public protests against police. Widely publicized incidents over the last few years have occurred in Baltimore, Maryland; New York City; Baton Rouge, Louisiana; Cleveland and Cincinnati, Ohio; North Charleston, South Carolina; St. Paul and Minneapolis, Minnesota; and Kenosha, Wisconsin, to name a few (Poon and Patino 2020). So, while it remains worthwhile to consider the general impact of negative media coverage about police on police officers across the 18,000 law enforcement agencies operating in the United States and elsewhere, it is also beneficial to place emphasis on investigating how officers from the departments at the center of the scrutiny manage to cope and what the community impact is. This is an issue faced by large and small departments alike. The protests in Ferguson were a catalyst for protest movements across the nation (Arora, Phoenix, and Delshad 2019). The questions I consider in this chapter include: (1) When the protest and the news coverage is about an officer's own jurisdiction, to what extent do officers experience the Ferguson effect? (2) What qualities or conditions helped officers to deflect the Ferguson effect? and (3) What other consequences to policing have arisen from the Ferguson protest experience?

The challenge presented to officers by the Ferguson effect in the heart of the controversy is put bluntly by Andre, a St. Louis County officer we spoke to, who explained, "You can't 'mother f*** me' and say you want to kill my family and rape my girlfriend and then want me to help you." Officers' experiences during the protests inspired lasting impressions. Chapter 1 of this book describes the experiences of police officers while they served on skirmish lines and attempted to create or maintain order. During an intensive three-week period and lasting intermittently for months, police officers and supervisors described 12–14-hour shifts without days off, canceling scheduled vacations, working in a tumultuous and sometimes violent environment featuring conflict with rioters, often without clear direction and major uncertainty, with changing directives and policies, and even changing leadership. Officers and their families were threatened and experienced a barrage of criticism on Facebook, Twitter, and the syndicated media. As a group, the officers we spoke to reported suffering from physical and emotional exhaustion stemming from their time conducting protest policing in Ferguson. Extremely stressful working conditions during the protests compounded by extensive and prolonged negative media coverage framing the protests in Ferguson gave rise to concerns about the Ferguson effect within St. Louis County Police Department and its potential consequences for county residents.

Theoretical Process Underlying the Ferguson Effect

Job Demands-Resources Model

The job demands-resources model explains the theoretical consequences of workplace stress that produce what has since been labeled by scholars, the Ferguson effect. The model outlines a pathway in which accumulated job strains lead to burnout, reduced job satisfaction, and withdrawal behaviors, among other negative consequences. In any job context, but specifically in policing, high job demands that produce stress can come in the form of role ambiguity, external pressures, conflict, competing obligations, work conditions, and work overload. Officers encountered all these workplace demands during the protests. The job demands-resources model explains that, especially combined with inadequate resources or insufficient support to address the demands, the strain imposed by these demands promotes burnout. Burnout is a psychological syndrome that manifests in cynicism about the value of the work, exhaustion, emotional distress, and reduced professional efficacy—the ability to solve problems at work (Demerouti and Verbeke 2004). Cynical, burned out officers tend to be less motivated, less productive, less satisfied, more distrusting of the public, and are more likely to use force (Kop, Euwema, and Schaufeli 1999; Martinussen,

Richardsen, and Burke 2007; Regoli, Crank, and Rivera 1990). Prior research supports the process outlined by the job demands- resources model, that experiencing burnout following job strains contributes to diminished job satisfaction, a desire to leave the job, poor family relationships, and withdrawal behaviors. Among police officers, burnout can even affect officers' responses to conflict and violence, when officers' attitudes toward the public become depersonalized and they feel less able to rely on cooperation from the public (Kop et al. 1999; Martinussen et al. 2007).

Applying the Job Demands-Resources Model to Policing Post-Ferguson

Studying policing in the United States post-Ferguson, Nix and Pickett (2017) outline a theoretical process whereby extensive negative media attention on policing imposes workplace strain capable of facilitating withdrawal and reducing proactivity of police officers. Complementary research provides indicators of the qualities and conditions that can operate like support resources to deflect the impact of the strain on the officers, mitigating the Ferguson effect.

Negative social media coverage that began within moments of Michael Brown's death expanded to network media and persisted in both formats throughout the Ferguson protests. Extensive hostile media attention imposed considerable strain on police officers as the public raged against police. The confidence crisis persisted with the deaths of Freddie Gray, Alton Sterling, Philando Castile, George Floyd, and others. Media coverage is expansive for sensational stories, like the relatively rare event of a police officer shooting an unarmed suspect. Citing past research, Nix and Pickett (2017) contend that police believe that public perceptions are heavily influenced by the media, even though news stories are often inaccurate or skewed, sometimes leading the public to believe that police misconduct and racism are pervasive in American policing and eroding public confidence in police (Weitzer 2015). As a case in point, a study by Ron Weitzer (2002) showed that public opinion about police declined considerably following extensive media coverage about incidents of police misconduct in New York City and Los Angeles. As discussed in chapter 3, I found similar declines among Black residents of

St. Louis County in the aftermath of Brown's death (Kochel 2019). The Community Callout at the end of this chapter discusses the long-term impact of Brown's death and the protests on county residents' confidence in police.

Public opinion matters to police. Nix and Pickett (2017) attest that police officers are highly sensitive to the public image of police—fearing scandal. When officers perceive media coverage of an event is hostile, they assume that the public, influenced by the media coverage, opposes police. The theory applied to policing suggests that officers' belief in public opposition to police—the view that police are giving of themselves but not receiving back from clients, referred to in the job demands-resources model as lack of reciprocity—causes officers to feel alienated from the public, and officer morale declines. When this occurs, officers actively seek to avoid situations that may further generate sensational news stories that negatively portray police and harm public perceptions. Officers reduce their interactions with the public and hesitate to use levels of force that the law permits to defend themselves. Officers' attempts to circumvent potentially problematic situations is a self-preservation function, adopted to avoid occupational strain (Nix, Wolfe, and Campbell 2018). By limiting their interactions with the public, officers reduce their chances of being scrutinized and possibly even assaulted by members of the public. However, another likely consequence of reduced community engagement and reduced officer proactivity is that residents in disadvantaged minority communities may become even more prone to victimization and feel more mistrustful, as officers pull back.

INTERSECTIONS WITH OFFICER SELF-LEGITIMACY

This process, when it occurs in policing, has important intersections with the concept of police legitimacy. Bottoms and Tankebe's (2012) dialogic model of officer self-legitimacy describes that the public forms and re-forms opinions about police authority legitimacy—the rightfulness and appropriateness of police authority—by observing police interactions with citizens, which may occur in-person or via social or news media. Police officers continuously reassess public perceptions about their legitimacy based on public reactions to police. During the protests, visual displays of disrespect for police authority were prolific in the form of signs, chants, throwing items at police, spitting on police, and vandalizing and setting police vehicles on fire. The media did not focus much airtime or screen time on these behaviors, so they were most likely to impact officers with direct protest experiences and when retold to other officers. The dialogic model would suggest that upon interpreting these negative signals, officers' confidence that the public respects and will adhere to their authority will decline. Research evidence supports that both public confidence in police and officer self-legitimacy were adversely impacted following Brown's shooting and the protests (Kochel 2019; Nix and Wolfe 2017). As the job demands-resource model theorizes, diminished self-legitimacy is correlated with an officer's willingness to engage with the public and to apply procedural justice during encounters with the public, as well as an officer's use of force (Bradford 2014; Tankebe and Meško 2015; Wolfe and Nix 2016).

In other words, diminished self-legitimacy compounds feelings of cynicism, emotional exhaustion, and burnout to reduce police officers' interactions with the public following public demonstrations against police. Yet it is important to keep in mind that while officer self-legitimacy was a casualty of negative media coverage and hostile public attitudes toward police, self-legitimacy is also a potential resource, a protective factor against the Ferguson effect. The job demands-resources model and available research infer that officers who believe that citizens respect police authority, even in the context of negative media criticism of police, may be less afflicted by the Ferguson effect, that self-legitimacy mitigates the consequences of occupational strain.

ORGANIZATIONAL JUSTICE AS SUPPORT

Organizational justice is also a potential mitigator and important resource and support to police officers (Bradford et al. 2014; McCarty et al. 2019; Nix and Wolfe 2016; Trinkner et al. 2016; Wolfe and Nix 2016). Organizational justice refers to procedurally just treatment by the police department toward officers and other employees. It entails procedures, policies, and actions within the police agency that are consistently and equitably applied across employees in an effort to promote fair and neutral decisions and treatment of police employees. Adherence to the policies creates a view among employees that the organization can be trusted to support them. Importantly, prior research suggests that procedural justice and fairness within police organizations promote external procedural justice when officers interact with citizens, as well as promote better officer morale and job satisfaction (Murphy and Tyler 2008). Organizational justice has also been found to diminish development of PTSD (Post Traumatic Stress Disorder) symptoms and emotional exhaustion among officers following a crisis event (Maguen et al. 2009; McCarty et al. 2019). Thus, organizational justice is a likely protective factor against the effects of occupational strain on officers, with the capacity to diminish the degree of negative consequences. The question is, among St. Louis County officers who felt treated fairly by the department, did this help protect them from the cynicism and reduced proactivity bound up in the Ferguson effect?

OTHER POTENTIAL RESOURCES THAT MAY MITIGATE BURNOUT

Other protective factors or supportive resources that could potentially mitigate the Ferguson effect by reducing the strain on officers or improve their ability to handle it include officers' competencies and training to handle crisis situations, years of experience as an officer, and their educational background, race, and possibly gender. Past research does not provide a clear answer (McCarty et al. 2019; Trinkner et al. 2016), but knowledge, skills, and experience have the potential to equip officers to better handle the protests and the workload strain, and curtail burnout. Cultural values and norms inherent in race or gender could bring perspective and coping strategies. Also, chapter 3 of this book reported that Black police officers experienced greater self-legitimacy, so being a Black officer may mitigate the Ferguson effect via elevated self-legitimacy. One indication of this potential is provided in a study by Morash and Haarr (1995). They found less workplace stress among Black officers than White officers.

Evidence of the Ferguson Effect

Research conducted since the Ferguson protests in 2014, largely by researchers Justin Nix, Scott Wolfe, and their coauthors, provides support that police officers have been impacted by the extensive negative media coverage of officer-involved shootings of Black suspects and protest policing in Ferguson and elsewhere (Deuchar, Fallik, and Crichlow

2019; Morin et al. 2017; Nix and Wolfe 2016, 2017; Shjarback et al. 2017). First, there is evidence to support that when officers perceive widespread news media are scrutinizing fatal police encounters with Black citizens, it has lessened public opinion of police. Because of the publicity, officers have reported feeling less confident that citizens view their authority as legitimate (Nix and Wolfe 2017). Nix and Pickett (2017) surveyed 251 officers in a large police agency in the Southeastern United States. They found that officers who believed the media coverage of police had been hostile toward police over the prior three years were more likely to believe that citizens had since become more distrustful of police, and those officers were more fearful of having false allegations waged against them by members of the public. A majority of the command personnel surveyed by Nix and colleagues (2018) also reported that from 2014 to 2016, citizens had become less cooperative and more willing to assault police officers, describing the situation as a "war on cops." Similarly, in-depth interviews conducted by Deuchar and colleagues (2019) of 20 police personnel from two agencies in the southern United States revealed that officers believed social media condemned police actions based on very little evidence. Officers in their study thought that younger people are especially persuaded by this information and tend to lose trust in police, whereas disadvantaged, marginalized communities became even more distrustful than previously. Deuchar and colleagues refer to the process of negative media altering public opinion as the "demonization of policing."

Consequences that followed from officers' beliefs in declining public confidence and support include poor officer morale, hesitancy to be proactive, and reluctance to use force even when policy supports that it is justified and appropriate. At a 2015 national summit of more than 100 police chiefs and politicians, Chicago Mayor Rahm Emmanuel was quoted by the *Washington Post* as saying of Chicago police officers in the year after Ferguson, "They have pulled back from the ability to interdict . . . they don't want to be a news story themselves, they don't want their career ended early, and it's having an impact" (Davis 2015). For example, a *Chicago Tribune* news story showcased how concern about public scrutiny led a Chicago police officer—during the two years following Brown's death—to fail to draw her gun at a traffic stop, despite being attacked and fearing for her life. Because of her apprehension of being scrutinized for using force, the officer was beaten unconscious by the suspect, without ever drawing her weapon (Gorner and Dardick 2016). A detective interviewed by Deuchar and colleagues (2019: 1052) explains that, "you can shoot a guy with a gun in his hand pointed at you right now and you may still be on the front page of the paper." Adams (2019: 1755) reported similar findings from his in-depth interviews with nine rural officers in Virginia. Officers expressed concern that "citizens form quick, non-factual opinions based on negatively portrayed law enforcement actions in the media." Adams's interviews revealed that concerns about racial tension and mistrust made officers cautious about how they interacted with people, fearful of stopping people, and reluctant to act in the presence of a threat. Adams quoted one officer as saying, "I really hope he doesn't produce a weapon . . . Just because of what I might face on the backside of that" (p. 1754).

The Ferguson effect predicts that fear of public scrutiny will reduce proactivity. As predicted, Shjarback and colleagues (2017) found declines in proactivity among Missouri police departments following Brown's death and the prolonged, racially charged protests in Ferguson. The highest declines in proactive police stops occurred in communities with more Black residents. Furthermore, officers suffering from the Ferguson effect are less willing to engage in community partnerships (Wolfe and Nix 2016).

However, research also supports that organizational justice, being treated fairly by the organization and supervisors, has a consistent and positive influence on police. Conducting a meta-analysis of 61 studies, Lee and Ashforth (1996) learned that support from supervisors and co-workers helps ward off emotional exhaustion and depersonalization. Nix and Wolfe (2016) found that organizational justice mitigates reduced motivation associated with the Ferguson effect. Organizational justice also improves morale and job satisfaction (Murphy and Tyler 2008) and increases an officer's trust with citizens, responsiveness toward citizens, engagement with citizens, and procedural justice during encounters (Bradford et al. 2014; McCarty et al. 2019; Nix and Wolfe 2016; Trinkner et al. 2016; Wolfe and Nix 2016). Organizational justice presents as a highly promising mitigating factor in past research.

To synthesize, available research affirms that police officers in the United States have reacted to recent widespread negative media coverage of police in the ways predicted by the job demands-resources model and applied to policing as the Ferguson effect. After Ferguson, officer morale declined, and officers became more cynical. Officers reduced their proactivity and disengaged from the public, especially in Black communities. However, prior research supports that police organizations can mitigate some of the impact by treating its employees with fairness and respect.

Seeing the Public through the Lens of Protest Police

In the aftermath of the Ferguson protests, officers described two notable shifts among residents of St. Louis County. Officers noticed a steep decline in public trust and in public cooperation with police. According to the officers we interviewed, the public was emboldened by the protests and became aggressive and antagonizing during interactions with police. Below, I recount officers' experiences that gave rise to this view.

Almost half of interviewed officers (42 percent) talked about increased tension and mistrust as a major issue for policing post-Ferguson. The protests brought the racial tensions between the police and the public to the foreground. For some community members, the demonstrations reinforced their concerns and frustrations about the nature of policing in general, and in their communities in particular. For others, the protests brought new awareness. Supervisor Lucas talked about how racial tensions and mistrust of police especially increased among the Black community in St. Louis County. Probably the most disheartening example of deteriorated trust was shared by Hugh, who worked in North County prior to the protests. Hugh described how he regularly talked with five or six youth pre-Ferguson; they knew his name. He would pull up in the patrol car and talk with them about school and whatever was going on in their lives, and he said that the kids would vent to him about what was happening in their lives. He felt that he had a bond, a mutual relationship with these kids from North County. However, after the protests, that changed. Hugh said, "Access was denied . . . We had to rebuild that, because in their eyes, the media told them that we are the bad guys, no matter what they saw or what they knew about us prior, it didn't matter anymore. We became an enemy and it became a constant struggle of trying to figure out, what is our role now?" Despite the foundation he had built with the youths prior to the Ferguson protests, that basis was insufficient to withstand the repetitive portrayal of police in the media and on the streets as the opposition. His relationship with the youth crumbled, and as he said, he was less clear on what role he could and should play in these youths' lives post-Ferguson. Related to this example, officer Owen described that when police talked to adolescents on the street post-Ferguson, crowds gathered out of concern that the police were harassing the kids. He said, "It happens fairly often."

The following is another example of public mistrust after the protests. Officer Ryan told a story about responding to a larceny complaint and being told by the complainant that he could not go inside the house, where the property reportedly was taken. When officer Ryan asked why he could not come in, the complainant told him, "You guys been shooting people." Officer Ryan also said that another resident who called the police told him that she had heard about a homicide in her neighborhood, and that she and others believed that the police had killed the person and framed some suspects. Officer Ryan was astonished that residents had seemingly come to believe, following the news coverage about Brown's death and the protests, that police shootings, including unjust police shootings, were becoming common. Supervisor Mason said that after the protests, residents did not believe the police nor accept what they say.

The impact of this mistrust, according to police officers like Karen, Joshua, Dylan, and Lisa, led to reduced cooperation from the public, including a reduction in calls for service and residents not coming forward to provide information about crimes, even homicides. Officers claimed that post-Ferguson, citizens in the area became more vocal and more aggressive in the form of social media posts, official complaints, referencing Michael Brown during encounters with police, threatening to make complaints, speaking about their rights, and gathering in crowds around police. More than half of police interviewees (51 percent) described this community reaction to the protests. Officer Teresa was frustrated about the reactions of stopped motorists that she described would immediately say, "Please don't kill me" or who would refuse to talk to her, claiming they knew their rights, and she could talk with their lawyer. Black officer Andre described that during traffic stops in North County, post-Ferguson, crowds formed and yelled at the officers. As officer Owen explained, crowds raise the danger level for officers and make maintaining order challenging. He complained that in the aftermath of the protests, at homicide scenes, "People are coming out by the hundreds . . . they are getting hostile toward us, and then it's making our job more difficult."

Officer Sebastian said that when he tried to talk to people post-Ferguson, "They're like, you're harassing me . . . who is your supervisor . . . I'm going to file a complaint." He told a story about a resident who on multiple occasions post-Ferguson called to file a report about an incident, and when the officers arrived on scene, she videotaped the call, narrating, "They're harassing me." Supervisor Lucas divulged that he received vague and unsubstantiated complaints from citizens who said that they were fearful of being the next Michael Brown. When he asked one complainant the basis of this concern, the complainant replied, "His demeanor. I just saw it in his eyes." When Lucas pressed the complainant for specifics such as whether the officer took out his gun or had his hand on the gun, the answers were no. These experiences led officers interacting with citizens post-Ferguson to realize that the public was looking at police through a new more distrustful, negative lens, and consequent to the bold public response after Michael Brown's death, they too felt emboldened, even hostile, in their behaviors toward police and were less likely to seek help from police.

The Ferguson Effect among St. Louis County Officers

St. Louis County officers did not remotely observe the extensive negative media coverage of Brown's death and protest policing. These officers experienced protestors first-hand, provided protection to the media while they covered the events, and then underwent community members' reactions to their protest policing experiences in the aftermath of Ferguson.

Officers' descriptions of the media coverage in chapter 2 make plain the officers' perspectives that the media did not accurately and fairly cover their actions during the protests and instead featured visuals that reinforced the public's and even the government's questioning of the appropriateness of the police response to the protests. St. Louis County officers went to work for several months, confronting crowds of demonstrators standing feet away holding critical and inflammatory signs, shouting rebukes, and even lobbing projectiles at police. So, it is not unreasonable to assume that the level of workplace strain imposed on protest policing officers was more intense than that measured across police in the United States and discussed in prior research by Nix, Wolfe, and their colleagues.

Thirty-eight of the 43 St. Louis County sworn personnel (88 percent) interviewed, when asked about the consequences to policing brought about by the protests in Ferguson, raised concerns related to the Ferguson effect. Chief Belmar explained that he was aware in the aftermath of Ferguson that his officers underwent considerable stress. When we talked, about a year after the protests, he knew his officers still feared that they could end up in a use of force situation that draws public scrutiny, which could end an officer's career, or worse, land them in prison. He recognized that officers' apprehension about public scrutiny affected officers' approaches to policing post-Ferguson. I can say that based on our discussions with his officers and supervisors, Chief Belmar did have his hand firmly on the pulse of the officers. Officer Owen synthesized what I heard many officers say during the year following the protests, "Everyone now is so quick to judge you. We're assumed to be the bad guy." The prolonged, impassioned protests coupled with large-scale media critiques about police were interpreted by police as the public being critical and unsupportive of police, widening the divide between us and them.

Each of the consequences of burnout described in the literature as the Ferguson effect came up during the interviews with police personnel. The most common post-Ferguson impact on policing raised by the officers was reduced proactivity, meaning officers engaged in fewer self-directed policing activities. In equal proportion, officers spoke of feeling apprehensive about using force and feeling cynical. The remaining aspects of the Ferguson effect, feeling less motivated at work and finding less enjoyment in law enforcement as a career, were also both discussed by officers as consequences of the Ferguson protest experience.

Reduced Proactivity

Most of the police (70 percent) we interviewed reported reductions in proactivity in the aftermath of Ferguson. Supervisor Noah explained that it was not an issue limited to patrol, but evident in other areas of policing as well, even narcotics. He said enforcement activity declined. Investigating minor infractions declined. After months of protests, officers began avoiding physical contact with suspects, according to officer Henry. Officers attributed much of the reduced proactivity to cynicism, frustration, and burnout triggered by engaging in protest policing and by the adverse media coverage. But, some of the reduced proactivity was motivated by a sense that making stops would be futile and ineffective— that the justice system would not process them. Officers were cognizant that in Ferguson and in some other jurisdictions, in response to critiques about court fines, fees, and failure to appear warrants, courts offered amnesty for offenses (Eligon and Smith 2015).

Reduced proactivity presented in a variety of ways. Officer Karen relayed an incident post-Ferguson when she limited her investigative efforts in response to a call about a suspicious man in an apartment complex. Officer Karen saw a man who matched the dispatcher's description in response to a request to "be on the look-out." So, she rolled down the car window and asked him, "Hey man, what's going on?" In response, the man said, "F*** you. I have the right to be here. I am a grown-ass man. F*** you." Officer Karen's response was to roll up the window and drive away, thinking, "You're right. You are a grown-ass man. You have the right to be here." The officer stated, "we don't challenge people." She said, "You didn't want to be the next Michael Brown story and you didn't want to have to go through what Darren Wilson went through. You had to, you thought about your family, you thought about yourself and your own well-being . . . You kinda weighed, okay, is this gonna be worth this possibly happening? And it's not."

Officer Henry described that post-Ferguson, officers responded like firefighters, just waiting to be called, even though, he said, "That's not our job; our job is to be out in the public and protecting people on an everyday basis." Lincoln agreed. He proclaimed to me that, "Progressive, professional police departments are proactive." Yet, a clear majority of the officers we spoke to were not proactive post-Ferguson. They limited or eliminated patrol activities, did not conduct traffic enforcement, did not vigorously investigate incidents, did not stop to talk to residents or check on abandoned properties. They stalled, at least for a time.

Lucas, a supervisor, explained that the back in forth in an officer's mind might be like this: "Yeah, why don't you just answer the radio?

Why do you want to stop the kids walking down the street at 10 a.m. on a school day? He's not hurting anybody. Why would you? [Response:] . . . Well, he should be in school. And if he's not in school, what is he doing?" People in the community, he explained, "are going to have different opinions on that. Do you want the police department to be stopping and talking to that kid to find out if he's truant from school or do you want them to turn the car around and drive the other way?" Officers weighed whether to take actions that they thought might help to control crime and delinquency, given the possible backfire effect on police-community relations. They were trying to anticipate what the public preferred that they do. For at least a time, officers prioritized perceived community preferences over crime control. Officer Andre said that it took him about two months after the protests before he even conducted a single traffic stop. Looking back, although most of the St. Louis County officers did experience a period of reduced proactivity post-Ferguson, a few officers viewed this period of reduced proactivity as harmful. Like officer Jack said, "Why do you catch people with guns? You stop people." The underlying message is that by not being proactive and not stopping people, there is a risk that guns and crime will abound in the area.

Supervisors suggested several possible motivations for the reduced proactivity. They believed that some officers sought retribution for the animosity they felt from the public, the media, and even government. Officers were exhausted. Officers were fearful and were protecting themselves from harm and further critique. They thought some officers felt disillusioned with the justice system and how the role of police fits into that system. One officer even questioned whether proactivity was the best thing for the community, since the Ferguson Police Department had been called out by the US Department of Justice Civil Rights investigation for using ticket-writing as a primary revenue source to run the government rather than for the purpose of protecting public safety (US Department of Justice Civil Rights Division 2015). Officer William questioned, "Are we writing tickets for the right reason or are we writing them because that's something to generate productivity? What are we doing, what's the actual goal out there? Our purpose is just to go out there and police, but we didn't have a unified kind of idea of what that was, and I think we're struggling to kind of find that." Supervisor Larry saw the reduced proactivity as a decompression phase for officers, because "our respect was taken away." He thought that officers were not respected by the public as humans, let alone respected for police authority. However, he strongly believed that "We have got to get back to doing what we do." Larry stated that police had an ethical obligation to do the job.

Supervisor Larry observed that officers felt frustrated and bitter, seeing their role as upholding the law, yet having to act on orders to stand down, which they felt conveyed the message to the public, "It is okay to loot, okay to say, 'I hope your kids die, I hope your wife gets raped.'" As discussed in chapter 2, police like Larry believed that officers felt as if they were being kept from performing their role during the protests and felt unsupported by the community. One officer, Kathie, explained that "people don't respect us and they don't appreciate us, so why should we put the extra effort in." Sometimes, post-Ferguson, when officers were handling an incident, officer Karen told me that people at the scene would say things like, "Hands up don't shoot" or "Oh, you gonna shoot me like Michael Brown." Supervisor Larry told me that he had overheard officers talking post-Ferguson, saying, "If you don't think I am doing the right thing, I won't do anything." He approximated that in the aftermath of the protests, officers' self-initiated activities had declined by about 40 percent. He thought that officers had lost faith in the system—in law and justice and public regard for law and justice—and so they withdrew from proactivity.

Lucas, a supervisor, explained that another reason that officers felt frustrated and cynical was because during the unrest, officers had their identities stolen, which drastically affected their credit and caused personal financial problems. Officer Jack found that even officers that he would previously have described as 'hard chargers'—very proactive and hard-working officers, "shut it off," thinking to themselves, "You know what? Those people that hate me are the people that live here and they're gonna suffer, not me, so screw them . . . They're gonna pay in the long term by having more crime and more killings in their community." Supervisor Oliver told me that staying put and not being aggressive was a way to protect officer safety—that families at home implored officers to minimize proactivity. Officer Levi raised the question, "Why would I go and stop a car for a bad license plate when it could be some dude just waiting to blast me?" Apart from dejection, confusion about their roles, and frustration, officers also pointed out that reduced activity stemmed from being worn out—simply being mentally and physically drained.

Officer Sebastian said, "I think we're just tired." So, several motives provided the basis of reduced proactivity, but the shared experience clearly demonstrated that reductions in proactivity were common among St. Louis County protest policing officers.

The passage of time helped with the issue of reduced proactivity among St. Louis County officers. Officer Jack heard some lieutenants and captains say, "Put miles on the cars, guys. Stop sitting." But, he said, "officers wouldn't." Eventually, though, it seems that they did. Officer Karen confirmed that it was about three or four months after Ferguson before supervisors really started pressing officers, "If you're gonna be here, then be here and do your job. If you're not, then leave." Officer Joshua said it was about February 2015, almost three months after most of the protests ended, before he finally said, "I gotta do something here." A few officers said that this period of reduced activity for them was only weeks long, not months.

Self-reported activity data supported the officers' perceptions. St. Louis County Police Department, concerned that their officers may have been struggling with the Ferguson effect, provided me with officer self-initiated activity log data. I compared self-initiated activity levels for the eight months preceding Michael Brown's shooting in Ferguson (January–August 2014) to the eight months that followed (September 2014–April 2015). See table 4.1. Across the county, I found that officers logged less self-initiated activity, fewer stops, fewer moving and non-moving citations, fewer Driving While Intoxicated (DWI) stops, and fewer felony and misdemeanor arrests after Brown's death. Declines in activity were especially evident among officers working in North County, where the protests had occurred. In North County, stops declined by 40 percent, moving citations declined by 50 percent, as did summonses in lieu of citations, field investigations, and guns seized. These behavioral outcomes indicate that following the demonstrations, at least some of the St. Louis County police officers, who conducted much of the protest policing efforts in Ferguson, did struggle with outcomes associated with the Ferguson effect. This, while the calls from the public for police assistance remained fairly stable, declining only 7 percent countywide and 8.7 percent in North County.

Some officers, of course, did not become less proactive post-Ferguson. One supervisor, Wyatt, noted that, "There's other officers that they still

TABLE 4.1 Self-Reported Police Activity Data Before and After the
Ferguson Protests

	Countywide			North County		
	January–August 2014	September 2014–April 2015	Percentage Change	January–August 2014	September 2014–April 2015	Percentage Change
Self-Initiated Activities	141,782	121,640	−14.2	29,513	21,479	−27.2
Stops	42,412	30,152	−28.9	6256	3761	−39.9
Moving Violation Citations	14,097	8,960	−36.4	2241	1114	−50.3
Nonmoving Violation Citations	22,767	15,072	−33.8	5267	2941	44.2
Summonses in Lieu of Citation	6,793	4,248	−37.5	1462	693	−52.6
Felony Arrests	3,739	2,963	−20.8	999	749	−25.0
Misdemeanor Arrests	9,173	6,370	−30.6	2503	1522	−39.2
Field Interrogation Report	4,369	3,113	−28.7	1,166	547	−53.1
Driving While Intoxicated	567	395	−30.3	57	40	−29.8
Guns Seized	700	414	−40.9	361	160	−55.7

handle themselves the exact same way that they did August 8th. August 9th, you know, they still gonna go out there and just still gonna do what they can do, you know, to enforce ordinances and laws and get involved." He did not think proactivity was based on how long the officer had been working as a police officer, nor was the difference based on age or gender. There was no clear pattern from what he observed to who persisted in being proactive and who stopped. One supervisor, Gabe, acknowledged,

> We still have to address those people in the community that are committing crimes. We can't not do that. Uh, you know law enforcement still serves that purpose. I mean that's our job. We can't not do that. That's the first thing that I think needs to be understood by everybody, is that we still have a job to do . . . The general public, they want to feel safe, they want us to protect them and that requires us to do our job.

Chief Belmar spent the better part of a year after the protests consulting with other police agencies. He told me that in the months following the protests, in the St. Louis area, reduced proactivity was common across departments, many of whom also engaged in protest policing in Ferguson. Yet, officers across the country, not just in St. Louis County, were less proactive, according to the Ferguson effect studies. One year after the initial shooting incident, Chief Belmar predicted, "That is the number one challenge that police chiefs across the country are going to be grappling with as we move forward over the next few years, is, how are we going to develop strategies to be proactive . . . and have these police officers feel like it's worth it for them to get out there and do that."

The implications of reduced proactivity, he said, are that "We are going to harm the very neighborhoods that we profess to try to protect the most." Even officers who felt hesitant to act simultaneously expressed concern that de-policing, as numerous officers called reduced proactivity, may result in increased crime and violence in the area. Officer Sebastian noted, "even the word on the street is that, you know, there's a lot of guns and dope on the streets right now because cops aren't doing anything." Officer Henry cited Cincinnati (probably in reference to the police shooting of Black motorist Samuel DuBose on July 15, 2015 by officer Raymond Tensing) as an example of how officer withdrawal following an officer-involved shooting led to increases in homicides (see Baldwin [2016]). Officer Jack said that this same problem with reduced proactivity occurred in Baltimore as well, after Freddie Gray died in police custody. However, available research does not support that crime or homicides increased following the Ferguson protests, except in a few select cities (Pyrooz et al. 2016; Rosenfeld 2016b, 2016a). The same thing cannot be said post–George Floyd protests, however. About three dozen large cities in the United States have seen increases in homicides by as much as 30 percent during the last year (Bauman and Chakrabarti 2021).

Apprehension about Using Force

A second consequence to policing in the aftermath of Brown's death and the Ferguson protests was officers' apprehension about using force or a hesitation to use force, even when a situation warranted it. More than one-quarter (28 percent) of sworn personnel raised this issue—that they were apprehensive and hesitant to use appropriate force. Officer Jack noted, "When you have the legal authority to kill somebody, yes, obviously you should have a little more scrutiny. But when you get, you just get butchered in the media, I mean it just, it makes you hesitant, and it makes you hesitate, and you could get killed." Although a minority of police interviewed for the study raised this concern, one officer I spoke to, Fred, believed that the concern about public scrutiny over police use of force had a nearly universal impact on officers in the aftermath of Brown's death. He said, "I think a lot of the cops out here, probably 99 percent of them, are very mindful of not being the next one to foul up and get put on video and it goes viral." How does this look in practice? Officer Nathan relayed a story about a fellow officer who had been involved in a shooting post-Ferguson, and the first few shots fired at him, the officer did not shoot back, "Because he didn't want to be the next Darren Wilson." Officers' hesitancy to use force even when faced with deadly force posed a challenge for police and public safety post-Ferguson.

Cynicism

Prior research suggests that cynicism is a major consequence of burnout. So, I was surprised that only about one-quarter of protest policing officers (28 percent) spoke during the interviews about feeling cynical following the protests. In contrast, Luke, a supervisor, told me that for the officers under his command, cynicism was rampant post-Ferguson. Officer Sebastian tried to describe the feeling. He said that it isn't anger toward the public or feeling like "you deserved it," rather, "There was no sympathy for really anyone now. You go on calls and you see awful things . . . But it just doesn't register anymore . . . you really don't care. People will be making pleas to you about how awful it is, and you're like, okay, what's your name?" Officer Isaac described it as being "numb," whereas officer Thomas described the feeling as becoming "calloused." Post-Ferguson, officers fell out of touch with the empathy that had led so many to become police officers. No fewer than 14 police personnel, 33 percent of those interviewed, mentioned during their interview that they became police officers or value being a police officer because they can help people, help communities, and to be on the side of the just and righteous. This is not a question we asked, rather something officers felt strongly enough about to raise on their own. So, feeling calloused or not feeling at all was a considerable departure.

What does cynicism look like? It took several forms. Three officers talked about how police try to help, try to do their jobs, but this effort goes unnoticed, unappreciated, or even triggers a negative reaction from the public in the aftermath of the Ferguson protests. One cynical supervisor, Luke, relayed to me, "No good deed goes unpunished," and told a story about how post-Ferguson, a woman protested a groundbreaking for the Urban League. They were constructing a new building, the Ferguson Community Empowerment Center, to provide services on the land previously occupied by the QuickTrip in Ferguson, the convenience store burned down by protestors. Luke and his team had been at the groundbreaking to help with traffic. Reflecting on her protest, he explained that, "It's just hard to watch that happen and get up the next day and tell yourself, I'm doing this for the good of the people, for the good of the community. Here is an organization that's trying to help the community, and the people that live in the community that they are [trying] to help are protesting. Is there anything that anyone won't protest?" Luke said that the incident was disheartening and explained, "it can tend to break a law enforcement officer's spirit." Another officer, Karen, reacting to a little kid telling her, "My daddy told me never to talk to a police officer and never trust the police," said that she felt "like throwing her hands up in the air and being like, Ugh, You guys wanna do this job, then you guys can do it yourself." The consequence of feeling chastised for trying to do the job, trying to help, according to officer Ryan, is that it turned cops bitter. He said, "It's the fact that they turned around and pointed the finger at us when we were just doing our job, trying to keep a town from burning, keep stores from being looted, keep people from getting shot." "It's the thing that really just kinda turns the younger enthusiastic cops bitter and the bitter cops super bitter."

Reduced Motivation at Work

Related to becoming cynical, 16 percent of police said they felt less motivated at work following Ferguson. Officer Karen claimed, "You just, you lose patience, and you lose hope, and you lose desire to help anybody, and you kind of lose track of why you started doing this job in the first place." Officer Ryan noted, "I found I was taking off work a lot because I just didn't want to go." He said that he had to find reasons to keep going. Logan, a supervisor, described how difficult it was for him to attend community meetings after the protests, because of criticism by attendees. He recalled one man saying to him, "Well, if police have their guns, I have my guns" and this frustrated the supervisor, because he had hoped that the meeting would include open discussion between the community members and police, but he felt as if instead "It was just one attack after the other" until he said, "I give up, I can't do this." Officer Lisa echoed the sentiment, saying, "so like post-Ferguson stuff, it got to the point where it was hard to come to work some days because I felt like I wasn't making an impact anymore." Officer Caleb said, "I just didn't want to deal with people." But, as a little time passed, some officers spoke of recovering their motivation.

Less Enjoyment from the Law Enforcement Career

With the increased challenges of policing a mistrustful, emboldened public, alongside officers who felt unmotivated, cynical, and fearful of using force, even when the circumstances dictate its use, it is not surprising that more than half of police we interviewed (53 percent) spoke about how after policing the protests in Ferguson, it was difficult to enjoy their career in law enforcement. Some left policing. At the time we spoke in September 2015, Chief Belmar estimated that he lost an average of 1.6 officers each week, double what he lost prior to the protests in Ferguson. He did not think all officers who left the department had quit law enforcement as a career; some employees merely sought better pay or chose to work elsewhere. However, he was confident that the numbers leaving had increased post-Ferguson. Three or four interviewees told us that Ferguson-motivated departures sometimes took the form of early retirements, moving into security jobs, or moving to a smaller, less active community, rather than leaving policing entirely.

Among St. Louis County police who conducted protest policing, losing interest in their law enforcement career was not merely a reaction to the media critiques, but also a repercussion from actively engaging in protest policing. On a personal level, supervisor Noah talked about how directly handling the unrest in Ferguson led him to doubt his career choice, doubts he had not experienced before. He vividly explained,

> It wears you out and it really makes you sit down sometimes at night and you know, when you tuck your kids in, and you kiss them goodnight, and you pull the covers up to their necks and you go, you really sit down and go, is the money I'm making and what I'm doing every day, is it worth it? If I go do this and I take a bullet in Ferguson tomorrow night in this riot, is it worth it? Is it worth it to me, will it be worth it to them? And I've never had those thoughts before that.

This sense of exhaustion, burnout, and frustration as the unrest wore on was repeated across many interviews. Supervisors (e.g., Al, Dylan) and officers (e.g., Henry, Anthony) told us that quite a few officers, those with little experience and those near retirement, had second thoughts about being in law enforcement post-Ferguson, and they knew of several officers who left the department since Ferguson.

One officer who left told me that the Ferguson experience made her feel introspective, and she realized that working in North County for several years—both before and during the Ferguson protests—was changing her as a person in a way that she did not approve. She found herself thinking or doing things that prior to working as a police officer in North County she would have told herself, "Snap out of it." She was particularly concerned about developing racial prejudice or bias after the protests, and so she left.

Officer Anthony raised the important question, "What are we replacing them with?" In other words, what kind of person wants to become a police officer post-Ferguson? What does that person look like compared to the eager recruit in 2013? We don't have research that answers that question at this time. But officer Nathan said that if he were advising a new recruit, he would say, "Go find another job."

Anecdotally, numerous officers explained that they persisted during the unrest and afterwards stayed in law enforcement out of a sense of pride and confidence in the department, especially the leadership in the department, and a team spirit of standing together with their colleagues and keeping each other safe. Officer Fred noted that police worked alongside one another through the toughest of experiences, and in hindsight it became absolutely clear that they take care of each other. He thought, "That is awesome." Officers were both motivated and reassured by the solidarity that they felt with each other.

Certainly, while the riots in Ferguson led some officers to question their choice of careers and to leave that career, not all officers with doubts left law enforcement. For example, although officer Lisa lamented that a long time passed after Ferguson where she did not feel satisfied with her job, when I spoke to her one year after the protests had ended, she explained that recently she had some experiences where she felt that she had helped people, so she again felt satisfied with her job. She said, "The good times feel that much better, because I guess I had gotten hard." Officer Henry reflected on when he contemplated leaving the profession and said he is glad he did not leave, that he would have regretted that decision. Officer Fred made a point of saying that he remained proud to be a police officer, even post-Ferguson. Officer Caleb's perspective was that, "The unrest in Ferguson either made good cops better, or caused officers that were not really that much into policing to leave." During his interview, supervisor Hugh said much the same.

During the interviews, St. Louis County officers provided ample evidence that they struggled with the Ferguson effect. They acknowledged that their experiences conducting protest policing in Ferguson inspired feelings of cynicism and reduced motivation at work, reduced their enjoyment in the law enforcement career, and imbued apprehension about using force. Most officers also reported that they and their colleagues were less proactive at making stops, investigating minor offenses, and engaging with residents in the aftermath of the protests. Their claims appear substantiated by data as well. So, the important next question is what conditions or qualities facilitate or mitigate officers' experiences with the Ferguson effect.

Conditions that Predict or Protect Officers Against the Ferguson Effect

To answer that question, I analyzed data from the officer survey of 218 St. Louis County police personnel who were directly involved in protest policing in Ferguson (see the appendix for methodological details about the survey and variable operationalization). This survey, administered about one and a half years after the Ferguson protests concluded, asked officers to self-report about their experiences and perceptions.

I made a concerted effort to define and operationalize the concepts consistent with how prior research has represented and measured these same ideas. To that end, the Ferguson effect captures the view that an officer believes that negative publicity about law enforcement since Ferguson has made it difficult to be motivated at work, caused apprehension about using force, made the officer less proactive, and made law enforcement as a career less enjoyable. Organizational justice refers to an officer's opinion that St. Louis County Police Department makes consistent decisions, gives employees a voice in decisions, has a fair evaluation system, is concerned about employee well-being, and is operating such that employees who work hard can get ahead. Furthermore, a favorable assessment about organizational justice means that the officer perceives that command staff in the department considers employee viewpoints, explains reasons for their decisions, treats subordinates respectfully, and treats employees the same across gender and race. The study integrates a variable, prepared, that reflects that prior to the protests, the officer felt prepared and competent to handle uncertainty, difficult situations, and confrontation, while also being capable of keeping their composure and maintaining sensitivity to people and the surroundings. Last, self-legitimacy in this study means that the officer perceives that members of the public respect the officer's authority, will obey directives, will accept decisions, and trust the officer to make decisions that are right for the community. See table A.1 in the appendix for additional information about the measures.

To best understand the potential ways that officers' backgrounds and characteristics facilitate or mitigate their experiences with the Ferguson effect, I analyzed the data in two parts. First, I examined how qualities like the background of the officer (years of experience, education, gender, and race), feelings of competence and preparedness prior to Ferguson, along with the officer's views about self-legitimacy and organizational justice directly relate to the officer's sensitivity to the Ferguson effect. Second, because as explained in chapter 3, I learned that Black officers tend to have higher levels of self-legitimacy post-Ferguson, I added a statistical test of an indirect effect to see whether an officer's race impacts their self-legitimacy assessment and in turn, their experience with the Ferguson effect. Results are displayed in figures 4.1 and 4.2.

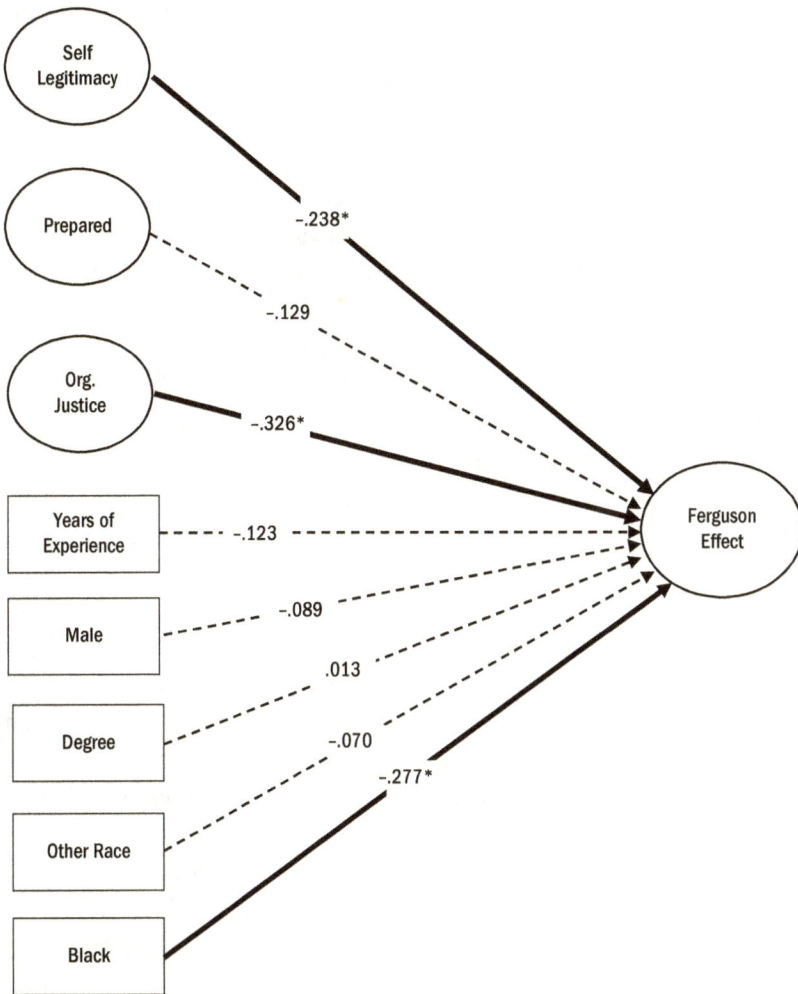

Figure 4.1 Predictors of the Ferguson Effect. Note: *p≤.05, standardized coefficients are presented.

Figure 4.1 shows that information about officer race, self-legitimacy, organizational justice, preparedness/competence, years of experience, college degree, and gender explains 36 percent of the variation across officers in their experiences with the Ferguson effect. In other words, these qualities do a fair job of explaining officers' experiences with the Ferguson effect. Three qualities were important (statistical significance is denoted by bolded lines, dashed lines reflect non-significant associations). Self-legitimacy, organizational justice, and being a Black officer (versus being a White officer) are inversely associated with the Ferguson effect. Across these three predictors, organizational justice had the strongest effect, followed by being a Black officer, and then self-legitimacy. Black officers, officers with greater confidence in their self-legitimacy, and officers who felt that the police organization and supervisors supported them and treated them fairly, experienced greater resilience against the Ferguson effect.

Figure 4.2 adds the indirect path between race and the Ferguson effect, testing how the officer's race contributes to their confidence in self-legitimacy and subsequent experience with the Ferguson effect. This model is an improvement over the model in figure 4.1, explaining more of the variation across officers in their sensitivity to the Ferguson effect. The proportion of variation explained across officers improves by 19 percent (from 36 percent explained in figure 4.1 to 43 percent explained in figure 4.2). The three important factors from figure 4.1 remained significant (statistical significance is denoted by bolded lines, dashed lines reflect non-significant associations). In the model in figure 4.2, however, self-legitimacy is the strongest mitigator of the Ferguson effect, followed by the belief that St. Louis County Police Department operates using organizational justice, and then being a Black police officer. Also, in this model, feeling prepared and competent prior to Ferguson showed significant but slightly less resilience than the direct effect of being a Black officer. Officers who believe that the public respects and will adhere to their authority, and officers who believe their organization is operating with procedurally just principles, are less impacted by the Ferguson effect. Additionally, officers' greater competence and preparedness in advance of the protests mitigated the Ferguson effect. Finally, Black officers were more confident in their self-legitimacy, and the indirect effect of officer race through self-legitimacy on the Ferguson effect was statistically significant (β=-.086, p=.005). Black officers have higher levels of self-legitimacy, which in turn provides resilience against the Ferguson effect. The direct effect of officer race is stronger than the indirect effect.

These findings paint a different picture than those reported by Nix and Wolfe (2016), when they surveyed sheriff's deputies in a large southeastern department that had not personally been engaged in protest

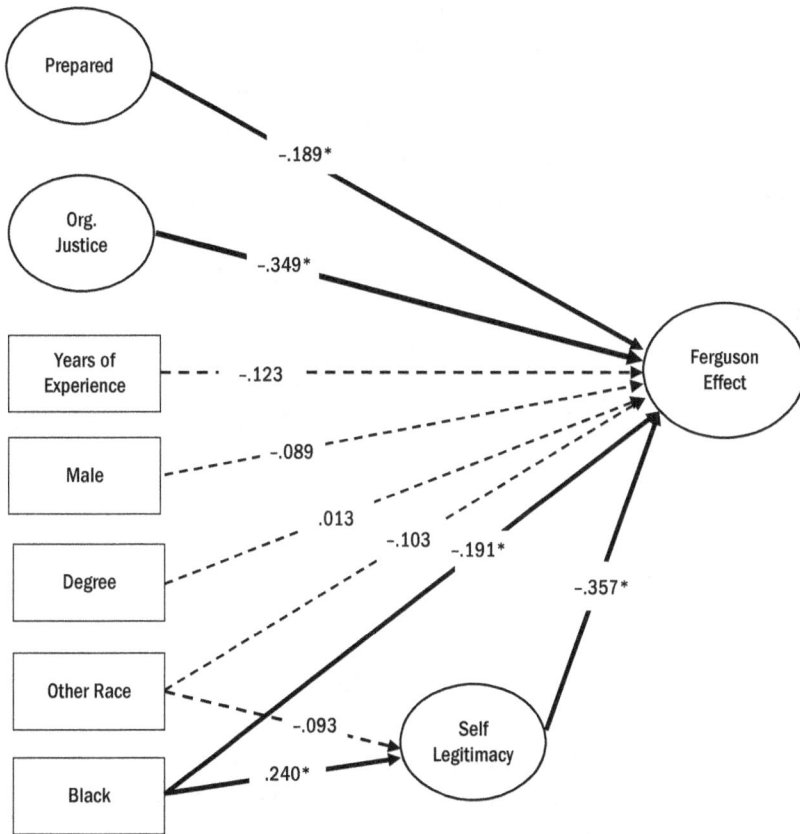

Figure 4.2 Predictors of the Ferguson Effect, with Race Operating through Self-Legitimacy. Note: *$p \leq$.05, standardized coefficients are presented.

policing. A key difference between the studies is that Nix and Wolfe isolated the impact of negative media attention on officers' motivation at work, rather than a more comprehensive measure of the Ferguson effect used in my analyses. That decision could help explain the differences. What the studies have in common is that officers' assessments that their agency practiced organizational justice mitigated the Ferguson effect. Unlike in my study, Nix and Wolfe did not find significant links between the officers' race or self-legitimacy and the Ferguson effect. However, the direction of the effects on these variables in their study were negative, as they were in my study. One speculation about the different results in the two studies is that the factors that provide resilience among officers directly involved in the media attention and in protest policing differ from the qualities that help mitigate the Ferguson effect among officers who only view the issues on the news or at a distance via social media. This was an important rationale motivating my study. To that end, Nix and Wolfe did not incorporate a measure of competence and preparedness to handle the civil disturbance, which, of course, the officers in their study did not have to do. However, figure 4.2 shows that competence and preparedness are important mitigators against the Ferguson effect among officers who do engage in protest policing.

A study by Hoffman, Hinkle, and Ledford (2021) examined Atlanta police officers' experiences with the Ferguson effect, overlapping two time points when Atlanta experienced several days of protests against officer-involved shootings that took place in other jurisdictions (Alton Sterling in Louisiana, Philando Castile in Minnesota, Terrence Crutcher in Oklahoma, Keith Lamont Scott in North Carolina). Like I found among St. Louis County protest policing officers, they found that White officers are more susceptible to the Ferguson effect. In their study, race had a strong influence, superseded only by an officer's heavy workload, which facilitated the Ferguson effect, and job autonomy, which mitigated the Ferguson effect. A sense of cohesiveness among an officer's peers was important, but not as important as race in mitigating the Ferguson effect. Their study straddles the gap between Nix and Wolfe's study of officers who did not conduct protest policing and my research with St. Louis County officers who were faced with protests against local police agencies. Hoffman and colleagues did assess some aspects of organizational justice, but this was not a significant predictor of the Ferguson effect in their study. They did not study self-legitimacy or preparedness as possible mitigators of the Ferguson effect.

The takeaways from my investigation into the Ferguson effect among St. Louis County officers who handled the protests are that the officers, en masse, did struggle with reduced motivation at work, cynicism toward the public, reduced proactivity, hesitancy to use appropriate levels of force, and feeling less enjoyment from their careers following the protests and negative publicity. This consequence for officers translated to fewer stops, tickets, arrests, and guns seized in the county, and especially in the part of the jurisdiction where the protests occurred. However, the impact of the Ferguson effect was lessened among officers who felt supported and treated fairly by the department and their supervisors, among Black officers, among those who felt that they were competent and well-prepared to handle civil disturbance pre-Ferguson, and among officers who felt confident that the public still respected and would abide by police authority. Based on my admittedly limited comparisons with the Nix and Wolfe (2016) and Hoffman et al. (2021) studies, it seems that mitigating the Ferguson effect among officers who police protests against their local police is more complex than among officers who observe a great deal of negative media coverage or protests about other police officers.

To examine this further, using the same officer survey, I compared the components of the Ferguson effect for officers who had worked for the St. Louis County Police Department during the protests in 2014 (n=252) versus those who took the survey in 2016 but had not worked for the St. Louis County Police Department at the time of the protests (n=11). Mann-Whitney U tests (see table A.7 in the appendix) revealed that officers who had worked for the St. Louis County Police Department during 2014 were significantly more likely than officers who had not to report that they felt less motivated to do the job (79 percent versus 40 percent), were less proactive (72 percent versus 46 percent), and found their career in law enforcement less enjoyable (85 percent versus 46 percent) as a result of the negative publicity surrounding Ferguson. There was not a significant difference in officers' hesitancy to use force. Sixty-four percent of officers who worked for the county during the protests and 45.5 percent of the officers who did not reported feeling apprehensive about using force even when it may be necessary. This simple comparison provides additional support that it is important to recognize the specific impact on officers who engage in protest policing, because they undergo a greater impact than police who do not. Yet the study also showed that police in general experienced a time of uncertainty about using force regardless of their involvement in the protests. I draw these conclusions tentatively, however, because there were very few officers in my sample who had not worked in the county during the protests—only 11.

Community Callout

In chapter 2, I reported that residents living near Ferguson had differed by race in their views about the protests and about police. Notably,

Black residents' trust in police declined by 26 percent and police legitimacy declined 8 percent within the first two months following Brown's shooting death. Meanwhile, non-Black residents' views remained stable. Feedback from residents led me to conclude that racial disparities were amplified by the media coverage and were motivated by accumulated negative experiences with police among Black Americans in my sample. Black residents felt connected to their racial social identity, related to Brown's experience as something that could have happened to them, and viewed his death as another injustice in a series of police stops, searches, and other negative encounters with police. Despite robust public opinions about police that generally persist over time, Brown's death was a critical incident that devastated Black residents' diffuse support for police.

Prior research shows similar trends following critical incidents involving Blacks. Two decades earlier, Lasley (1994) had similarly found dramatic declines among Black inner-city residents in their opinions of police following the beating of Rodney King by police in Los Angeles. Jefferis and colleagues (1997), who studied a high-profile use of force incident against a Black arrestee in Cincinnati, also found that minority residents' assessments of police were drastically impacted by the incident. Studying four incidents of police misconduct involving Black suspects (Love killing in 1979; King beating in 1991; Vasquez/Flores beating in 1996; and Rampart Division misconduct incidents involving 70 officers in 2000), Weitzer (2002) too reported initial dramatic declines in Black residents' confidence in police in the immediate aftermath of these incidents. Importantly, he also found that public regard for police tends to recover to pre-incident levels with time.

During the community survey in September and October 2014, we asked St. Louis County residents what would improve their confidence and trust in police. Figure 4.3 shows residents' responses by race. There was widespread agreement by race across the eight items. The two factors that received the most support across both racial groups include police using body or dash cameras and police organizing focus groups of residents. Roughly 80 percent of residents told us that police doing those things would improve their confidence and trust. Among Black residents, 75 percent thought that increasing the number of minority officers would improve their trust, while only 54 percent of non-Black residents

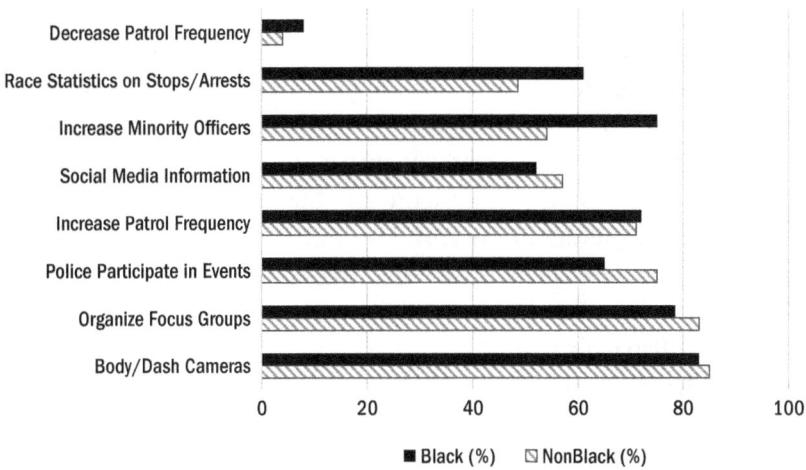

Figure 4.3 Factors to Improve Confidence and Trust in Police, by Race.

supported this strategy. Similarly, Black residents were more optimistic than non-Black residents that police providing racial breakdowns of their stop and arrest statistics could improve confidence and trust. Other strategies that at least half of Black and non-Black residents thought would help to restore confidence in police include police participating in community events, increasing the frequency of police patrols, and police using social media to share information with the public. Indeed, many of these reform strategies were adopted into the Ferguson Consent Decree, the agreement between the US Department of Justice and the City of Ferguson to improve policing and criminal justice post-Ferguson, and they also appear in the recommendations for twenty-first-century policing. Neither racial group thought that by decreasing police patrols, their confidence and trust in policing would improve. Yet, according to police and to available stop data, this did happen.

St. Louis County police implemented several recommendations supported by residents in the first year or so after the protests. Those changes are described in the next section titled, "Other Changes in Policing in the Aftermath of Ferguson." Body cameras and police-community engagement were priority initiatives adopted to promote trust and confidence in police. These initiatives had begun by the time I resurveyed residents in 2015, just under one year after Brown's death.

In early summer 2015, when we asked residents what tactics police had changed since the grand jury verdict in fall 2014, the most common response was that tactics had not changed—39 percent of the respondents claimed police had not changed their tactics. One Black woman said, "The police here are already doing a good job. They take care of us here in St. Louis County," but she thought that changes had been made in other municipalities in the area. One in ten residents surveyed said that police presence had increased since the fall, something not well supported by the stop data. However, police presence could have assumed a form other than enforcement activity (e.g., vehicle stops, arrests), rather, as one older man said, "They ride out here more often . . . [They] ask about the changes in the neighborhood." Four percent of residents said that police presence had decreased.

After references to police presence, the next most common theme was that police reactions since fall 2014 had greatly improved, were good, or that police could be said to be working to fix things. Nine percent of residents made comments such as "They have been very fair since the incident," police are "concerned about the neighborhood and what's going on," that police are more involved in the community, doing things like playing basketball with kids and holding police-community meetings, that police are more respectful, police are "warmer and more sensitive and approachable," "friendly," and they have a "calmer tone" toward youth. One resident described an incident she saw, a hostage situation involving a gun, where she said police were patient and negotiated for hours, but that they did have to shoot the man. Despite the outcome, she said that the incident showed that "Things have changed."

Seven percent of residents said that police profiling, aggression, and misconduct declined since fall 2014. Residents told us that there was "less police activity toward Blacks" and that they had observed greater diversity in who police stopped. One Black female told us that police were not out looking for minor or nuisance violations (e.g., not having specific community stickers on the vehicle). Residents' comments overall tended to be favorable or neutral about how tactics had changed since fall 2014.

Also during the follow-up survey of residents in early summer 2015, we again asked residents what strategies they thought police could adopt to improve confidence and trust in police. The most favored responses across the eight items remained police using body or dash cameras and police engaging the public in focus groups. Two strategies that we asked about showed increased support between the 2014 protest surveys and by summer 2015. In 2015, a higher proportion of residents thought that involvement of police officers in community events would improve trust and confidence (78 percent in summer 2015 versus 68 percent in fall 2014), and more residents supported using social media to inform the public (67 percent in 2015 versus 54 percent in 2014). The latter shift could have been motivated, in part, by the departments' substantial increase in use of social media communication between the two surveys.

We also asked residents an open-ended question about changes that they wish police would make in tactics or the way that police interact with the public. The most common responses reflected procedurally just practices. More than one-quarter of residents (27 percent) offered that they would like police to focus on being respectful, professional, empathetic, and friendly during interactions with the public. Additionally, 13 percent of residents talked about the importance of treating Black residents equally to other races or simply treating Black residents better. Other requests included police engaging with the public (12 percent) and police using less force (12 percent). None of the recommendations included abolishing policing as an institution.

The results of the 2015 community survey showed significant improvement in Black residents' trust in police. Black residents had initially experienced the largest drop in trust (26 percent) in September and October 2014, but by summer 2015, Black residents' trust in police improved by 19 percent. Police legitimacy among Black residents, which had declined 8 percent following Brown's death, improved by 11 percent in the year after the protests. Black residents did not report significant changes in how often they saw police using aggressive policing tactics, but the trend was downward. I speculate that the reasons Black residents' opinions of police showed improvement are likely to be similar to the reasons Weitzer (2002) offered in his study. As he reported, county residents' memories of Brown's death and the feelings it inspired may have lost a sense of urgency as time passed and media accounts waned, their opinions may have regressed toward the mean, as we see with most extremes, or most optimistically, changes that police made post-Ferguson may have improved police-community relations.

Between the initial impact survey and the long-term survey in summer 2015, a grand jury decided not to indict officer Wilson, exonerating him from wrongdoing in the death of Michael Brown. This could have improved public opinion about police, albeit the protests the night that the grand jury verdict was released were explosive, suggesting that is unlikely. The best explanation is probably related to the Ferguson effect. For months after the protests, officers reported declines in proactivity, especially within the predominantly Black neighborhoods in North County, and police stop data support this. Residents also reported seeing police less often in their neighborhoods. Leading up to Brown's death and even in the immediate aftermath, Black residents saw police an average of several times a week in their neighborhoods. By summer 2015, Black residents saw police an average of one or two times per month. At that time, 19 percent of Black residents reported that they had been stopped by police during the prior six months. At all three of the pre-Ferguson surveys, higher proportions of Black residents said that police had stopped them, ranging from 21 percent to 34 percent who had been stopped by police. Fewer encounters between Black residents and police translates into fewer negative experiences with police, a powerful antecedent to negative views about police (Skogan 2006).

Conversely, among non-Black residents, I only found one significant change in opinion about police since the protests. Non-Black residents' willingness to cooperate with police declined by 5 percent. The remaining trends among non-Black residents, while not major shifts, also were not favorable, showing a trend toward declining levels of trust and reporting more frequently seeing aggressive policing tactics. There was no change in perceived legitimacy among non-Black residents. It strikes me that as non-Black residents became exposed by the protests to concerns about racial disparities in experiences with police among Black residents, diffuse support for police was impacted, if only slightly, as non-Black residents no longer viewed critical incidents as a one-off, an isolated bad experience. Another speculative explanation is that in the aftermath of the protests, non-Black residents could have adopted a more critical view of police, making fewer assumptions based upon their lack of personal experiences and instead being more attentive to the experiences of others. See Kochel (2018b) for a detailed study about the long-term impact of Ferguson on residents.

TABLE 4.2 Reported Policing Improvements for Black Residents since 2014

	2020 (n = 97)	2021 (n = 244)
Black Residents	25%	44%
White Residents	35%	45%
Other Residents	17%	33%

Recently, in summer 2020 (five years after I measured the long-term effect of the Ferguson protests on public opinion), while protests over Black suspect George Floyd's death at the hands of Minneapolis Police were prevalent, I surveyed St. Louis County residents living in three high-crime neighborhoods in North County and asked, "Since Michael Brown's death and the public protests in Ferguson in 2014, do you feel that policing in the area has improved for African American residents?" Twenty-six percent of those surveyed (97 of 134 residents surveyed answered the question) reported that policing has improved for Black residents in their neighborhood. Seventy-four percent did not report improvements. One year after Floyd's death, in summer 2021, I conducted a follow-up survey in the same neighborhoods, using the same question. This period showed improvement; 42 percent of respondents (104/248) reported that policing has improved for Black residents since 2014. Nevertheless, the majority still disagreed (58 percent). I found it especially interesting that Black and White residents at both time points did not significantly differ in their opinion based on race. Table 4.2 presents the proportion of residents by race that affirmed that policing improved for Black residents since 2014. The appendix provides more information about these surveys, including that the response rate was low (16%) for the 2020 survey, because it was conducted during the COVID-19 pandemic, diminishing confidence that respondents do a good job of representing all residents of the neighborhoods.

Other Changes in Policing in the Aftermath of Ferguson

St. Louis County police adopted several formal and informal strategies to policing during the year or so after the protests, in response to what they saw as a more emboldened, mistrustful public, out of concern over officer safety and well-being, and in response to fractured police-community relationships. The department adopted strategies to promote transparency, to facilitate police-community engagement and trust, and to improve officer safety and mental health.

Strategies to Promote Transparency

BODY CAMERAS

Supervisor Noah told me, "I want that trust back . . . I want that neighbor and I want those children to see me, to not see me as a militaristic armored vehicle storm trooper. I want them to know I'm a human being." A major initiative that St. Louis County police adopted to restore public trust entailed increasing transparency by adopting body cameras. A body camera is clipped onto the officer's uniform, and when activated, records audio and video of officers' interactions with the public, making the interaction available for future review and even sharing with the public. Before 2014, body camera use was not yet common in policing in the United States. Brown's death and the Ferguson protests prompted national discussion and movement toward their use. In fall 2014, Los Angeles and New York City Police Departments, reacting to Brown's shooting death and the Ferguson protests, piloted the use of body cameras (DeBonis and St. Martin 2014; Hermann and Weiner 2014). Nationally, in September 2015, the US Department of Justice announced $23.2 million in grants to fund 73 local police agencies to purchase body-worn cameras. By 2016, 47 percent of law enforcement agencies in the United States had purchased body-worn cameras (Hyland 2018). Writing for a technology magazine, Miller (2019) tracked the revenue of the country's largest body camera company, Axon (formerly known as Taser), and reported revenues from body-worn cameras rose from about $4 million in 2014 to over $40 million in 2018. Body-worn cameras progressed from being rarely used in policing to being commonplace in just a few years. The *New York Times* describes body-worn cameras as the legacy of the Ferguson protests (Smith 2019). However, Cobbina (2019) questions their efficacy for improving accountability and police-community relations.

Sixty-three percent of the police involved in protest policing in Ferguson viewed body camera use as a significant post-Ferguson impact on policing. Although officer Lisa had worn a camera during the

Ferguson protests, most St. Louis County officers did not have access to body cameras at that time. During our interviews in 2015, most police correctly predicted the reality that body cameras would be integrated into policing in the future as standard practice, becoming customary equipment like cars and radios. Supervisor Mason described, "A new level of transparency, let's say a new level of standard as far as being accountable for how you do things . . . Just accept it that that's the way it's going to be." During the interviews in 2015, a pilot program had already begun in the department in three police precincts, and those we interviewed viewed body camera use as inevitable. While they anticipated that the cameras would be a minimal disruption to policing, they also held limited expectations for their impact. Dylan, a supervisor, felt that officers resisted the cameras at first, but the resistance was short- lived. Several interviewees, like Jacob, a supervisor, talked about their potential utility to positively resolve citizen complaints against officers. Police realized that police-community interactions are likely to be recorded, if not by body cameras, then by bystanders' cell phones, according to Dylan and officer Fred. The only negative undertones we heard about the cameras included concern that a body camera could not present the complete accurate story as experienced on the scene, and so camera footage could be misleading in that way, per officers Jack and Nathan. Officer Ryan also thought that the body camera may symbolize to officers the perception that the community and/or the department does not trust the officer.

Line-level supervisors that we interviewed tended to favor the use of body cameras. Supervisors described body cameras as a means to demonstrate the professionalism of officers' interactions with the public. Supervisor Joseph explained, "As a policeman that knows when I was on the street that I went and did my job the right way every day, I don't mind if someone puts a body camera on my chest, because I'm not doing anything wrong." I heard this sentiment repeatedly. Interviewees agreed that their job was to behave professionally. Yet, even so, they were also cognizant, "When you have a little recording device that's vibrating on your hip, that's a good reminder that you better pick your words carefully," offered Lucas, another supervisor. This view was echoed by numerous officers. Officer Thomas, who had participated in the pilot program said,

I loved it. You would see people's attitude change drastically when they noticed you had the body camera on. You would get out of the car and somebody's yelling, screaming "I'm videotaping you" and they got their camera phone in your face. And you're like, "Yeah I got my camera on too." And then people just kind of start leaving. The crowds would start dispersing, and people that weren't directly involved in it would kinda start wandering off in a different direction. And even the people we were talking to would immediately start calming down, knowing that they were on camera. Now, sometimes it didn't help at all. Some people just didn't care.

INFORMATION SHARING AND COMMUNICATION WITH THE PUBLIC

A key shortcoming of the protest policing in Ferguson, as observed by numerous police personnel, was communication. St. Louis County police eventually recognized the need to swiftly get information to the public. Social media had been overlooked as a tool for proactive and reactive information sharing, recognized Andre. Officer Henry explained,

> We've learned [the value] of getting as much information and video out and, you know, audio out and all that stuff just right away, just to dispel, you know, us trying to hide anything because it's not the case, even in the first place, that we did that, you know. But it's always a conspiracy, you know, "Police department is not saying anything because they're hiding something." Well, no, we're not, we're not hiding anything. We just gotta do a complete investigation before we release anything.

As mentioned in chapter 1, after the Ferguson protests, by November 2014, St. Louis County police hired a social media coordinator and the department used social media to engage with the public and share information about what they were doing in communities. Civilian police personnel, Pamela, offered that the department's goal through social media was to humanize the officers by talking about what they do. By way of example, she described how one precinct commander made a practice of cleaning up neighborhoods on weekends when he was not scheduled to be at work, and that officers volunteered to join him and help. She said that the department has given kids gifts to give to their mothers on Mother's Day for years. Now, these types of activities are the subject of social media posts, aiming to showcase police "as the human beings they are." Supervisor Dylan explained, "Let's be transparent. There's nothing to really hide, we do good work."

One example of how the department benefited from this lesson in communication occurred on Christmas Eve morning 2014. The department had a video of Antonio Martin, a Black teenager, pulling a gun on a police officer and the officer then pulling his weapon and shooting in response. Prior to the Ferguson protests, such a video would not have been made public. Having learned the importance of sharing the facts quickly, within hours of the shooting, the public could see for themselves what happened. In officer Henry's words, "So, obviously before Michael Brown, that would never have been released, ever. But people started forming at that gas station [scene of the shooting]; they started protesting. They started trying to get that narrative out there again, and that was when we released that video. I think four hours after that shooting with what happened that night and it went away."

POLICY CHANGES TO IMPROVE TRANSPARENCY

Other efforts to promote transparency adopted post-Ferguson by St. Louis County police, according to the officers we interviewed, included putting departmental policies online for public access. Those remain publicly available today. Supervisor Mason told us of a shift in policy to keep track and make available detailed information about tear gas deployment. The department also updated their bias-free policing and traffic stop procedures to describe the importance of intolerance against biased actions, the need to maintain the public's respect and to outline detailed procedures for tracking and evaluating stop statistics against concerns about bias. Officer Lisa and supervisor Jacob explained that they began tracking pedestrian and investigative stops, not just traffic stops, based on race and sex. This was a strategy supported by the community survey.

Police-Community Engagement

The county adopted formal and informal changes to police-community engagement, nearly half (46 percent) of police we interviewed told us. A leader within the department, Dylan, espoused, "Community engagement is really the most important thing right now. It's gonna be that way for the next several years." He stressed that following the strained interactions during the protests, it is essential to purposefully interact with the public to "get to where people don't fear the police anymore." He described a posture of service and help, for instance, being a department that links the public to resources rather than administering code violations or other sanctions. Furthermore, he explained, when the department is helping the community, the media will be less likely to run negative news about police, because the public will have positive things to say.

Renewed efforts to engage with the public took several forms, as described by officers Teresa, Henry, and Jason, and supervisor Hugh, including informing the public about what police do via social media, holding press conferences immediately if something happens of interest to the public, reaching out to the public through door-to-door contacts and coffee with a cop, participating in community meetings, playing basketball with kids, throwing footballs to kids, and engaging in impromptu chats at the local convenience store, for example. The goal of these casual contacts, Jason said, is to get a dialogue going and "see if you can get them to smile and look at you, that you're not this robot racist police officer, that you're just a human being." Officer Malorie saw colleagues reaching out to help citizens post-Ferguson who were not doing that before, such as helping people find jobs. Officer William said he goes out of his way to just be nice to people while wearing his uniform. Officer Teresa provided a dramatic optic, describing a day when a commander, working at a precinct near Ferguson, hauled his desk out to the street and and stated that members of the public should approach and talk with him. In this same spirit, supervisor Mason said that he thought that command staff, whom he felt were open-minded before, became more cognizant of police-community relations and especially receptive post-Ferguson to hearing critiques from the public and making changes to policing.

Coupled with increasing the quantity of interaction with the public, St. Louis County police realized the importance of the nature and content of that interaction for improving police-community relationships and trust. About one in five officers (19 percent) said that they thought that a post-Ferguson consequence for policing was procedurally just policing. Officer Karen described that she learned that by talking calmly and respectfully to people, even while they are yelling, will help the citizen calm down and have a conversation, helping to de-escalate the situation. She said that she also realized the value of taking the time to listen to community members, to better understand their perspective. Similarly, supervisor Al said that post-Ferguson he was intentional about explaining his actions to the public. He gave an example of a time, post-Ferguson, when he was part of a team that executed a felony arrest warrant at a subject's house. A large crowd of neighbors had gathered to watch, but afterward, he took time to explain to the neighbors what the officers had done. Through that experience, he realized the benefit of explaining police actions—that it is important that the public not get the wrong impression about what police are doing. He saw this as a change for the better in policing post-Ferguson. After he explained the situation to the neighbors, they thanked him. Logan, another supervisor we interviewed, also found that explaining things to the public, helping them understand why they were stopped, produces positive results. He advocated that "We have to do a better job of communicating any and all that we do." Officer Lucas spoke about the importance of being able to actively reassure the public of fair and honest reviews of all complaints against officers, that complaints are investigated and taken seriously, and if misconduct occurs, that the offending officer will be punished. In these efforts, officers became more active in delivering procedurally just policing.

By about July 2015, nearly one year after Brown's death, officer Kathie said that she saw changes in the community's attitude toward police. She said that in responding to calls, people were more kind and grateful, rather than immediately yelling at the police. Post-Ferguson, but prior to summer, she described getting out of the patrol car at the scene of a call and people immediately yelling and verbally attacking her as the responding officer. In contrast, as time passed after the protests, more and more people became appreciative of their help. One example that she shared was a story about a grandma who called 911 to report her grandchild missing. When officer Kathie and the other officers on scene searched inside the grandma's home, they found the child curled up under a sweatshirt in the house. At this, Kathie said that the grandma hugged her and was very grateful. Gratitude became more common in North County by summer

2015, and we heard from multiple officers that after some time passed, citizens in the county became more actively supportive of police than they had been even prior to Ferguson. Twenty-one percent of officers described positive reactions and support from citizens post-Ferguson. Supervisor Oliver reported taking citizen calls to say that officers are doing a good job. Officers and supervisors like Teresa, Jack, Dylan, and Connor reported favorable interactions with citizens at gas stations, convenience stores, high school basketball games, barber shops, and restaurants, residents thanking the officers—even more than before the protests. Notably, though, only a minority of those officers worked in North County, where Ferguson is located.

Of course, officers also told negative stories about the ongoing status of police-community relations even a year after the protests. Officer Caleb felt as if youth (ages 17–22, he said), who did not truly care about what happened to Michael Brown, merely used Brown's death as a reason to be ignorant and disrespectful toward police. Officer Fred described an encounter he had in summer 2015 when a motorist leaned out of his window while driving down the highway to scream at the officer "F*** you pig! F*** you pig." When officer Fred subsequently stopped the motorist for unsafe driving, the driver was belligerent and threatening, saying, "You just wanna kill me don't you?" Despite this negative encounter, Fred agreed with his colleagues that for some county residents, the Ferguson experience increased their appreciation of police.

Engaging with the public improved officers' attitudes toward citizens. For example, supervisor Dylan described a conversation that he had with an officer that drew parallels with his experience in Afghanistan serving in the military. Initially, the officer said that he was aware that the public did not want the troops, based on the way the public treated the troops. However, at some point, the officer told Dylan, he saw that the people in Afghanistan were not bad people, because he observed changes in how they treated him. He paralleled the experience to residents in St. Louis County after the protests. Dylan retold the officer's story:

> At first it didn't seem like people cared about us . . . they may have thought we were the enemy, but after it was all over with, you can see people see you at restaurants, "Hey, thanks for your service." And next thing, you get

up, he says, "Hey, someone took care of your meal for you." You know, you're like, wow. So that's what makes you say, okay, North County's not that bad. There's still some good people in North County.

Dylan recognized through this story that police-community relations are dynamic and that citizens, just like police, cannot all be placed together in one group.

Policies Affecting Police-Community Relations

In the year after the protests, St. Louis County adopted several policy changes in response to the protests and Collaborative Reform Report (Norton et al. 2015) recommendations. Officers mentioned changes to training, tactical uniforms, and to the K-9 deployment policy, all designed to improve police-community relations.

IMPLICIT BIAS TRAINING TO REDUCE BIASED BEHAVIORS

The department added training requirements to minimize discrimination and promote procedurally just policing. Annually since Ferguson, the department has required officers to complete a form of implicit bias training. During each of the last four years (2018 to 2021), I evaluated the impact of the implicit bias training on officers' knowledge about implicit bias and how it works, officers' ability to recognize implicit bias in themselves, and awareness about strategies to help counteract implicit bias during encounters with the public. Each of the training evaluations showed improvements among the officer trainees, especially when the training topics extended beyond cultural diversity to incorporate skills-based training (Kochel 2022). Prior to 2021, the implicit bias trainings were limited to online training. In spring 2021, the department's Diversity and Inclusion unit delivered an in-service implicit bias training. The 2021 training was the most effective training, showing the greatest increases between pretest scores to posttest surveys of officer trainees.

The training focused on how the brain functions during decision-making. Key topics included what is implicit bias, how individuals' backgrounds and experiences help shape identity and bias, awareness about one's diversity of experiences, and strategies to manage implicit bias. These strategies included proper sleep, eating, and exercise; slowing down decision-making; combat breathing; preparation and practice to promote predictability, reduce stress, and increase control in situations; reframing one's thinking; listening to hear all voices; evaluating experiences with empathy; and assessing interactions for procedural justice and police legitimacy. Pre- and post-officer surveys of 234 trainees showed significant improvement across five of six outcomes measured. (1) Trainees reported increased knowledge about how implicit bias works. They learned that bias is unconscious, affects even well-meaning people, bias can form when limiting interactions to people who are like oneself, and that stereotypes impact behaviors. (2) Trainees showed increased knowledge about the consequences of implicit bias and ways that they can overcome them, including that policing based on stereotypes can make police unsafe and harm police-community relationships, as well as that the first step to overcoming implicit bias is recognizing how it can affect perceptions and behavior. (3) After the training, officers more highly valued applying procedural justice during citizen encounters. They more highly valued citizens feeling respected and that police care about them. (4) Trainees more highly valued using exposure to stimulus techniques (e.g., spending time with people who were not like the officer to reduce implicit bias) following the training. (5) Trainees were more likely to prepare for citizen encounters by implementing tactics such as talking with colleagues about how to handle calls, practicing de-escalation strategies, employing combat breathing techniques, and taking steps to slow down decision-making.

POLICIES TO IMPROVE THE PUBLIC IMAGE

Two policy changes were motivated by a desire to improve the optics and image of St. Louis County Police Department when conducting protest policing. First, in direct response to the media images of the K-9 dogs in the midst of the protest crowds, and in response to the Collaborative Reform Report criticism about K-9 deployment (Norton et al. 2015), police leadership saw that K-9 use for crowd control provided a negative image that they wished to avoid in the future. The revised policy does not permit K-9 teams to be deployed for crowd control, and the dogs are expected to be secured (e.g., in a patrol vehicle) and out of view of a crowd, when possible. For similar concerns of negative optics, the department also purchased new uniforms for the tactical teams, replacing camouflage, military-looking uniforms with navy blue uniforms.

Policies Supporting Officer Safety During Interactions with the Public

Several policy changes focused on improving officer safety while policing demonstrations. One policy change adopted during the months following Brown's death sought to protect officers against identity theft and personal attack. The county shifted to using an officer's badge number, rather than his or her last name, on the uniform name plate. Prior to Ferguson, this personal touch was probably meant to create a sense of familiarity with the public, but the Ferguson protests turned this into a point of fear and financial consequence for quite a few officers. It is important for accountability purposes for the public to be able to distinguish one officer from another, but the badge number allows for that accountability without putting officers at risk.

Guidelines were adapted to allow officers to wear plate carriers at their discretion, providing increased protection from gunfire. A plate carrier is an exterior vest that, when loaded with armor plates, can withstand gunfire from higher caliber weapons and rifles, providing additional safety precautions for officers beyond the standard issue bulletproof vest. After the Ferguson protests, the department received a donation of 410 plate carriers from The Police Foundation and a group called Civic Progress. These donations provided enough funding to outfit every patrol car with the vests and ceramic plates (Byers 2016).

Post-Ferguson, the department altered access into police headquarters, significantly increasing security. Previously, anyone could walk directly into the building from at least three different entrances. I did so many times. Post-Ferguson, the county limited public access to one entrance and deployed security guards and metal detectors to screen admission. These provisions remain in place. Post-Ferguson, officers also received enhanced training on Community Disaster Response, including annual role-playing on skirmish lines, to maximize officer preparedness for handling future demonstrations.

Officers also informally adopted safety precautions. A quarter of officers (26 percent), all of whom were line-level officers working the streets, talked about being more cautious in their approach to policing post-Ferguson. For example, officers spoke about being quick to provide backup to other officers on traffic stops and avoiding putting themselves in questionable situations. Officer Caleb said that he did not want to "get into a situation where I am attacked or ambushed by someone who does not like police." So now he routinely calls for backup when dealing with citizens. Officer Andre raised concerns about being ambushed also. Discussions about being ambushed may have been prompted by the March 2015 shooting of two police officers outside of the Ferguson Police Station. Chief Belmar was quoted by the press, calling it an ambush, underscoring that "These police officers were standing there and were shot . . . just because they were police officers" (Berman 2015). As described in chapter 1, the officers were seriously injured in the attack, but not killed. A *Washington Post* article provided historical context, that 15 officers were killed during ambush attacks during 2014 (ibid.). Ambushes of police are relatively rare but costly encounters. About eight months after most of the interviews were completed, there was a major ambush attack in Dallas, Texas, resulting in the deaths of five Dallas police officers and injuries of nine others, when Micah Xavier Johnson shot them during a Black Lives Matter Rally for Alton Sterling and Philando Castile.

Officer Isaac said he is less comfortable talking with citizens post-Ferguson, that "Like, even the person that's being nice to me, I now think that they could change at the drop of a dime. I'm not as trusting anymore as I used to be." Officer William also reported that he is hesitant and guarded during his interactions with the public, careful about what to say and how to say it. I heard this from several officers.

Provisions for Officer Mental Health

It is impossible to overlook that 42 percent of officers spoke about the harmful impact of protest policing on their mental health. Mental illness is stigmatized in policing, just as it is in society. Mental health is an issue that has not received the attention it deserves in policing. During the unrest, the department's Critical Incident Team had prepared and distributed a flyer to officers that described signs and symptoms to look for on- and off duty—indicators of mental health concerns. The flyer provided information about resources, such as the employee assistance program and contact information for mental health professionals. During the protests, a chaplain also prayed for officers at the command post and remained on hand for officers.

Following the Ferguson protests, providing mental health treatment and counseling to the officers became a departmental priority. Initially, according to Wyatt, a supervisor, a counselor attended roll calls and conducted officer ride-alongs, and the department conducted mandatory after-action debriefings for all employees starting in January 2015. The debriefings operated within rank, rather than across different ranks, trying to make participating in the discussion as comfortable as possible. Discussions were facilitated by the Critical Incident Stress Management Team. At first, Elijah said, there was pushback from people, saying, "Are you kidding me? We're tough guys, you're going to make us sit in a room and hold hands and sing Kumbaya. That's the dumbest thing I've ever heard." And Theo agreed, it is hard to speak out in a group setting when "you're supposed to be a tough cop." But officer Caleb described the debriefings as "very effective, and I would like to see these group talks continue. It feels good to talk about stuff." The sentiment was echoed by Dylan, who described the discussions and help from counselors as enlightening and beneficial. Hugh felt that for the officers who were able to speak in the group, it was beneficial. He realized that the debriefings worked against the police culture that advised officers to "suck it up" and be tough, but he recognized, "This is different." The mandatory debriefings were a mechanism designed to touch every employee, knowing that police culture makes officers hesitant to proactively seek counseling for themselves. Around this time, the department also began developing a peer crisis intervention initiative, according to Lincoln.

Despite these efforts, officers spoke about traumatic effects that they endured. Officer Lisa described an incident that occurred eight months after Brown's death that involved a large crowd of people. A call went out on the radio that the responding officer needed aid. The crowd was too large for the number of officers on scene to control. Officer Lisa described that as she drove to the scene, her leg kept shaking from adrenaline, just like it had while she stood on the skirmish line during the protests. She tried to describe the feeling, "I don't want to say flashback, but the memory between that and like getting surrounded in Ferguson . . . and the amount of people coming at you at one time, and not feeling safe or secure. It all hit me like a brick wall, and for the rest of the night, I sat in a parking lot and I couldn't move on from it . . . I couldn't move on that night. I could not make that distinction."

Police adopted personal coping mechanisms that they felt improved their mental health in the aftermath of the protests. Officer Caleb shared that engaging in volunteer work at his child's school helped him wrestle with the lingering emotions left by the disconnect between how police were portrayed during the protests versus his reason for becoming a police officer being to help people. Officer Wendy explained that after Ferguson, she became involved with Big Brothers and Big Sisters in North County. She wanted to do it, she said, to keep from getting jaded about the residents in North County. Looking back, she shared how impactful the experience was for her. She reflected that "Maybe it's kept me from being a totally horrible person in the way that I think about society now . . . She's [her 'little sister'] really kind of kept me from being too closed off." She added, "I am ashamed that I never thought to do it prior to that [the Ferguson protests]."

CONSENT DECREE IN FERGUSON

Although the focus of this book is on the experiences of St. Louis County police officers, I would be remiss if I did not also acknowledge that many of these same reforms were subsequently also integrated into the consent decree between the US Department of Justice and the City of Ferguson, approved by the City Council on March 15, 2016 (and also into the 2017 consent decree with Baltimore, Maryland). The city of Ferguson committed to increasing community engagement, including with youth, adopting policies supportive of community policing, procedural justice, and bias-free policing, and altering policies about searches, stops, and arrests to reduce investigatory stops, consent searches, and negative encounters with police. They agreed to minimize the use of force and adopted specific constraints on neck holds, retaliatory force, shooting, force against restrained individuals, canines, and less lethal force, and outlined a plan for a use of force review board. The consent decree also addressed numerous training policies and expectations, expectations for body-worn and in-car cameras, supervision and early-intervention approaches, officer assistance and support, annual assessments for disproportionate impact by race, and established a civilian review board to review police misconduct complaints and recommend disciplinary and corrective actions.

Since Ferguson, the city elected its first Black mayor, Ella Jones. She proclaimed, "The consent decree is working . . . We have community engagement with the police and the stakeholders and the people sit down and talk about what's going on and how they can bring [policy changes]" (Patrick and Harris 2021). In addition to adopting changes in policing, Ferguson now has a sitting city council composed predominantly of Black members, and St. Louis County elected its first Black American prosecutor, Wesley Bell, to replace Bob McCulloch.

Conclusions

Police who faced prolonged protest against police brutality and discrimination and hostile media coverage interpreted and internalized the message that the public loathed police and viewed them scornfully as the bad guys. In response, police became burned out and cynical, adapting their approach to policing—becoming less proactive and more distant from the community. Officers' accounts show that their experiences with the public drastically affect how they view the public, themselves, police authority, the job, and their willingness to do the job a certain way. Policing in the aftermath of a protest is complicated. Police leaders face intense challenges, trying to help police personnel to properly understand their role in communities, to recover from physical and mental impacts from the protest experience, to feel supported by and treated fairly by the police organization, and to adopt policing strategies than can help foster positive police-community relationships. Police leaders are tasked with adopting practices that facilitate transparency, fairness, police-community engagement, and a respectful approach when interacting with community members. Some of these strategies might even help prevent future critical incidents and protests.

Sixteen percent of police we interviewed, including the chief, thought that having undergone the experience of policing the Ferguson protests and learning from what went wrong and what went right, that county officers became more experienced, informed, and positioned to handle nearly anything that they face on the job. Supervisor Wyatt told his subordinates that, "You're better than you were before, because you had that experience." Officer Caleb agreed. He said that he became a better officer, more patient and also tougher. Things do not bother him as much anymore. He feels that police officers who remained in the department post-Ferguson are stronger and more cohesive. Command staff also felt that they emerged from the experience with qualities like improved leadership skills, according to Larry. So, despite considerable challenges faced during the protests and in the aftermath of the protests, police in St. Louis County report numerous improvements in policing and in the police themselves that have come from the experience.

5

Conclusion

Interviewer: What has been the impact of the shooting and protests?

Respondent: Awareness of the relationship of the community with the police . . . It's a good thing that people are talking and trying to relate, not just Black people and White people, but all people. The conversations that are starting are good. I do respect the police, but the relationship with the community could improve.
—54-year-old Black female resident of St. Louis County

We hope this tragic incident is going to turn into something better for our police department and for our communities throughout our area. It's because I think it opened everybody's eyes up. . . . You know, even though at the time they probably don't like certain members of the police department, or still have that trust issue with police, I still think that opened up their eyes enough to realize police departments are needed and relationships with police departments are definitely needed with our youth and community. And I think that's why, um, this tragedy of Michael Brown's death hopefully turns into a good future for our area.
—Henry, White police officer

The introduction to this book asserted that during an era when protesting against police has become frequent, it is important to explore what led to the Ferguson protests, to understand the police and public response to them, and to use this knowledge to improve policing. In this pursuit, I applied the revised flashpoints model to explain the etiology of the Ferguson protests. A compilation of evidence from the

US Department of Justice Civil Rights Investigation, resident surveys, and interviews with police showed that collective discontent among marginalized Black residents in Ferguson arose from Black residents feeling discriminated against, treated poorly by police, and being disproportionately impacted by court fines and fees, collected as a primary revenue stream for the city. Their experiences weakened diffuse support for police and perceptions of police legitimacy. So, when Michael Brown was shot and killed and lay in the street for four hours, it triggered a shock of injustice that resonated within the Black community and unified people to collectively protest against police.

Ferguson demonstrated that priorities compete for police attention during protests. Police valued maintaining social order, enforcement against illegal behaviors like burglary, vandalism, and arson, officer and public safety, and police-community relations, but the goals of officer safety and public safety, law enforcement and crime prevention, and facilitating police legitimacy in the eyes of the public often suggested different and competing tactics to police. Competing priorities led to oscillating protest policing approaches in Ferguson from "standing down" to aggressive police responses to communication and community engagement. The Ferguson experience was the epitome of the paradox of violence described by Bittner and Klockars. Throughout the protests, police wrestled with the need to apply coercion to ensure order and safety, but when they did use force, they experienced social reticence against coercion. The major challenge police faced was adopting protest policing tactics that balanced the right to peaceful assembly and petition to redress grievances relative to police goals like safety and order. These tensions led to shifts from brutal to soft tactics, from repressive to tolerant approaches, and from diffuse to selective policing strategies, trying to find the balance.

Policing goals are challenging to balance under normal circumstances, but under conditions of intense threat of danger, chaos, and fast-changing circumstances, making decisions and clearly communicating them with subordinates and even a cadre of other police agencies with different radio channels is extremely difficult. At least initially, there did not appear to be time to slow down the police decision-making process or carefully consider the dialogic nature of actions and reactions between the public and police. Complicating the challenge, the many police agencies involved in protest policing in Ferguson brought multiple organizational ethos—made blatantly apparent by the shift in priorities and tactics when the Missouri Highway Patrol assumed command from St. Louis County Police.

Officers working at the protests felt confused and frustrated by unclear goals, conflicting priorities, and switching tactics. Thus, police fell back on the occupational culture to help make sense of their circumstances. The occupational culture is a tool that police use to help them deal with a complex, fast-paced, and uncertain work environment. The police occupational culture provides a lens to quickly identify danger and classify trouble, defines a central role for police that is righteous, and simultaneously helps officers cope with the paradox of violence. For example, in Ferguson, the occupational culture symbolically assigned certain situations as dangerous and threatening to public or officer safety, such as large, loud, and moving crowds. However, the cultural role of police as the valiant protector of society was tainted and confused by the challenges to the social identity of police.

Social identity was an important element to the Ferguson protests for both police and the protestors. The police observed protestors' vehemence toward police and personal attacks on police and began to question their righteous task of defending the public against bad guys. Officers questioned whether they were the "good guys" and who they were trying to protect. Media coverage and social media were central to the Ferguson protest policing experience, helping inform the social identities of police and the crowd. Officers spent a great deal of time watching news and social media platforms to obtain information about public opinion, providing a feedback loop about the social identity of police. Officers interpreted the media coverage to mean that everyone was against the police, creating a sense of isolation and increased solidarity among police.

The Ferguson protests painted a vivid picture of the cultural concept of us versus them. For police, the definition of "them" grew much larger in Ferguson than they were accustomed to handling. Rather than criminals and jerks being the important "them" opposed to the goals of police and society, during Ferguson, it felt to police as if everyone was against police and so media, politicians, protestors, and often residents all felt like "them," unified in their opposition to police, increasing the isolation and solidarity among police. To cope with the condemnation and isolation, police adapted by applying precepts of the occupational culture, helping each other, pulling their weight, and framing the situation as one focused on individual officer accountability—that of officer Wilson, rather than commentary about the profession overall.

Residents conveyed how protestors and residents reacted to the actions of police. Police supplied symbols that the public interpreted, just like the public and others provided signals interpreted by police. The symbols provided a silent dialogue in which each group responded to the other. Much like the police understood projectiles, large nighttime crowds, and young men with bulges in their waistbands as threats to their safety, to police authority, and to social order, the public interpreted riot gear, skirmish lines, and tear gas clouds as oppressive and threatening. The protestors saw themselves as victims of police and the criminal justice system. A shared racial group identity and a perceived shared accumulation of negative experiences with police united the Black community in the area and then across the nation. This perspective allowed protestors and some residents to justify the zealous collective pursuit of social justice and racial equality, including in some cases using violent means. As with police, cultural frames situated protestors' and residents' views about Brown's shooting, the police response, and the protests, and then that interpretation motivated their behaviors (see figure 1.2).

Officers' accounts about the protests provide support that their ability to remain present, professional, and composed on the skirmish line and to cope with feeling isolated, betrayed, and cynical was motivated in part by officer solidarity, in small ways by empathy for the social cause of the Black community, and in large part by organizational justice, by feeling as if police leaders and their supervisors were supportive of the officers and treated them fairly. Prior research has shown that organizational justice has also facilitated officers' procedurally just treatment of the public. The experiences of officers in Ferguson underscore the benefit of police organizations adopting procedures that ensure their treatment of officers is fair and supportive.

A proactive approach that police leaders and officers proclaimed helped change the dynamics of the protests was direct communication. With insufficient direct communication, the conditions in Ferguson created a silent dialogue as both police and protestors interpreted the actions of the other and responded. A more effective dialogue came in the form of Chief Belmar walking among and talking with protestors, of supervisors talking to people on the skirmish lines, of timely press conferences, and especially of social media use by the department. Providing timely and accurate information to the public and protestors helped diffuse potentially volatile encounters and de-escalate the protests.

From the officers' perspective, residents' communication with them in the form of cards, contributions of food, drink, supplies, prayers, standing up for police on the skirmish line, and thanking them in stores conveyed a critical message that helped diffuse the feeling of isolation and gave police someone to protect. Residents' kindnesses and expressed appreciation or understanding (primarily after some time had passed) helped restore officers' altruistic motives and motivate officers to provide services and help the community.

Ferguson underscored five fundamental features in policing. (1) Police use of force is abhorred by the public, even when justified and necessary; (2) Diffuse support for police tempers the public response to a shocking incident involving police use of force; (3) Police actions are interpreted by the public, just as police interpret public actions, applying a cultural lens that frames and taints actions with meaning informed by cultural norms, values, and beliefs; (4) Police have agency to shape the interpretation of their own actions; (5) The police posture toward the public affects their approach to policing the public. The implications are that police should proactively adopt a posture with the public that encourages support and cooperation from the public and therefore minimizes the need for police to use force, attenuates the social distance between the police and the public, and encourages diffuse support by the public for police. Thus, police-community relations appear central to the etiology of the protests, the impetus to de-escalate the protests, and there is strong incentive that working toward enhancing relationships, trust, and legitimacy should be the primary goal in the aftermath of the protests.

Lessons to Learn and Apply Post-Ferguson

Officers' stories made clear that policing the Ferguson protests was arduous and challenged officers and leadership beyond any circumstance that they had previously encountered. The protest experience challenged residents, the media, and politicians as well. It is dismal to think of the many other communities that have had similar experiences since Ferguson, as protests, including violent demonstrations with looting and arson, have become more common. This begs the question raised in the introduction: What can be learned to improve policing going forward? Key implications center on fair treatment and pursuit of positive police-community relations.

The Ferguson experience showcases the importance of trust and confidence in police and strong police-community relations as a foundation to prevent flashpoint events from taking hold following even justified police uses of force. The silver lining is that severe harm to public opinion following Ferguson was not enduring. Efforts to restore confidence and trust in police by re-engaging with the public, applying procedural justice during encounters, using body cameras for accountability and transparency, and minimizing behaviors grounded in implicit bias resonated with residents in the County. Within a year after the initial protests, Black residents saw trust in police improve, and their comments suggested that they noticed police efforts to improve.

Easton's (1976) theory of diffuse support, which helped explain residents' different reactions toward police by race after Brown's shooting, encourages police to position themselves to receive diffuse support by the public, even across racial groups and other groups with historically less favorable opinions of police. Feedback in this study from police and residents supports pursuing legitimacy and trust, in part by hiring more police that look like the communities where they spend much of their time. Legitimacy and confidence in police authority may also be advanced by direct communication through social media and other formats, as applied (eventually) in Ferguson. Available research supports that the public feels more confident about police legitimacy when they are treated respectfully, fairly, when they have input and a chance to understand police behaviors, and when they feel that police decisions are neutral and unbiased. This is the impetus behind implicit bias and procedural justice training. County residents across multiple time points and across racial groups advocated for several strategies to help improve trust and confidence, including use of body or vehicle cameras during interactions with the public to promote accountability and trust and holding meetings with the public to discuss concerns and strategies to provide community voice. Police organizations can create an organizational environment in which officers feel supported and treated fairly, which translates into better treatment of the public. These are steps that police might take to promote police legitimacy, trust, and positive police-community relations. For society and government more broadly, the challenge is to alter the structural circumstances that create feelings of injustice and illegitimacy, conditions that disadvantage and marginalize groups of people.

Current Debate over the Role of Police in Society

The protests in Ferguson and the many major protests since Ferguson have been at least somewhat effective at drawing attention to the concerns and goals of the Black community, according to 55 percent of Americans surveyed in a 2020 Pew Research poll (Parker, Horowitz, and Anderson 2020). Largely in response to the protests about Brown's death in Ferguson and other more recent police killings involving Black suspects, such as George Floyd, scholars, practitioners, and politicians have reopened the debate regarding the proper role for police in society.

Some activists have called for the total abolition of police as an institution, advocating that reform is insufficient, because policing is fatally flawed as an inherently racist tool of social control that in any form will oppress the poor and perpetuate racial inequality. Among abolitionists, the call to reform is to replace police with "empowered communities working to solve their own problems" (Vitale 2018: 30). The movement condemns procedural justice approaches to reform, including an emphasis on community policing, body cameras, and improved policing training. The replacement for police focuses on provision of substance use and mental health services, youth programs, employment opportunities—including for youth, and restorative justice practices (Vitale 2018). However, thus far, communities in the United States have not taken the approach of abolishing police.

An alternative perspective, offered by former New York City and Los Angeles Police Commissioner Bill Bratton, is that policing should be reimagined, including narrowing the responsibilities allocated to police (The Marshall Project 2020). This view raises the debate of whether the role of police is currently too broad, whether police should continue to handle all situational exigencies (things that ought not to be happening and about which someone better do something right now). Responding to the protests about police, during the last two years, at least 30 state legislatures and Washington, DC have enacted police reform legislation, largely narrowing police responsibilities and increasing police accountability (Gause 2022; Subramanian and Arzy 2021).

Narrowing the responsibilities of police includes tasks like handling mental health crises, for example. Post-Ferguson, San Francisco, California, Eugene, Oregon, and Chicago, Illinois, among other jurisdictions, adopted approaches whereby crisis response teams including mental health professionals and paramedics respond to mental health or behavioral health calls in lieu of police officers (or alongside unarmed police officers in Albuquerque, New Mexico) (Butler and Sheriff 2020; Struet 2021; Subramanian and Arzy 2021; Westervelt 2020). Several states, including Alabama, Arkansas, Colorado, Maryland, and Oklahoma, enacted legislation making provisions for police to transport individuals who are intoxicated, mentally ill, possessing drugs, or in crisis to treatment facilities in lieu of arrest (National Conference of State Legislatures, 2021). Reducing the role of police would simplify the challenges to police who have limited options (hospitalization, arrest, or informally handling) and high social responsibility when encountering mentally ill subjects (Teplin 2000). However, a challenge to narrowing the scope of expectations and role for police is that Bittner's basic presumption about why police have been given this broad responsibility remains. Since the threat of noncompliance, disorder, and violence remains in situational exigencies, it seems unlikely society will successfully *fully* reassign responsibility to handle emergencies elsewhere.

Many ongoing reform strategies aim to address the pillars twenty-first-century policing, advocated by then President Obama's task force and released in May 2015. The pillars include:

1. Building trust and legitimacy in the communities that police serve.
2. Adopting and abiding policies, such as use of force, that reflect community values.
3. Using technology and social media to facilitate transparency and accountability.

4. Implementing community policing to engage residents in co-producing public safety.
5. Improving and expanding officer training and education on crisis intervention, implicit bias, procedural justice, and other topics.
6. Instituting policies and practices to promote officer safety and wellness.

Several of these pillars seek to improve police-community relationships. Two key approaches include striving to reduce police use of force and increasing police oversight and accountability. Chapter 4 describes the widespread adoption of body-worn camera technology that emerged from the Ferguson protests. Camera use was meant to achieve both goals. A recent meta-analysis examining 32 studies about body-worn cameras in places like New York City, Phoenix, Denver, Boston, and Miami-Dade provides encouraging results, finding that police use of force was lower by 10 percent and complaints against police were 17 percent lower when police agencies adopted body-worn cameras (Williams et al. 2021).

Nearly as quickly implemented as body-worn cameras was a policy shift to limit police use of militarized equipment, which portrayed an image to the public of police as warriors or invaders in a community. In direct response to protest policing in Ferguson, then President Obama released an executive order (13688) that sought to restrict police use of military surplus equipment that had previously been made available through the Federal 1033 program (although Obama's order was then rescinded in 2017 by former President Trump). The move aimed to limit police access to military vehicles and some weapons. The reform was initiated amidst discussion, which continues, of altering the image, cultural position, and perceived role of policing from warrior (fighting an enemy) to guardians (protect, serve, and build cooperation and trust) in communities. The police role of guardian has shifted the emphasis from crime fighting to trust-building through procedurally just treatment and community policing.

Limiting and monitoring police use of force has been central to recent police reforms. In the last two years (2020–2021), 16 states and Washington, DC have adopted legislation to limit law enforcement use of neck restraints or chokeholds. Other legislation has focused on mandating officers to intervene when they witness excessive use of force by another officer, requiring officers to report excessive force, instituting civilian review boards and other oversight mechanisms to investigate use of force incidents, and increasing reporting requirements of incidents involving officers' use of force (National Conference of State Legislatures 2021; Widgery 2021). In the last two to three years, targeted reforms have sought to limit lethal force to only when necessary to prevent death or serious bodily injury and to increase officer accountability to this standard. For example, in Connecticut (2021 CT H 6462) a police officer is required to determine that they have no available reasonable alternatives to lethal force. In Hawaii, the law enforcement standards board was granted the right to revoke officer certification and to establish statewide policies for the use of force (2019 HI H 285). Maine enacted legislation to require that investigations of police use of deadly force be completed within 180 days (2020 ME H 1095). The trend has been toward introducing legislation to advocate alternatives to lethal force and to increase individual accountability of police officers for their use of force decisions. A recent national study found that 59 percent of policing bills introduced by states between 2013 and 2016 focused on increasing police accountability (Arora et al. 2019). Officer Derek Chauvin's murder conviction for George Floyd's 2020 killing was paramount in this regard. Few police officers involved in shootings have been convicted in criminal court and made to serve prison time. In stark contrast, Chauvin received an enhanced sentence of 270 months (22.5 years), compared to the 150 months (12.5 years) outlined by the Minnesota sentencing guidelines (Lempert 2021).

As described in the introduction to this book, police rarely use force. About 1 percent of the US population experiences police use of force during any one year (Harrell and Davis 2020). Police even more rarely apply lethal force. The Mapping Police Violence Project reported that police killed 1,126 people in 2020 ("2020 Police Violence Report" 2021). This includes people who died following police use of both lethal and nonlethal types of force, including shootings, taser use, physical force, and police vehicles. This figure is tragic. Put into perspective, in the most recent year that police-public contact information is available, 61.5 million people had contact with police during a year (Harrell and Davis 2020). That means that in one year, police kill 0.0018 percent of people whom they encounter. This is an extraordinarily rare occurrence. The point I wish to make is that focusing on minimizing police use of lethal force is likely to have a miniscule impact on abating discontent, feelings of injustice/ discrimination, and negative outcomes of police encounters in Black communities.

Apart from structural conditions, the greater underlying issues motivating disparities and racial tension involving police are strategies and behaviors police use that can inspire negative opinions of police or negative consequences in a community. In his book, *Uneasy Peace*, Sharkey (2018) outlines an uncomfortable fact that many effective policing strategies that have been able to suppress violence are aggressive, proactive, and intense (e.g., hot spots policing, focused deterrence) and focused within disadvantaged, high-minority communities. Crime declines often come with a cost, such as intense police scrutiny and mass incarceration, that some communities may be unwilling to pay. This is not to say there are not alternative or additional approaches that could prevent violence, rather to point out that the strategies police choose should consider their effectiveness against crime as well as broader issues in community well-being and the impact on police-community relationships and police legitimacy (Kochel 2011).

Drawing from the police and public experiences in Ferguson alongside the empirical and theoretical knowledge that informed my interpretation of that experience suggests that police and communities who seek to prevent similar occurrences or recover from them must place high value on creating and maintaining strong police-community relationships, including within Black communities. The solution is more ambitious than merely police reform. But to focus on policing, some potential strategies, which align well with the pillars of twenty-first-century policing, include implementing policing strategies that reduce crime without creating other negative community consequences, actively engaging the public in communication—sharing information and giving them voice, striving to deploy police personnel into communities where they are a reflection of that community's culture—including racial parity, avoiding acting on implicit bias and intentionally applying procedural justice during encounters, adopting policies and practices that promote organizational justice and mental health within the police organization, and persistently striving to minimize police use of force through training, transparency, and accountability. Available evidence supports the expectation that these strategies will further the goals of twenty-first-century policing, including improving police-community relations and reducing racial tension (Lum et al. 2016).

ACKNOWLEDGMENTS

Credit for this book belongs with the St. Louis County police personnel who made themselves vulnerable and gave detailed and personal accounts of their experiences conducting protest policing. Their ability to do this reflects the leadership provided by former Chief Jon Belmar, who provided every opportunity and encouragement for participation in the research. Due to confidentiality assured as part of the human subjects' research, I will not use names, but I am truly indebted to each person who shared their story with me. Every single interview contributed to the telling of the protest policing experience in Ferguson, and I could not have succeeded in writing this book without even one of these personal accounts. Several members of the St. Louis County Police Department were instrumental in helping to initiate the research (William Howe, Pete Morrow) and to organize and arrange the interviews (John Wall). It was a great deal of work for them, and much appreciated. I feel blessed and honored at the trust this department bestowed in me to share this story.

I am also grateful for the assistance of numerous former graduate students who worked diligently to help collect, transcribe, and code the data. Thank you especially to Karla Keller Avelar, Joseph Pashea, Allison Heater, Elle Teshima, Karen Gunderman, and Charern Lee. I am also thankful for the funding provided by Southern Illinois University Carbondale and the Charles Koch Foundation to defray the cost of travel, equipment, and interviewers.

Finally, I am thankful for the many friends, family, and mentors who supported me in conducting the research and writing of the book. It was a massive effort made easier with your encouragement. Thank you Steve Mastrofski, Devon Johnson, Wes Skogan, and Jennifer Cobbina for your helpful feedback on the development of the book concept.

Study Methods, Data Sources, and Variables

The research and data collection efforts that support this book were conducted in response to the protests in Ferguson, Missouri in August 2014. However, these data were not collected in isolation. Prior to Ferguson, I had partnered with St. Louis County Police Department on several research projects, since 2005. In August 2014, when Michael Brown was killed and the protests began, we had just completed research for a National Institute of Justice (NIJ) funded study examining how different policing approaches in hot spots of crime impacted hot spot residents' perceptions of police (SCHIRA: St. Louis County Hot Spots in Residential Areas). As part of that study, I had conducted three waves of household surveys in spring 2012, winter 2012–2013, and summer 2013, across 71 crime hot spots in the County, most of which were located in North County (see Kochel and Weisburd 2017; Kochel, Burruss, and Weisburd 2016; Kochel and Weisburd 2019). Ferguson is located in North County (see figure I.1 in the introduction). Perceiving an opportunity to build on that knowledge, leadership within St. Louis County Police Department approached me during the first week of the protests and asked whether I could study how the protests impacted police-community relations and what county residents thought police could do to improve their confidence and trust in police. The research for this book emanated from that discussion.

Survey data from the NIJ hot spots study provided a baseline from which to examine community perceptions of police and how they were impacted by the Ferguson protests and police response. The research partnership that I formed with St. Louis County provided a basis of familiarity and trust, which yielded access to important data sources. The primary data sources that inform this book include in-depth qualitative interviews with police officers who conducted pro-test policing, a web-based survey of St. Louis County police officers, and two community surveys conducted as follow-ups to the hot spots surveys. One analysis draws on surveys in 2020 and 2021, conducted as part of the St. Louis County Police Department's Community Based Crime Reduction project, funded by the US Department of Justice, Bureau of Justice Assistance, and for which I am the research partner. I also describe the results of four evaluations of implicit bias training, 2018–2021, funded by the US Department of Health and Human Ser-vices, Office of Minority Health, under the Minority Youth Violence project, for which I am a research partner. Each of the training stud-ies included pre- and post-officer trainee surveys, but only the 2021 implicit bias training results are detailed, and so only those surveys are described herein. The Southern Illinois University Institutional Review Board reviewed and approved all research protocols and in-struments used in the study.

To clarify the parameters and responsibilities for the research, I en-tered into a Memorandum of Understanding with Chief Jon Belmar specifying the details. Creating written documentation of expecta-tions was instrumental to the successful research partnership. Chief Belmar's outspoken support of the data collection for the book and his own participation were instrumental in securing officer interviews and surveys.

On my part, the research was motivated by a desire to learn as much as possible from the traumatic experience and to be a resource to the police profession. I was determined to proceed even without funding. However, Southern Illinois University provided a small internal grant ($3,000) to pay telephone interviewers in support of the 2014 com-munity follow-up survey, and the Charles Koch Foundation provided funding ($37,979) to support administration of the 2015 community fol-low-up survey, officer interviews, and the web-based officer survey. The funds allowed me to pay community surveyors and audio transcrip-tionists, purchase audio recording equipment, and cover the expense of traveling the more than 100 miles from Southern Illinois University Carbondale to the St. Louis area to conduct in-person interviews across seven precincts and one city in the county, which spanned 500 square miles. Much was accomplished on a shoestring budget. By comparison, the NIJ funded hot spots study cost $395,481 (2011-IJ-CX-007).

For the officer interviews, I used snowball sampling to identify potential interview subjects. A key informant identified eight principal subjects to start. When those subjects agreed and participated, they too were asked to recommend others that could serve as key informants about protest policing in Ferguson. Interviews were scheduled and conducted in private, one-on-one, while officers were on duty, and conducted in their workspace (e.g., conference room, roll call room, office). When a subject consented to be audio recorded, the interview was audiotaped and transcribed. When a subject opted against audio recording (n=3), the interviewer took detailed notes and typed them immediately following the interview. The protocol included approximately 30 openended questions asking police personnel about their role in handling the protests, experiences they had, challenges they faced, moments that stood out, what the public and media did, how the police handled the protests, how the experiences impacted the officer and their family and colleagues, the impact of the protests on the organization, on policing, and on citizens, and lessons learned. I completed the interviews, along with one doctoral student. Before releasing the doctoral student to conduct solo interviews, he observed me and assisted me with three interviews.

Together, a doctoral student and I completed 45 interviews of St. Louis County police personnel. Interviews lasted up to two hours. Most interviews were completed between September 2015 and November 2015, but a few were completed as late as June 2016. Interviews included 43 sworn personnel and two civilians. We interviewed 38 males and six females, 11 Black personnel and 34 White personnel. Police rank ranged from officer to the chief. We interviewed 22 line-level personnel and 21 police ranked sergeant and above. Police ranged in experience from less than one year on the job through 29 years. Table I.2 in the introduction provides officer demographics for the police interviewees as well as for sworn personnel in the department.

Subjects were assigned an identification code to protect their identity, and only that anonymized code was attached to audio recordings and transcribed files. After the interviews were transcribed, they were imported into NVivo software, along with classification data. The qualitative coding employed an integrated approach, both deductive and inductive strategies. First, I created a broad start list of codes that reflected the conceptual framework of the interview protocol (e.g., initial role; environmental conditions; interactions with public; family and friends' reactions; tactics to handle unrest; mental and emotional impact). Subsequently, a graduate student read the transcribed data to develop the specific codes under the broad categories and further refine the coding, allowing the data to drive the codes. She applied an iterative process, returning repeatedly to already coded interviews to update them as the coding evolved. Afterward, a second graduate student and I went back through the coded interviews to review and update the coding as needed to be comprehensive. The themes identified by the coding process are the basis of the framework for this book.

WEB-BASED SURVEY OF ST. LOUIS COUNTY POLICE

In June and July 2016, all St. Louis County sworn personnel received an email inviting their participation in an online survey. The survey contained approximately 80 questions and asked officers about police legitimacy and police-community relations, officers' skills related to protest policing, experiences with protest policing, and impacts from protest policing. The response rate was 31 percent (266/872 sworn at the time). Of the 266 respondents, 218 police had worked for St. Louis County in 2014 and were directly involved with protest policing in Ferguson (e.g., responding to the original scene, serving on a skirmish line, command post, crowd control). Analyses within this book draw primarily from the 218 respondents who were directly involved in handling the unrest in Ferguson. One analysis in chapter 4 conducts one analysis comparing the Ferguson effect for officers who worked for St. Louis County police in 2014 versus 11 respondents who did not work for the department in 2014, but who took the survey in 2016.

The demographics of the subsample of 218 officers who conducted protest policing in Ferguson included 88 percent males; 89 percent White, 7.5 percent Black, 3.5 percent other; 75 percent at the rank of officer; 70 percent with a bachelors or graduate degree; and an average of 15 years on the job. The demographics of the sample approximated the population of sworn officers at the time. See table I.2 in the introduction for the comparison. In this book, the police survey data are used to compare Black versus White officers on seven outcomes and to assess whether being a Black officer, among other critical factors, provides resilience against the Ferguson effect.

Questions from the officer survey were used to operationalize latent variables discussed in chapter 3, "Being Black in Blue," and chapter 4, "Policing in the Aftermath of Protests." I first utilized exploratory factor analysis with all question items of interest (n=45). I then ran a confirmatory factor analysis (CFI=.960, TLI=.956, RMSEA=.045) and saved the factor scores.

Table A.1 describes the outcomes and provides reliability estimates. All measures show good internal reliability.

2021 IMPLICIT BIAS TRAINING SURVEYS OF OFFICER TRAINEES

To evaluate the impact of the 2021 in-service implicit bias training, in-person pretest surveys were administered to all trainees at their in-service training held between February and April 2021 at the St. Louis County and Municipal Police Academy. After concluding the training, officers took a posttest that asked the same questions. Demographics for the trainees and survey respondents are provided in table A.2. Most trainees took the surveys, so respondents are a good representation of the trainees. Most trainees are male, White, and work at the rank of police officer. The majority of police trainees surveyed had more than ten years of experience.

To create outcome measures for the evaluation, I utilized multiple indicators and created latent variables. I first used exploratory and then confirmatory factor analysis. The model fit was good for the confirmatory factor analysis (CFI: .949; TLI: .941; RMSEA: .014). The indicators for the outcome variables are summarized in table A.3 below. The Cronbach's alphas show reasonably good reliability, ranging from .680 to .836.

COMMUNITY SURVEYS

Within weeks of Brown's death and while protests remained ongoing, we conducted telephone surveys of St. Louis County residents to study

TABLE A.1. Outcome Measures from the Police Officer Survey

Time	Variable	Meaning and Indicators	Cronbach's Alpha	Range (Mean)
Before	Prepared/ Competence	Felt prepared before Ferguson to handle uncertainty, difficult situations, and confrontation, while keeping composure and maintaining sensitivity to people and surroundings. Prior to August 9, 2014, I was capable of . . . Q18. adjusting quickly to cope with changes over which I had no control. Q19. recovering quickly from setbacks. Q20. I had a sensitivity and awareness of my surroundings, and particularly people. Q21. responding quickly without detailed explanations of orders or events. Q22. calming myself down in the minutes before an anticipated aggressive confrontation. Q23. controlling myself and keeping my composure in difficult situations.	0.880	−2.94–1.56 (−0.07)
During	Leadership	During the unrest, felt effective at making decisions, setting priorities, motivating, and guiding others, and resolving problems. During the height of the unrest, August 9, 2014 to December 2, 2014, how effective were you at . . . Q28. making decisions without having all of the relevant information. Q29. choosing what your top priority should be. Q30. motivating and guiding others. Q31. anticipating and resolving potential problems.	0.891	−2.36–1.55 (−0.04)
During	Procedural Justice	During the unrest, felt effective at behaving professionally, being impartial and fair, restraining the use of force, and upholding the SLCPD standards of conduct. During the height of the unrest, August 9, 2014 to December 2, 2014, how effective were you at . . . Q32. controlling yourself and acting professionally at all times. Q33. upholding the qualities and standards of the St. Louis County Police Department. Q34. being impartial and fair no matter what situation was presented. Q35. restraining yourself from using no more force than the situation called for.	0.830	−2.3–1.42 (−0.09)
During	Mental and Emotional Impact	During the unrest, experienced anxiety, stress, lack of energy, slowed responses, poor concentration, difficulty sleeping. During the height of the unrest, August 9, 2014 to December 2, 2014, level of agreement or disagreement: Q40. Situations in which I felt uncertainty caused me anxiety. Q41. I experienced levels of excessive worrying. Q42. As stress compounded, I felt tired and had less energy sooner. Q43. As stress compounded, my reflexes and physical responses were slower. Q44. I had poor levels of concentration. Q45. I had trouble falling/staying asleep or sleeping too much.	0.873	−1.73–1.76 (0)

After	PTSD-like Symptoms	0.933	−2.03–2.59 (0.03)	Experience panic without reason, avoid situations that remind me of stressful past experiences, have physical and emotional reactions when encounter similar past stressful experience. At the present time (Spring 2016), level of agreement or disagreement: Q48. Situations that remind me of the unrest cause me anxiety. Q49. I feel that I am close to panic without any good reason. Q50. I avoid activities or situations because they remind me of a stressful experience from the past. Q51. I feel very upset when something reminds me of a stressful experience. Q52. I have physical reactions when something reminds me of a stressful past experience.
After	Ferguson Effect	0.860	−2.23–2.32 (−0.01)	Negative publicity about law enforcement since Ferguson has made it difficult to be motivated at work, caused apprehension about using force, made me less proactive, and made law enforcement as a career less enjoyable. Negative publicity about law enforcement since Ferguson . . . Q53. made it difficult to be motivated at work. Q54. caused me to be less proactive on the job than in the past. Q55. caused me to be more apprehensive about using force even though it may be necessary. Q56. made it less enjoyable to have a career in law enforcement.
After	Self-Legitimacy	0.877	−1.8–1.92 (0)	Members of the public respect officers' authority, will obey directives, will accept decisions, and trust me to make decisions that are right for the community. Level of agreement or disagreement (2016): Q3. If I give a directive to members of the public, they will obey even if they disagree. Q6. In my assigned community, citizens respect my authority as a police officer. Q9. Residents in the community where I work trust me to make decisions that are right for the people there. Q10. I feel that residents will obey my directives because they see that as the proper or morally right response. Q11. Residents accept my decisions even when they do not understand my reasons behind them.
After	Organizational Justice	0.933	−2.08–2.0 (−0.02)	SLCPD: Makes consistent decisions, gives employees a voice in decisions, has fair evaluation system—if you work hard, you will get ahead, and is concerned about employee well-being. Command staff: Considers employee viewpoints, explains reasons for decisions, treats individuals respectfully, treats same across gender/race. Level of agreement or disagreement (2016): Q57. SLCPD policies provide standards so that decisions are made with consistency. Q58. SLCPD policies are designed to allow employees to have a voice in agency decisions (e.g., assignment changes, discipline). Q59. SLCPD performance evaluation system is fair. Q60. If you work hard, you can get ahead. Q61. SLCPD is concerned about my mental and emotional welfare. Q62. The culture within SLCPD is accepting of officers' use of employee assistance resources for emotional or personal issues. Q63. SLCPD would defend me against public scrutiny, if my actions are justifiable. Q64. SLCPD command staff consider employees' viewpoints. Q65. SLCPD command staff clearly explain the reasons for their decisions. Q66. SLCPD command staff treat employees with respect. Q67. SLCPD command staff treat employees the same regardless of gender or race.

TABLE A.2 2021 Implicit Bias Trainee Versus Survey Respondent Demographics

	Trainees	Survey Respondents
	n = 279	n = 234
Gender		
Male	87%	85%
Race		
White	88%	81%
Black	10%	13%
Other	2%	6%
Rank		
Officer	91%	86%
Sergeant	9%	14%
Work Experience		
0–3 years	—	15%
4–6 years	—	16%
7–10 years	—	12%
> 10 years	—	57%

the impact of Brown's death and police handling of the unrest on public opinions about police. We contacted residents who had been surveyed as part of the hot spots policing study. Although the hot spots study adopted in-person surveying, interviewer safety concerns due to the protests and monetary resources restricted this follow-up to telephone surveys. We had collected telephone numbers from respondents at the end of the in-person survey.

The pre-Ferguson community surveys asked residents their opinions about policing in their neighborhoods. Having established baseline views about police prior to Brown's death and the protests, I re-surveyed 390 residents in September and October 2014, while protests remained ongoing. Of the residents we called during the protests, 48 percent participated in the survey. Just over one-quarter of those we surveyed (26 percent) lived within two miles of where Brown was killed, 46 percent lived within four miles, and 77 percent lived within ten miles. Despite the county covering more than 500 square miles in size, all survey

TABLE A.3 Implicit Bias Training Evaluation Outcome Measures

Understands How Implicit Bias Works (α = .751)

Level of agreement:

Even well-meaning people may have biases
My biases do not affect my behavior (reverse coded)
Implicit bias does not affect our actions because it is unconscious (reverse coded)
Spending most of my time with people who are a great deal like me reinforces stereotypes about people who are different from me
Bias in the police profession is merely a fiction produced by the media (reverse coded)

Knowledge of Implicit Bias Consequences and How to Overcome Them (α = .680)

Level of agreement:

Policing based on stereotypes or biases can make police unsafe
First step toward overriding implicit bias is recognizing how it can affect perceptions and behavior
Implicit bias can harm police-community relationships

Values Procedural Justice (α = .824)

How important is it to you:

That citizens feel respected by you?
To express empathy to citizens during your interactions with the public?
That citizens you interact with feel like you care about their concerns?

Favors Exposure to Stimulus to Reduce Implicit Bias (α = .836)

How important is it to you to:

To spend time with people who are not like you?
To spend time in places where you stand out because you are different?

Applies Skills to Prepare for Encounter (α = .792)

How likely are you to:

Use combat breathing techniques when responding to a call or handling an emergency?
Take steps to slow down your decision-making process when handling a call?
When not on a call, talk with coworkers about ways to best handle different types of calls?
Informally practice with other officers ways to de-escalate intense situations?
Spend time after a call evaluating how the call made you and the other people involved feel?

Applies Procedural Justice (α = .765)

How likely are you to:

Encourage all people at a scene to tell their side of events?
Tailor your language, manner, or tone to make a citizen feel more comfortable interacting with police?
Explain your actions and decisions to people that you stop?
Explain your actions and decisions to people during a call for service?

respondents lived within 20 miles of the location on Canfield Drive where Brown was killed (see figures 0.1 and 1.3 for a map of the county and of the shooting location, respectively). That part of the county tended to show elevated levels of crime.

Since residents surveyed were from high crime areas in the county, they do not represent county residents as a whole. Study residents lived in highly disadvantaged neighborhood contexts, two-thirds of which were multifamily housing. The hot spots, only an average of 0.1 square miles in size, experienced an average of 2.25 hours of police presence each week at the outset of the NIJ study—suggesting that they were accustomed to police presence. Table I.1 in the introduction compares the respondents of the community surveys to demographics of county residents. Follow-up survey respondents are predominantly Black (70 percent), never married (44 percent), and with lower incomes than the average in the county (48 percent made less than $25,000 per year). Only one-third of the residents we surveyed during September and October 2014 owned their residence.

In this follow-up survey, we asked all the same questions as in the prior surveys for the NIJ funded study. However, we added open- and closed-ended questions to allow us to gather details about how Brown's death and the protests affected the residents. We asked residents about their familiarity with the shooting, their views about the public's response and about the police response, their participation in protest activities, and what strategies residents thought would improve confidence and trust in police.

In April and May 2015, we conducted a final survey follow-up with St. Louis County residents who had been part of the hot spots study. We conducted the survey by phone and in-person, completing 259 surveys. As shown in table I.1, although residential mobility and other factors resulted in attrition, demographics at this final wave approximated those who responded during the height of the protests in 2014. Respondents were predominantly Black, female, never married, older, did not own their homes, earned modest incomes, and had some college experience, but most did not earn a college degree. Once again, we asked the same questions as with the NIJ funded survey. In addition, as with the September and October 2014 surveys, we also asked

TABLE A.4 Outcome Measures from the Community Surveys

	Scale	Cronbach's α	NIJ Study		2014		2015	
			n	Mean (s.d.)	n	Mean (s.d.)	n	Mean (s.d.)
Police Legitimacy	0–100	.738	587	69.1 (26.1)	367	64.1 (27.9)	220	70.1 (25.1)
I/you should								
. . . do what the police tell you to even if you disagree.								
. . . accept decisions made by area police, even if I do not understand the reasons.								
. . . obey police directives because that is the proper or right thing to do.								
Procedural Justice and Trust	0–100	.932	588	64.6 (27.3)	378	52.5 (29.5)	219	59.2 (27.6)
Area police								
. . . try to help citizens solve their problems.								
. . . address citizens in a respectful manner and appropriate tone.								
. . . can be trusted to make decisions that are right for the people in this area.								
. . . treat people fairly.								
. . . provide the same quality of service to all citizens in the area.								
. . . explain their actions to people.								
. . . take the time to listen to people.								
For the most part, area police are honest.								

residents, again, what might improve their confidence and trust in police. We added two open-ended questions asking residents what changes they had observed in policing since the grand jury decision and what changes they would like to see police make in terms of tactics and services. Table A.4 provides the description of the outcome variables measured across the NIJ, 2014, and 2015 community surveys and presented in this book.

Finally, one analysis in the book draws from a summer 2020 survey and a follow-up summer 2021 survey of St. Louis County residents from three high crime neighborhoods in North County. We administered the 2020 survey during the COVID-19 pandemic, which presented challenges, even beyond those encountered when trying to survey residents of high crime areas (Pashea and Kochel 2016). In general, high crime areas have depressed response rates due to vacancies, language barriers,

TABLE A.5 Demographics 2020 Survey of Three St. Louis County High Crime Neighborhoods

	2020 Survey Respondents (n = 124)	2021 Survey Respondents (n = 274)	Census
Males	40%	40%	45%
Home Ownership	60%	45%	51%
Mean Age	52	48	—
Race			
Black	68%	74%	84%
White	22%	14%	14%
Asian/Pacific Islander	1%	<1%	1%
Other	5%	6%	1%
Multi	3%	4%	2%
Hispanic	1%	1%	1%

residential mobility, and mistrust of strangers and government (Groves and Couper 2012). Due to constraints imposed by government officials during the pandemic, initial efforts to survey residents entailed telephone surveys. Response rates to the telephone survey were low, and so as soon as permissible and feasible, we switched to in-person surveys, which generally garner a higher response rate than telephone surveys. However, due to COVID-19 exposure concerns, we halted in-person surveys after two weeks and switched to a mailed survey approach, which also tends to have a lower return than in-person surveys. In 2020, we obtained 124 completed household surveys. The overall response rate was 16% (41% completed by telephone, 32% completed in person, 27% completed by mail). Our experience was, unfortunately, typical among surveys conducted during the pandemic. Prior research has found that the pandemic significantly lowered survey response rates, especially among lower income groups (Rothbaum and Bee 2021).

The follow-up summer 2021 survey was in person and more successful. Although the COVID-19 pandemic had not fully subsided and interviewers had to wear face masks, we were able to conduct the surveys in person. The response rate was 32 percent, with a 47 percent cooperation rate, obtaining 274 completed surveys. Table A.5 provides the demographics of the respondents to both surveys compared to census data available for the areas. The 2020 sample was 40 percent male, with a mean age of 52 years, 60 percent owned their homes, and the majority were Black (68 percent). The 2020 sample slightly underrepresents Black residents and renters, hard-to-reach groups. The 2021 sample was similar. The sample was 40 percent male, with a mean age of 48 years, and the majority were Black (74 percent). While the 2020 sample somewhat underrepresented renters, the in-person surveys of 2021 did a better job incorporating renters.

APPLICATION OF THE DATA

In this book, I rely most heavily on the detailed qualitative interviews with 45 police personnel who conducted protest policing to tell the story about officers' experiences. Each of the chapters integrates themes and quotes from these interviews. The online survey of police involved in the protests provides the basis of the empirical tests in chapters 3 and 4, comparing Black and non-Black officers on a variety of outcomes and assessing the impact of officers' characteristics and self-legitimacy on the Ferguson effect. The community surveys are the basis of the community callouts within each chapter. Most of the details about the analyses and findings are described within the relevant chapters. However, I wished to provide a few analytical tables within the appendix as reference or support for the text.

In chapter 3, I compared Black versus White police officers on seven outcomes. Table A.6 provides the t-test results, which are described in narrative form in the text and are depicted in figures 3.1 and 3.2.

TABLE A.6 T-Test Results by Officer Race (Black versus Non-Black)

Outcomes	t	Black Officers mean (s.d.)	Non-Black Officers mean (s.d.)
Prepared/Competence	1.709†	0.232 (.799)	−.108 (.738)
Leadership	1.566	0.260 (.668)	−.064 (.778)
Procedural Justice	1.459	0.143 (.670)	−.111 (.647)
Mental and Emotional Impact	−3.137**	−.516 (.673)	0.026 (.642)
PTSD-like Symptoms	−2.730**	−.520 (.824)	0.072 (.807)
Self-Legitimacy	3.261**	.556 (.749)	−.056 (.694)
Ferguson Effect	−3.450**	−.692 (.746)	0.047 (.801)

NOTE: † $p \leq .10$, * $p \leq .05$, ** $p \leq .01$.

TABLE A.7 Mann-Whitney U Tests, Officers Who Worked for the County During 2014 (252) versus Those Who Did Not (11)

Negative publicity surrounding law enforcement since Ferguson has . . .	Mann-Whitney U	Z
Made it more difficult to be motivated at work	661	2.62**
Caused me to be less proactive on the job than previously	686	2.87**
Made it less enjoyable to have a career in law enforcement	483	3.97***
Caused me to be more apprehensive about using force, even though it may be necessary	1154.5	0.80

NOTE: *p≤.05, **p≤.01, ***p≤.001.

Briefly in chapter 4, I described the contrast between officers who worked for St. Louis County Police Department in 2014 and those that did not work for the department in 2014, but who took the 2016 survey. I compared the officers on the four measures I collected that compose the Ferguson effect and found that in three of the four outcomes, officers employed by the department in 2014 fared more negatively than those who did not. Table A.7 is the reference table for that comparison, using Mann-Whitney U nonparametric tests to compare independent groups on ordinal outcomes.

REFERENCES

"2020 Police Violence Report." 2021. *2020 Police Violence Report.* Accessed June 30. https://policeviolencereport.org.

ACLED. 2020. "U.S. Crisis Monitor Releases Full Data for Summer 2020." Princeton, NJ: Bridging Divides Initiative, Princeton School of Public and International Affairs' Liechtenstein Institute on Self-Determination.

Adams, Joshua L. 2019. "'I Almost Quit': Exploring the Prevalence of the Ferguson Effect in Two Small Sized Law Enforcement Agencies in Rural Southcentral Virginia." *Qualitative Report* 24 (7): 1747–64.

Alex, Nicholas. 1969. *Black in Blue: A Study of the Negro Policeman.* New York: Appleton.

Anonymous. 2014a. "Ferguson Day Three Wrap Up: Calls for Justice." *St. Louis Post-Dispatch*, August 12. www.stltoday.com.

——. 2014b. "#Ferguson in Pictures." *St. Louis Post-Dispatch.* August 31. www.stltoday.com.

Arora, Maneesh, Davin L. Phoenix, and Archie Delshad. 2019. "Framing Police and Protesters: Assessing Volume and Framing of News Coverage Post-Ferguson, and Corresponding Impacts on Legislative Activity." *Politics, Groups, and Identities* 7 (1): 151–64. doi: 10.1080/21565503.2018.1518782.

"Attorney General Eric Holder's Statement on Developments in Ferguson, MO." 2014. US Department of Justice Office of Public Affairs. August 21. https://www.justice .gov.

Baker, David, Simon Bronitt, and Philip Stenning. 2017. "Policing Protest, Security and Freedom: The 2014 G20 Experience." *Police Practice and Research* 18 (5): 425–48. doi: 10.1080/15614263.2017.1280674.

Baldwin, Michael. 2016. "Homicides, Shootings Increase in Cincinnati; Overall Violent Crime Down." Fox 19 Now, January 20. www.fox19.com.

Barlow, David E., and Melissa Hickman Barlow. 2018. *Police in a Multicultural Society: An American Story.* Long Grove, IL: Waveland Press.

Bauman, Anna, and Meghna Chakrabarti. 2021. *America's Crime Surge: Why Violence Is Rising, and Solutions to Fix It.* On Point. www.wbur.org.

Berestycki, Henri, Jean-Pierre Nadal, and Nancy Rodriguez. 2015. "A Model of Riots Dynamics: Shocks, Diffusion and Thresholds." *Networks and Heterogeneous Media (NHM)* 10 (3): 443–75. doi: 10.3934/nhm.2015.10.443.

Berman, Mark. 2015. "Two Police Officers Shot, Seriously Injured in Ferguson 'Ambush.'" *Washington Post*, March 12. www.washingtonpost.com.

Bittner, Egon. 1970. *The Functions of the Police in Modern Society*. Chevy Chase, MD: US National Institute of Mental Health, Center for Studies of Crime and Delinquency.

———. 1990. *Aspects of Police Work*. Boston, MA: Northeastern University Press.

Blumer, Herbert. 1958. "Race Prejudice as a Sense of Group Position." *Pacific Sociological Review* 1 (1): 3–7. doi: 10.2307/1388607.

Bolger, P. Colin. 2015. "Just Following Orders: A Meta-Analysis of the Correlates of American Police Officer Use of Force Decisions." *American Journal of Criminal Justice* 40 (3): 466–92. doi: 10.1007/s12103-014-9278-y.

Bolton, Kenneth, and Joe Feagin. 2004. *Black in Blue: African-American Police Officers and Racism*. New York: Routledge.

Bottoms, Anthony, and Justice Tankebe. 2012. "Beyond Procedural Justice: A Dialogic Approach to Legitimacy in Criminal Justice." *Journal of Criminal Law and Criminology* 102 (1): 119–70. doi: 0091–4169/12/10201–0119.

Bradford, Ben. 2014. "Policing and Social Identity: Procedural Justice, Inclusion and Cooperation between Police and Public." *Policing and Society* 24 (1): 22–43. doi: 10.1080/10439463.2012.724068.

Bradford, Ben, Paul Quinton, Andy Myhill, and Gillian Porter. 2014. "Why Do 'the Law' Comply? Procedural Justice, Group Identification and Officer Motivation in Police Organizations." *European Journal of Criminology* 11 (1): 110–31. doi:10.1177/1477370813491898.

Brandl, Steven G., and Meghan S. Stroshine. 2013. "The Role of Officer Attributes, Job Characteristics, and Arrest Activity in Explaining Police Use of Force." *Criminal Justice Policy Review* 24 (5): 551–72. doi: 10.1177/0887403412452424.

Butler, Stuart M., and Nehath Sheriff. 2020. "Innovative Solutions to Address the Mental Health Crisis: Shifting Away from Police as First Responders." Washington, DC: Brookings Institution.

Byers, Christine. 2016. "St. Louis-Area Police Concerned Whether Their Body Armor Provides Enough Protection." *St. Louis Post-Dispatch*, July 25. www.stltoday.com.

CBS This Morning. 2014. *State Police Captain Ron Johnson Speaks at Michael Brown Rally*. www.youtube.com/watch?v=3-KmLQXQIpg.

Cobbina, Jennifer E. 2016. "The Point, after All, Is to Change the World. Ferguson Residents and Protesters Views about Police Perceptions of Race and Crime." *Berkeley Journal of Sociology*. http://berkeleyjournal.org.

———. 2019. *Hands Up, Don't Shoot: Why the Protests in Ferguson and Baltimore Matter, and How They Changed America*. New York: NYU Press.

Cobbina, Jennifer E., Soma Chaudhuri, Victor M. Rios, and Michael Conteh. 2019. "'I Will Be Out There Every Day Strong!' Protest Policing and Future Activism Among Ferguson and Baltimore Protesters." *Sociological Forum* 34: 409–33. doi: 10.1111/socf.12503.

Cobbina, Jennifer E., Michael Conteh, and Collin Emrich. 2019 "Race, Gender, and Responses to the Police Among Ferguson Residents and Protesters." *Race and Justice* 9 (3): 276–303. doi: 10.1177/2153368717699673.

Cobbina, Jennifer E., Akwasi Owusu-Bempah, and Kimberly Bender. 2016. "Perceptions of Race, Crime, and Policing among Ferguson Protesters." *Journal of Crime and Justice* 39 (1): 210–29. doi: 10.1080/0735648X.2015.1119950.

Cochran, Joshua C., and Patricia Y. Warren. 2012. "Racial, Ethnic, and Gender Differences in Perceptions of the Police: The Salience of Officer Race within the Context of Racial Profiling." *Journal of Contemporary Criminal Justice* 28 (2): 206–27. doi: 10.1177/1043986211425726.

Colgan, Beth. 2015. "Policing and Profit." *Harvard Law Review* 128 (6): 1723–46. http://cdn.harvardlawreview.org/.

Crank, John P. 2014. *Understanding Police Culture.* New York: Routledge.

Davis, Aaron C. 2015. "'YouTube Effect' Has Left Police Officers under Siege, Law Enforcement Leaders Say." *Washington Post*, October 8. www.washingtonpost.com.

DeBonis, Mike, and Victoria St. Martin. 2014. "D.C. Police Will Wear Body Cameras as Part of Pilot Program—The Washington Post." *Washington Post*, September 24. www.washingtonpost.com.

Decker, Scott H., and Russell L. Smith. 1980. "Police Minority Recruitment: A Note on Its Effectiveness in Improving Black Evaluations of the Police." *Journal of Criminal Justice* 8 (6): 387–93. doi: 10.1016/0047-2352(80)90114-2.

della Porta, Donatella, and Herbert Reiter. 1998. *Policing Protest: The Control of Mass Demonstrations in Western Democracies.* Vol. 6. Social Movements, Protest and Contention. Minneapolis: University of Minnesota Press.

Demerouti, Evangelia, and Willem Verbeke. 2004. "Using the Job Demands–Resources Model to Predict Burnout and Performance." *Human Resource Management* 43 (1): 83–104. doi: 10.1002/hrm.20004.

Deuchar, Ross, Seth Wyatt Fallik, and Vaughn J. Crichlow. 2019. "Despondent Officer Narratives and the 'Post-Ferguson' Effect: Exploring Law Enforcement Perspectives and Strategies in a Southern American State." *Policing and Society* 29 (9): 1042–57. doi: 10.1080/10439463.2018.1480020.

Drakulich, Kevin M., Kevin H. Wozniak, John Hagan, and Devon Johnson. 2021. "Whose Lives Mattered? How White and Black Americans Felt about Black Lives Matter in 2016." *Law & Society Review* 55: 227–51. doi: 10.1111/lasr.12552.

Drury, John, and Steve Reicher. 2009. "Collective Psychological Empowerment as a Model of Social Change: Researching Crowds and Power." *Journal of Social Issues* 65 (4): 707–25. doi: 10.1111/j.1540-4560.2009.01622.x.

Earl, Jennifer. 2003. "Tanks, Tear Gas, and Taxes: Toward a Theory of Movement Repression." *Sociological Theory* 21 (1): 44–68. doi: 10.1111/1467-9558.00175.

Earl, Jennifer, and Sarah Soule. 2006. "Seeing Blue: A Police-Centered Explanation of Protest Policing." *Mobilization: An International Quarterly* 11 (2): 145–64. doi: 10.17813/maiq.11.2.u1wj8w41n301627u.

Earl, Jennifer, Sarah A. Soule, and John D. McCarthy. 2003. "Protest under Fire? Explaining the Policing of Protest." *American Sociological Review* 68 (4): 581–606. doi: 10.2307/1519740.

Easton, David. 1965. *A Framework for Political Analysis*. Vol. 25. Englewood Cliffs, NJ: Prentice-Hall.

———. 1976. "Theoretical Approaches to Political Support." *Canadian Journal of Political Science* 9 (03): 431–48. doi: 10.1017/S0008423900044309.

Eggert, Nina, Ruud Wouters, Pauline Ketelaars, and Stefaan Walgrave. 2018. "Preparing for Action: Police Deployment Decisions for Demonstrations." *Policing and Society* 28 (2): 137–48. doi: 10.1080/10439463.2016.1147565.

Eligon, John, and Mitch Smith. 2015. "Ferguson Announces an Amnesty on Warrants." *New York Times*, August 25. www.nytimes.com.

Engel, Robin Shepard, James J. Sobol, and Robert E. Worden. 2000. "Further Exploration of the Demeanor Hypothesis: The Interaction Effects of Suspects' Characteristics and Demeanor on Police Behavior." *Justice Quarterly* 17 (2): 235–58. doi: 10.1080/07418820000096311.

Executive Office of the President of the United States. 2020. "President's Commission on Law Enforcement and Administration of Justice: Final Report." NCJ 225565. Washington, DC: US Department of Justice.

Feldman, Lauren, P. Sol Hart, Anthony Leiserowitz, Edward Maibach, and Connie Roser-Renouf. 2017. "Do Hostile Media Perceptions Lead to Action? The Role of Hostile Media Perceptions, Political Efficacy, and Ideology in Predicting Climate Change Activism." *Communication Research* 44 (8): 1099–1124. doi: 10.1177/0093650214565914.

Gau, Jacinta M., and Rod K. Brunson. 2010. "Procedural Justice and Order Maintenance Policing: A Study of Inner-City Young Men's Perceptions of Police Legitimacy." *Justice Quarterly* 27 (2): 255–79. doi: 10.1080/07418820902763889.

Gau, Jacinta M., and Eugene A. Paoline III. 2017. "Officer Race, Role Orientations, and Cynicism toward Citizens." *Justice Quarterly* 34 (7): 1246–71. doi: 10.1080/07418825.2017.1380838.

Gause, LaGina. 2022. "Revealing Issue Salience via Costly Protest: How Legislative Behavior Following Protest Advantages Low-Resource Groups." *British Journal of Political Science* 52 (1): 259–79. doi: 10.1017/S000712340000423.

Gorner, Jeremy, and Hal Dardick. 2016. "Citing Beating of Officer, Chicago's Top Cop Says Police Are 'Second-Guessing Themselves.'" *Chicago Tribune*, October 7. www.chicagotribune.com.

Governing. 2015. *Diversity on the Police Force: Where Police Don't Mirror Communities*. Washington, DC: Governing.

Groves, Robert M., and Mick P. Couper. 2012. *Nonresponse in Household Interview Surveys*. Hoboken, NJ: John Wiley & Sons.

Hansen, Glenn J., and Hyunjung Kim. 2011. "Is the Media Biased against Me? A Meta-Analysis of the Hostile Media Effect Research." *Communication Research Reports* 28 (2): 169–79. doi: 10.1080/08824096.2011.565280.

Harrell, Erika, and Elizabeth Davis. 2020. "Contacts Between Police and the Public, 2018–Statistical Tables." NCJ 255730. Washington, DC: US Department of Justice, Bureau of Justice Statistics.

Hawkins, Homer C. 2001. "Police Officer Burnout: A Partial Replication of Maslach's Burnout Inventory." *Police Quarterly* 4 (3): 343–60. doi: 10.1177/109861101129197888.

Hermann, Peter, and Rachel Weiner. 2014. "Issues over Police Shooting in Ferguson Lead Push for Officers and Body Cameras." *Washington Post*, December 2. www.washingtonpost.com.

Hoffman, Chrystina Y., Joshua C. Hinkle, and Logan S. Ledford. 2021. "Beyond the 'Ferguson Effect' on Crime: Examining Its Influence on Law Enforcement Personnel." *Crime & Delinquency*, 1–23. doi: 10.1177/00111287211052440.

Holdaway, Simon. 1991. "Race Relations and Police Recruitment." *British Journal of Criminology* 31 (4): 365–82. doi: 10.1093/oxfordjournals.bjc.a048135.

Hsiao, Yuan, and Scott Radnitz. 2021. "Allies or Agitators? How Partisan Identity Shapes Public Opinion about Violent or Nonviolent Protests." *Political Communication* 38 (4): 479–97. doi.org/10.1080/10584609.2020.1793848.

Hudson, David. 2014. "President Obama Issues a Statement on the Death of Michael Brown." *Whitehouse.gov*, August 12. https://obamawhitehouse.archives.gov.

Hunt, I. C., and Bernard Cohen. 1971. *Minority Recruiting in the New York City Police Department*. New York: Rand Institute.

Hyland, Shelley S. 2018. "Body-Worn Cameras in Law Enforcement Agencies, 2016." NCJ 251775. Washington, DC: US Department of Justice, Bureau of Justice Statistics.

Hyland, Shelley S., and Elizabeth Davis. 2019. "Local Police Departments 2016: Personnel." NCJ 252835. Washington, DC: US Department of Justice, Bureau of Justice Statistics.

Institute for Intergovernmental Research. 2015. "After-Action Assessment of the Police Response to the August 2014 Demonstrations in Ferguson, Missouri." Washington, DC: Office of Community Oriented Policing Services.

Jefferis, Eric S., Robert J. Kaminski, Stephen Holmes, and Dena E. Hanley. 1997. "The Effect of a Videotaped Arrest on Public Perceptions of Police Use of Force." *Journal of Criminal Justice* 25 (5): 381–95. doi: 10.1016/S0047-2352(97)00022-6.

Jones, Jeffrey M. 2021. "In U.S., Black Confidence in Police Recovers from 2020 Low." *Social & Policy Issues*. Washington, DC: Gallup Inc. https://news.gallup.com.

Kaminski, Robert J., and Eric S. Jefferis. 1998. "The Effect of a Violent Televised Arrest on Public Perceptions of the Police: A Partial Test of Easton's Theoretical Framework." *Policing: An International Journal of Police Strategies & Management* 21 (4): 683–706. doi: 10.1108/13639519810241692.

Kendzior, Sarah, and Umar Lee. 2014. "After Ferguson." *POLITICO Magazine*, August 26. www.politico.com.

King, Mike, and David Waddington. 2005. "Flashpoints Revisited: A Critical Application to the Policing of Anti-Globalization Protest." *Policing & Society* 15 (3): 255–82. doi: 10.1080/10439460500168584.

Klockars, Carl B. 1980. "The Dirty Harry Problem." *The Annals of the American Academy of Political and Social Science* 452 (1): 33–47. doi: 10.1177/000271628045200104.

———. 1985. *The Idea of Police*. Vol. 3. Beverly Hills, CA: Sage Publications.

Kochel, Tammy Rinehart. 2011. "Constructing Hot Spots Policing: Unexamined Consequences for Disadvantaged Populations and for Police Legitimacy." *Criminal Justice Policy Review* 22 (3): 350–74. doi: 10.1177/0887403410376233.

———. 2014. "Views by St. Louis County Residents Regarding the Police and Public Responses to the Shooting of Michael Brown in Ferguson, Missouri on August 9, 2014." http://opensiuc.lib.siu.edu.

———. 2015a. "Assessing the Initial Impact of the Michael Brown Shooting and Police and Public Responses to It on St. Louis County Residents' Views about Police." http://opensiuc.lib.siu.edu.

———. 2015b. "Ferguson's Long-Term Impact on Public Views about Police." http://opensiuc.lib.siu.edu.

———. 2018a. "Police Legitimacy and Resident Cooperation in Crime Hotspots: Effects of Victimisation Risk and Collective Efficacy." *Policing and Society* 28 (3): 251–70. doi: 10.1080/10439463.2016.1174235.

———. 2018b. "The Impact of the Ferguson, MO Police Shooting on Black and Non-black Residents' Perceptions of Police." In *Police-Citizen Relations Across the World: Comparing Sources and Contexts of Trust and Legitimacy*, 196–218. New York: Routledge.

———. 2019. "Explaining Racial Differences in Ferguson's Impact on Local Residents' Trust and Perceived Legitimacy: Policy Implications for Police." *Criminal Justice Policy Review* 30 (3): 374–405. doi: 10.1177/0887403416684923.

———. 2022. "Effectiveness of Online Implicit Bias Training: Evaluating Officer Outcomes from a Cultural Diversity Training versus a Skills-Based Course on Communication." In *Exploring Contemporary Police Challenges*, edited by Sanja Kutnjak Ivkovich, Jon Maskaly, Christopher Donner, Irena Cajner Mraovic, and Dilip Das. New York: Routledge.

Kochel, Tammy Rinehart, George Burruss, and David Weisburd. 2016. "Assessing the Effects of Hot Spots Policing Strategies on Police Legitimacy, Crime, and Collective Efficacy." Washington, DC: US Department of Justice.

Kochel, Tammy Rinehart, and David Weisburd. 2017. "Assessing Community Consequences of Implementing Hot Spots Policing in Residential Areas: Findings from a Randomized Field Trial." *Journal of Experimental Criminology* 13 (2): 143–70. doi: 10.1007/s11292-017-9283-5.

———. 2019. "The Impact of Hot Spots Policing on Collective Efficacy: Findings from a Randomized Field Trial." *Justice Quarterly* 36 (5): 900–928. Taylor & Francis. doi: 10.1080/07418825.2018.1465579.

Kochel, Tammy Rinehart, David B. Wilson, and Stephen D. Mastrofski. 2011. "Effect of Suspect Race on Officers' Arrest Decisions." *Criminology* 49 (2): 473–512. doi: 10.1111/j.1745-9125.2011.00230.x.

Kop, Nicolien, Martin Euwema, and Wilmar Schaufeli. 1999. "Burnout, Job Stress and Violent Behaviour among Dutch Police Officers." *Work & Stress* 13 (4): 326–40. doi: 10.1080/02678379950019789.

Kraske, Steve. 2014. "Gov. Jay Nixon: Protect Ferguson, Seek Justice, Restore Trust." *Kansas City Star*, August 20. www.kansascity.com.

Lasley, James R. 1994. "The Impact of the Rodney King Incident on Citizen Attitudes toward Police." *Policing and Society: An International Journal* 3 (4): 245–55. doi: 10.1080/10439463.1994.9964673.

Lasley, James R., James Larson, Chandrika Kelso, and Gregory Chris Brown. 2011. "Assessing the Long-Term Effects of Officer Race on Police Attitudes towards the Community: A Case for Representative Bureaucracy Theory." *Police Practice and Research* 12 (6): 474–91. doi: 10.1080/15614263.2011.589567.

Le Bon, Gustave. 1895. *The Crowd: A Study of the Popular Mind*. London: T. Fisher Unwin.

Lee, Raymond T., and Blake E. Ashforth. 1996. "A Meta-Analytic Examination of the Correlates of the Three Dimensions of Job Burnout." *Journal of Applied Psychology* 81 (2): 123–33. doi: 10.1037/0021-9010.81.2.123.

Lempert, Richard. 2021. "The Derek Chauvin Sentencing Decision: Is It Fair?" *Brookings*, July 1. www.brookings.edu.

Lum, Cynthia, Christopher S. Koper, Charlotte Gill, Julie Hibdon, Cody Telep, and Laurie O. Robinson. 2016. "Evidence-Assessment of the Recommendations of the President's Task Force on 21st Century Policing: Implementation and Research Priorities." Alexandria, VA: Center for Evidence-Based Crime Policy and International Association of Chiefs of Police. www.ojp.gov.

Maguen, Shira, Thomas J. Metzler, Shannon E. McCaslin, Sabra S. Inslicht, Clare Henn-Haase, Thomas C. Neylan, and Charles R. Marmar. 2009. "Routine Work Environment Stress and PTSD Symptoms in Police Officers." *Journal of Nervous and Mental Disease* 197 (10): 754–60. doi: 10.1097/NMD.0b013e3181b975f8.

Maguire, Edward R., Maya Barak, Karie Cross, and Kris Lugo. 2018. "Attitudes among Occupy DC Participants about the Use of Violence against Police." *Policing and Society* 28 (5): 526–40. Routledge. doi: 10.1080/10439463.2016.1202247.

Maguire, Edward, Maya Barak, William Wells, and Charles Katz. 2020. "Attitudes towards the Use of Violence against Police among Occupy Wall Street Protesters." *Policing: A Journal of Policy and Practice* 14 (4): 883–99. doi:10.1093/police/pay003.

Manekin, Devorah, and Tamar Mitts. 2020. "Effective for Whom? Ethnic Identity and Nonviolent Resistance." *American Political Science Review*. Cambridge University Press, 1–20. doi: 10.1017/S0003055421000940.

Marschall, Melissa J., and Anirudh V. S. Ruhil. 2007. "Substantive Symbols: The Attitudinal Dimension of Black Political Incorporation in Local Government." *American Journal of Political Science* 51 (1): 17–33.

Martinussen, M., A. M. Richardsen, and R. J. Burke. 2007. "Job Demands, Job Resources, and Burnout among Police Officers." *Journal of Criminal Justice* 35 (3): 239–49. doi: 10.1016/j.jcrimjus.2007.03.001.

Maslach, Christina, and Susan E. Jackson. 1984. "Patterns of Burnout among a National Sample of Public Contact Workers." *Journal of Health and Human Resources Administration* 7 (2): 189–212.

Mastrofski, Stephen D., Michael D. Reisig, and John D. McCluskey. 2002. "Police Disrespect Toward the Public: An Encounter-Based Analysis." *Criminology* 40 (3): 519–52. doi: 10.1111/j.1745-9125.2002.tb00965.x.

McCarty, William P., Hani Aldirawi, Stacy Dewald, and Mariana Palacios. 2019. "Burnout in Blue: An Analysis of the Extent and Primary Predictors of Burnout Among Law Enforcement Officers in the United States." *Police Quarterly* 22 (3): 278–304. doi: Fox News. www.foxnews.com.

Moore, Doug. 2015. "Among the Ferguson Protests, a Young Woman Offers Herself as Police Shield." *St. Louis PostDispatch*, August 12. www.stltoday.com.

Moran, Matthew, and David Waddington. 2016. "The Revised Flashpoints Model of Public Disorder." In *Riots: An International Comparison*, edited by Matthew Moran and David Waddington, 15–38. London: Palgrave Macmillan UK.

Morash, Merry, and Robin N. Haarr. 1995. "Gender, Workplace Problems, and Stress in Policing." *Justice Quarterly* 12 (2): 113–40. doi: 10.1080/07418829500092591.

Morin, Rich, Kim Parker, Renee Stepler, and Andrew Mercer. 2017. "Behind the Badge: Amid Protests and Calls for Reform, How Police View Their Jobs, Key Issues, and Recent Fatal Encounters between Blacks and Police." Washington, DC: Pew Research Center. www.pewsocialtrends.org.

Muir, William Ker. 1977. *Police: Streetcorner Politicians.* Chicago: University of Chicago Press.

Murphy, Kristina, and Adrian Cherney. 2012. "Understanding Cooperation with Police in a Diverse Society." *British Journal of Criminology* 52 (1): 181–201. doi: 10.1093/bjc/azr065.

Murphy, Kristina, and Tom Tyler. 2008. "Procedural Justice and Compliance Behaviour: The Mediating Role of Emotions." *European Journal of Social Psychology* 38 (4): 652–68. doi: 10.1002/ejsp.502.

Nashrulla, Tasneem. 2014. "13 Powerful Signs Protesting the Death of Michael Brown in Ferguson." August 14, www.buzzfeednews.com.

National Conference of State Legislatures. "Legislative Responses for Policing-State Bill Tracking Database." 2021. *National Conference of State Legislatures*, October 8. www.ncsl.org.

Newburn, Tim. 2016a. "The 2011 England Riots in European Context: A Framework for Understanding the 'Life-Cycle' of Riots." *European Journal of Criminology* 13 (5): 540–55. doi: 10.1177/1477370816633726.

———. 2016b. "Reflections on Why Riots Don't Happen." *Theoretical Criminology* 20 (2): 125–44. doi: 10.1177/1362480615598829.

Nicholson-Crotty, Sean, Jill Nicholson-Crotty, and Sergio Fernandez. 2017. "Will More Black Cops Matter? Officer Race and Police-Involved Homicides of Black Citizens." *Public Administration Review* 77 (2): 206–16. doi: 10.1111/puar.12734.

Nix, Justin, and Justin T. Pickett. 2017. "Third-Person Perceptions, Hostile Media Effects, and Policing: Developing a Theoretical Framework for Assessing the Ferguson Effect." *Journal of Criminal Justice* 51 (July): 24–33. doi: 10.1016/j.jcrimjus.2017.05.016.

Nix, Justin, and Scott E. Wolfe. 2016. "Sensitivity to the Ferguson Effect: The Role of Managerial Organizational Justice." *Journal of Criminal Justice* 47 (December): 12–20. doi: 10.1016/j.jcrimjus.2016.06.002.

———. 2017. "The Impact of Negative Publicity on Police Self-Legitimacy." *Justice Quarterly* 34 (1): 84–108. doi: 10.1080/07418825.2015.1102954.

Nix, Justin, Scott E. Wolfe, and Bradley A. Campbell. 2018. "Command-Level Police Officers' Perceptions of the 'War on Cops' and De-Policing." *Justice Quarterly* 35 (1): 33–54. doi: 10.1080/07418825.2017.1338743.

Norton, Blake, Edwin E. Hamilton, Rick Braziel, Daniel Linkskey, and Jennifer Zeunik. 2015. "Collaborative Reform Initiative: An Assessment of the St. Louis County Police Department." Washington, DC: Office of Community Oriented Policing Services. www.policefoundation.org.

Paoline III, Eugene A., and Jacinta M. Gau. 2018. "Police Occupational Culture: Testing the Monolithic Model." *Justice Quarterly* 35 (4): 670–98. doi: 10.1080/07418825.2017 .1335764.

Paoline III, Eugene A., Stephanie M. Myers, and Robert E. Worden. 2000. "Police Culture, Individualism, and Community Policing: Evidence from Two Police Departments." *Justice Quarterly* 17 (3): 575–606. doi: 10.1080/074188200000 94671.

Paoline III, Eugene A., and William Terrill. 2013. *Police Culture: Adapting to the Strains of the Job.* Durham, NC: Carolina Academic Press.

Paoline III, Eugene A., William Terrill, and Michael T. Rossler. 2015. "Higher Education, College Degree Major, and Police Occupational Attitudes." *Journal of Criminal Justice Education* 26 (1): 49–73. doi: 10.1080/10511253.2014.923010.

Parker, Kim, Juliana Menasce Horowitz, and Monica Anderson. 2020. "Amid Protests, Majorities Across Racial and Ethnic Groups Express Support for the Black Lives Matter Movement." Washington, DC: Pew Research Center. www.pewre search.org.

Pashea, Joseph John Jr., and Tammy Rinehart Kochel. 2016. "Face-to-Face Surveys in High Crime Areas: Balancing Respondent Cooperation and Interviewer Safety." *Journal of Criminal Justice Education* 27 (1): 95–120. doi: 10.1080/10511253.2015 .1091487.

Patrick, Robert, and Taylor Tiamoyo Harris. 2021. " 'We Are Working Diligently to Change Ferguson,' Mayor Says on Anniversary of Brown's Death." *St. Louis Post-Dispatch*, August 10. www.stltoday.com.

Perry, Gali, Tal Jonathan-Zamir, and David Weisburd. 2017. "The Effect of Paramilitary Protest Policing on Protestors' Trust in the Police: The Case of the 'Occupy Israel' Movement." *Law & Society Review* 51 (3): 602–34. doi: 10.1111/lasr.12279.

Police Executive Research Forum. 2021. "Managing Demonstrations: New Strategies for Protecting Protesters and the Police." YouTube. April 15. www.youtube.com/watch ?v=WBAiuPucZQo.

Poon, Linda, and Marie Patino. 2020. "A Timeline of U.S. Police Protests." *Bloomberg CityLab*, August 28. www.bloomberg.com.

President's Task Force on 21st Century Policing. 2015. "Final Report of the President's Task Force on 21st Century Policing." Washington, DC: Office of Community Oriented Policing Services.

Pyrooz, David C., Scott H. Decker, Scott E. Wolfe, and John A. Shjarback. 2016. "Was There a Ferguson Effect on Crime Rates in Large U.S. Cities?" *Journal of Criminal Justice* 46 (September): 1–8. doi: 10.1016/j.jcrimjus.2016.01.001.

Raganella, Anthony J., and Michael D. White. 2004. "Race, Gender, and Motivation for Becoming a Police Officer: Implications for Building a Representative Police Department." *Journal of Criminal Justice* 32 (6): 501–13. doi: 10.1016/j.jcrimjus.2004.08.009.

Reaves, B. 2015. "Local Police Departments, 2013: Personnel, Policies, and Practices." Washington, DC: US Department of Justice, NCJ 248677.

Regoli, Bob, John P. Crank, and George F. Rivera. 1990. "The Construction and Implementation of an Alternative Measure of Police Cynicism." *Criminal Justice and Behavior* 17 (4): 395–409. doi: 10.1177/0093854890017004001.

Reicher, S., C. Stott, J. Drury, O. Adang, P. Cronin, and A. Livingstone. 2007. "Knowledge-Based Public Order Policing: Principles and Practice." *Policing* 1 (4): 403–15. doi: 10.1093/police/pam067.

Reiss, Albert J. 1967. "Career Orientations, Job Satisfaction and the Assessment of Law Enforcement Problems by Police Officers." In *Studies in Crime and Law Enforcement in Major Metropolitan Areas: Field Surveys III (Vol. 2)*, edited by the President's Commission on Law Enforcement and Administration of Justice. Washington, DC: US Government Printing Office.

Reynolds-Stenson, Heidi. 2018. "Protesting the Police: Anti-Police Brutality Claims as a Predictor of Police Repression of Protest." *Social Movement Studies* 17 (1): 48–63. doi: 10.1080/14742837.2017.1381592.

Rosenfeld, Richard. 2016a. "Documenting and Explaining the 2015 Homicide Rise: Research Directions." Washington, DC: US Department of Justice, National Institute of Justice.

———. 2016b. "Was There a 'Ferguson Effect' on Crime in St. Louis?" Washington, DC: The Sentencing Project.

Rothbaum, Jonathan, and Adam Bee. 2021. "Coronavirus Infects Surveys, Too: Survey Nonresponse Bias and the Coronavirus Pandemic." Washington, DC: US Census Bureau.

Ryan, William. 2010. *Blaming the Victim*. New York: Knopf Doubleday.

Schneider, Margaret. 2014. "The Story of North County: How America Is in a Perpetual State of Reconstruction." *Quartz*, September 14. https://qz.com.

Selden, Sally Coleman. 1997. *The Promise of Representative Bureaucracy: Diversity and Responsiveness in a Government Agency*. Armonk, NY: M.E. Sharpe.

Sharkey, Patrick. 2018. *Uneasy Peace: The Great Crime Decline, the Renewal of City Life, and the Next War on Violence*. New York: W.W. Norton.

Shjarback, John A., David C. Pyrooz, Scott E. Wolfe, and Scott H. Decker. 2017. "De-Policing and Crime in the Wake of Ferguson: Racialized Changes in the Quantity and Quality of Policing among Missouri Police Departments." *Journal of Criminal Justice* 50 (May): 42–52. doi: 10.1016/j.jcrimjus.2017.04.003.

Skogan, Wesley G. 1978. "Citizen Satisfaction with Police Services: Individual and Contextual Effects." *Policy Studies Journal* 7 (s1): 469–79. doi: 10.1111/j.1541-0072.1978.tb01795.x.

———. 2006. "Asymmetry in the Impact of Encounters with Police." *Policing & Society* 16 (2): 99–126. doi: 10.1080/10439460600662098.

Smith, Mitch. 2019. "Policing: What Changed (and Didn't) Since Michael Brown Died." *New York Times*, August 7. www.newyorktimes.com.

Snipes, Jeffrey B., Edward R. Maguire, and David H. Tyler. 2019. "The Effects of Procedural Justice on Civil Disobedience: Evidence from Protesters in Three Cities." *Journal of Crime and Justice* 42 (1) 32–44. doi: 10.1080/0735648X.2018.1559128.

Stott, Clifford, and Stephen Reicher. 1998. "Crowd Action as Intergroup Process: Introducing the Police Perspective." *European Journal of Social Psychology* 28 (4): 509–29. doi: 10.1002/(SICI)1099-0992(199807/08)28:4<509::AID-EJSP877>3.0.CO;2-C.

Struett, David. 2021. "Mental Health Clinicians Will Start Answering Some 911 Calls in Chicago—Instead of Cops." *Chicago Sun-Times*, July 13. https://chicago.suntimes.com.

Subramanian, Ram, and Leily Arzy. 2021. "State Policing Reforms Since George Floyd's Murder." New York: Brennan Center for Justice. www.brennancenter.org.

Sun, Ivan Y., and Brian K. Payne. 2004. "Racial Differences in Resolving Conflicts: A Comparison between Black and White Police Officers." *Crime & Delinquency* 50 (4): 516–41. doi: 10.1177/0011128703259298.

Sunshine, Jason, and Tom R. Tyler. 2003. "The Role of Procedural Justice and Legitimacy in Shaping Public Support for Policing." *Law & Society Review* 37 (3): 513–48. doi: 10.1111/1540-5893.3703002.

Tankebe, Justice, and Gorazd Meško. 2015. "Police Self-Legitimacy, Use of Force, and Pro-Organizational Behavior in Slovenia." In *Trust and Legitimacy in Criminal Justice: European Perspectives*, edited by Gorazd Meško and Justice Tankebe, 261–77. New York: Springer International. doi: 10.1007/978-3-319-09813-5_12.

Teplin, Linda A. 2000. "Keeping the Peace: Police Discretion and Mentally Ill Persons." *National Institute of Justice Journal*, July. Washington, DC: National Institute of Justice. doi: 10.1037/e528652006-002.

Terrill, William. 2003. "Police Use of Force and Suspect Resistance: The Micro Process of the Police-Suspect Encounter." *Police Quarterly* 6 (1): 51–83. doi: 10.1177/109861110 2250584.

Terrill, William, and Stephen D. Mastrofski. 2002. "Situational and Officer-Based Determinants of Police Coercion." *Justice Quarterly* 19 (2): 215–48. doi: 10.1080/0741882 0200095221.

The Marshall Project. 2020. "The Future of Policing." *The System*, October 23. www.themarshallproject.org.

The Policing Project at NYU School of Law. 2020. "Policing Protests to Protect Constitutional Rights and Public Safety." New York: The Policing Project at New York University School of Law. www.policingproject.org.

"The President Speaks on Iraq and Ferguson." 2014. *The White House: President Barack Obama.* August 18. www.youtube.com/watch?v=1RdIZ-IKR-Q.

Theobald, Nick A., and Donald P. Haider-Markel. 2008. "Race, Bureaucracy, and Symbolic Representation: Interactions between Citizens and Police." *Journal of Public Administration Research and Theory* 19 (2): 409–26. doi: 10.1093/jopart/mun006.

Trinkner, Rick, Tom R. Tyler, and Phillip Atiba Goff. 2016. "Justice from Within: The Relations between a Procedurally Just Organizational Climate and Police Organizational Efficiency, Endorsement of Democratic Policing, and Officer Well-Being." *Psychology, Public Policy, and Law* 22 (2): 158–72. doi: 10.1037/law0000085.

Tyler, Tom R. 2006. *Why People Obey the Law.* Princeton, NJ: Princeton University Press.

US Department of Justice Civil Rights Division. 2015. "Investigation of the Ferguson Police Department." Washington, DC: US Department of Justice Civil Rights Division. www.justice.gov.

Van Craen, Maarten. 2016. "Understanding Police Officers' Trust and Trustworthy Behavior: A Work Relations Framework." *European Journal of Criminology* 13 (2): 274–94. doi: 10.1177/1477370815617187.

Van Maanen, John. 1978. "The Asshole." In *Policing: A View from the Street*, edited by Peter K. Manning and John Van Maanen, 221–238. Santa Monica, CA: Goodyear.

Vitale, Alex S. 2018. *The End of Policing.* New York: Verso Books.

Waddington, David, and Mike King. 2005. "The Disorderly Crowd: From Classical Psychological Reductionism to Socio-Contextual Theory—the Impact on Public Order Policing Strategies." *Howard Journal of Criminal Justice* 44 (5): 490–503. doi: 10.1111/j.1468-2311.2005.00393.x.

Waddington, David P., Karen Jones, and Chas Critcher. 1989. *Flashpoints: Studies in Public Disorder.* New York: Routledge.

Weitzer, Ronald. 2002. "Incidents of Police Misconduct and Public Opinion." *Journal of Criminal Justice* 30 (5): 397–408. doi: 10.1016/S0047-2352(02)00150-2.

———. 2015. "American Policing Under Fire: Misconduct and Reform." *Society* 52 (5): 475–80. doi: 10.1007/s12115-015-9931-1.

Weitzer, Ronald, and Steven A. Tuch. 2004. "Race and Perceptions of Police Misconduct." *Social Problems* 51 (3): 305–25. doi: 10.1525/sp.2004.51.3.305.

Weitzer, Ronald, Steven A. Tuch, and Wesley G. Skogan. 2008. "Police–Community Relations in a Majority-Black City." *Journal of Research in Crime and Delinquency* 45 (4): 398–428. doi: 10.1177/0022427808322617.

Westervelt, Eric. (2020). "Removing Cops from Behavioral Crisis Calls: 'We Need to Change the Model.'" National Public Radio. WSIU Radio, Carbondale, IL: WSIU, October 19.

White, Michael D., Jonathon A. Cooper, Jessica Saunders, and Anthony J. Raganella. 2010. "Motivations for Becoming a Police Officer: Re-Assessing Officer Attitudes and Job Satisfaction after Six Years on the Street." *Journal of Criminal Justice* 38 (4): 520–30. doi: j.jcrimjus.2010.04.022.

Widgery, Amber. 2021. "Legislatures Address Police Accountability." *State Legislatures News*, April 21. www.ncsl.org.

Wilkins, Vicky M., and Brian N. Williams. 2008. "Black or Blue: Racial Profiling and Representative Bureaucracy." *Public Administration Review* 68 (4): 654–64. doi: 10.1111/j.1540–6210.2008.00905.x.

Williams, Morgan C., Jr., Nathan Weil, Elizabeth A. Rasich, Jens Ludwig, Hye Chang, and Sophia Egrari. 2021. "Body-Worn Cameras in Policing: Benefits and Costs." Cambridge, MA: National Bureau of Economic Research. www.nber.org.

Willis, James J. 2011. "Enhancing Police Legitimacy by Integrating Compstat and Community Policing." *Policing: An International Journal of Police Strategies & Management* 34 (4): 654–73. doi: 10.1108/13639511111180261.

Willis, James J., Stephen D. Mastrofski, and Tammy Rinehart Kochel. 2010a. "Recommendations for Integrating Compstat and Community Policing." *Policing* 4 (2): 182–93. doi: 10.1093/police/paq005.

———. 2010b. "The Co-Implementation of Compstat and Community Policing." *Journal of Criminal Justice* 38 (5): 969–80. doi: 10.1016/j.jcrimjus.2010.06.014.

Wolfe, Scott E., and Justin Nix. 2016. "The Alleged 'Ferguson Effect' and Police Willingness to Engage in Community Partnership." *Law and Human Behavior* 40 (1): 1–10. doi: 10.1037/lhb0000164.

Worden, Robert E. 1995. "The Causes of Police Brutality: Theory and Evidence on Police Use of Force." In *And Justice for All: Understanding and Controlling Police Abuse of Force*, Vol. 14, edited by A. William and H. Toch, 31–60. Washington, DC: Police Executive Research Forum.

Worden, Robert E., and Robin L. Shepard. 1996. "Demeanor, Crime and Police Behavior: A Reexamination of the Police Services Study Data." *Criminology* 34 (1): 83–105. doi:10.1111/j.1745-9125.1996.tb01196.x.

Young, Danielle. 2019. "Never Forget: 39 Unforgettable Images of People Protesting the Killing of Michael Brown." *Newone*, August 9. https://newsone.com.

Zhang, Zhiran, Dexuan Sha, Beidi Dong, Shiyang Ruan, Agen Qiu, Yun Li, Jiping Liu, and Chaowei Yang. 2020. "Spatiotemporal Patterns and Driving Factors on Crime Changing During Black Lives Matter Protests." *ISPRS International Journal of Geo-Information* 9 (11): 640–59. doi: 10.3390/ijgi9110640.

INDEX

ABOUT THE AUTHOR

TAMMY RINEHART KOCHEL is Associate Dean of Research, Diversity, and Personnel for the College of Health and Human Sciences and Professor of Criminology and Criminal Justice in the School of Justice and Public Safety at Southern Illinois University Carbondale.